Benston, Kimber
Baraka

Baraka: The Renegade and the Mask

B A R A K A

The Renegade and the Mask

Kimberly W. Benston

New Haven and London
Yale University Press
1976

Library of Congress catalog card number: 75–43302
International standard book number: 0–300–01958–0

Designed by Sally Sullivan
and set in Times Roman type.
Printed in the United States of America by
The Colonial Press Inc., Clinton, Mass.

Published in Great Britain, Europe, Africa, and Asia
(except Japan) by Yale University Press, Ltd., London.
Distributed in Latin America by Kaiman & Polon, Inc.,
New York City; in Australia and New Zealand by Book & Film
Services, Artarmon, N.S.W., Australia; in Japan by John
Weatherhill, Inc., Tokyo.

Acknowledgment is made to those mentioned below for permission to quote:

Imamu Baraka, for excerpts from the unpublished *A Recent Killing.*

The Bobbs-Merrill Company, Inc., Indianapolis, for excerpts from *Black Magic Poetry (1961–1967)*, copyright © 1969 by LeRoi Jones, reprinted by permission of the publisher, The Bobbs-Merrill Company, Inc.; and for excerpts from *In Our Terribleness*, copyright © 1970 by Imamu Amiri Baraka (LeRoi Jones) and Fundi (Billy Abernathy), reprinted by permission of the publisher, The Bobbs-Merrill Company, Inc.

Corinth Books, Inc., New Haven, for excerpts from *Preface to a Twenty Volume Suicide Note*, copyright © 1961 by LeRoi Jones. Reprinted by permission of Corinth Books.

The Sterling Lord Agency, Inc., New York, for excerpts from *The Dead Lecturer*, copyright © 1964 by LeRoi Jones. Used by permission of The Sterling Lord Agency.

Third World Press, Chicago, for excerpts from *It's Nation Time*, copyright © 1970 by Imamu Amiri Baraka (LeRoi Jones), reprinted by permission of Third World Press, 7524 South Cottage Grove, Chicago, Illinois 60619.

To My Family
And To
The Memory Of My Teacher
Elizabeth Hart

A renegade
behind the mask. And even
the mask, a renegade
disguise. Black skin . . .
natural
rhythms.

His head is
at the window. The only
part
that sings.

Imamu Amiri Baraka,
from "A Poem for Willie Best"

Contents

Foreword

This is a very tough book. It is the first really important study of the literature and cultural criticism of the controversial Black American poet, Imamu Baraka. Kimberly Benston has intentionally eschewed the more overtly sensational aspects of Baraka's career. Instead, he has attempted a systematic exploration of Baraka's literary themes and the attitudes toward culture that inform them. This is not journalistic sociology masquerading as literary criticism. Essentially, Benston has avoided the sociological trap which often ensnares black and white critics of Afro-American literature and culture.

An understanding of Baraka's work demands the analytical intelligence associated with modern critical technique, but it also demands something more, something beyond rhetorical display. That "something" we designate the "Black Ethos." There are quotation marks around this because we must keep in mind Albert Murray's stipulation that sometimes black is not really black, and white is not really white. But Murray would probably agree that there is a specific texture to Black American life and culture. In framing his study, Benston has kept this in mind. He not only locates Baraka in the general tradition of modern literature, but he also understands the compelling significance of the poet's specific cultural references. Benston has done an especially good job in exploring the links between Baraka's aesthetic and Afro-American music. This is extremely important, because Afro-American music has been a major internal force in the shaping of Afro-American culture and literary styles.

No serious critic can begin to grapple with the Black Ethos unless he first comes to grips with the psychic vortex, the emotional and mythic history that operates in the sub-text of the poet's aesthetic. For example, in the works of Baraka and many other writers in the Sixties—notably, Ishmael Reed, Askia M. Touré, and Henry Dumas—there is an awesome "double consciousness" of the dominant society. In their cosmologies America and the European idea which birthed her are at once objects of disdain and admiration.

The black poet sets forth like the storybook hero to engage in what George Kent terms the "Adventure of Western Culture." He learns the structure of Western thought and the Western terms in which the world is ordered. If he is lucky enough to receive a university education, and if he is interested in ideas, he literally inundates himself in the whole of Western culture. He passionately encounters the works of Dante, Goethe, Heine, Marx, Wittgenstein, Joyce, Beckett, Sartre, Pound, ad infinitum. And out of this encounter, which is, in fact, an encounter with tradition, the poet must fashion *his own* artistic image, his special ethos. He must, as the nameless narrator of Ellison's *Invisible Man* perceives, shape the "uncreated features of his face."

For some writers in the black diaspora the adventure led to a spiritual crisis. This is nothing new per se: all of the major explosions and innovations in so-called avant-garde art have taken place around a core of aesthetic and political crisis. What is new, however, is the particular manner in which the diasporic sensibility manifested itself within the Afro-American consciousness. Undoubtedly, the modern black writer's first problem centered on the issue of language and appropriate form. The distant but gnawing memory of a prior history before the enslavement and the dispersal demanded that he assume a special position with reference to Western language and culture. In the Sixties, the black activist/artist found himself engaged in a cultural revolution whose goal was the reclamation of authentic black cultures and the development of new aesthetic styles and values.

For many of the poets, this meant that so-called Western values had to be discarded. They declared that at the center of the Western cultural ethos there was a paralysis of the spirit, an atmosphere of decay and malaise which they loathed to embrace.

Perhaps, in this sense, they had really become Western men, the new Rousseaus and Rimbauds in search of Eden. And perhaps, too, they were Western men in that they had fixed their place in history—a possibility that both fascinated and angered them.

And what of history? Had not the West, some of them reasoned, literally invented History and then sallied forth to wield this invention like a weapon before the dispossessed of the Earth? This kind of questioning almost invariably forces a shift in perspective, a sense of having arrived at a disjuncture in the adventure. The West is seen as an arhythmical place preoccupied with death. (Recall Ling, Malraux's Chinese visitor to Europe in *The Temptation of the West*, remarking: "You have weighted the universe with anguish.") Wouldn't a fall outside of "history" really be, in fact, a fall outside of the Western idea of order? Isn't that what Tod Clifton in *Invisible Man* finally realizes? Ling or Clifton could symbolize any of the young displaced Negritude poets in Paris during the Thirties: Césaire, Senghor, Damas. The adventurer has suddenly become the stranded alien in a strange land.

We have entered a highly charged zone here. Now the poet finds himself foraging among the ruins of his diasporic past. He feels trapped by European culture. He even doubts whether the language in which he expresses his dilemma can ever, finally, sustain the force of his vision. And the very act of doubting takes on the quality of a lucid irrationality. For he may write elaborate treatises in impeccable French or English, denouncing the language of his oppressors, while he asserts the necessity for a new poetic symbology. He is both native and alien. He may be the displaced Jamaican poet in London or the Martiniquean writer in Paris. He may be the Afro-American poet situated in the United States where he experiences a sense of what scholar Mae Henderson calls "interior exile." The poet is both urban and urbane now. He quotes Pound, but he finally fears—the way only a poet fears—that he will lose the ability to sing the old songs and do the old dances. He dreads, in short, what T. S. Eliot called "the dissociation of sensibility."

This is the emotional atmosphere in which the search for the Holy Grail of "Blackness" ensues—"spirit," rhythm, and song pitted against "logic" and technology. Hipness pitted against corniness. The idiom of Charlie Parker poised against that of Glenn Miller. The suppleness and the inventiveness of black popular dance contrasted with the stiffness that seems to abound in the white community. The poet seeks Blackness/Negritude, the *élan vital,* the primeval and archetypal energy that seems manifest in what Janheinz Jahn called the "neo-African" cultures of the Western hemisphere. There is clearly a Herderian construct operating at the base of the black aesthetic ideology, but that finally is not important. Consider instead the idea of Blackness as a mythic construct with a nearly discrete cosmology, like the structures of Bantu or Dogon philosophy, or the phenomenology of the blues—a discrete cosmology with its own style, laws, and correspondences. Ishmael Reed's hoodoo novel *Mumbo Jumbo* comes to mind readily. There is nothing impenetrable about it, just as there is nothing truly impenetrable about a work like *Finnegans Wake* once we grasp its overall system and structure.

Much of Baraka's later work strives for a non-Western symbology and mythos. Like Ishmael Reed and Henry Dumas, he evokes the orishas and loas of the Yoruba and Haitian pantheons. He also tries to modulate the pull of Western culture by undertaking the study of Sanskrit, Arabic, Swahili, Amharic. He consciously attempts to create a mythology out of the symbols of a pre-Christian, non-European past—a past dominated by what the poet feels to be a more liberating and vibrant sensibility. So our adventurer in the Western realms of gold forays Southward toward the Sun and the place of rhythm:

> We are beautiful people
> with african imaginations
> full of masks and dances and swelling chants
> with african eyes, and noses, and arms,
> though we sprawl in grey chains in a place
> full of winters, when what we want is sun.
>
> [Imamu Baraka, from "Ka 'Ba"]

And here, in what Baraka calls the "black labs of the heart," the poet attempts the ritual enactment of his priestly role as artificer and oracle for his community (nation). He has come a long way to get home and still can't be sure whether he has found a real haven or just another kind of illusion. This is the conundrum, the tragic situation that confronts the diasporic artist as he attempts to liberate himself psychically from what he feels to be the death-oriented ethos of the West.

It is in this context that black music occupies a central place in black aesthetic ideology and vocabulary. For the music has never had to explain itself; it simply exists in all of its glory. In the churches, the fields, the juke joints, the chain gangs, and in the Mintons' and Savoys, the music had even developed its own craft procedures and critique. It forged a character all its own, and it apologized to no one. A famous musician involved in the so-called bebop movement at Minton's once remarked: "We wasn't giving lectures, we was making music."

It took a long time for black writers to develop a critical perspective on Afro-American music. After the pioneering efforts of Alain Locke, Sterling Brown, and John Work there was a hiatus in which very little critical work was done on Afro-American music by blacks themselves. So until Ellison's seminal essays in *Shadow and Act*, Baraka's *Blues People*, and A. B. Spellman's *Four Lives in the Bebop Business*, Afro-American musical criticism was generally left to perceptive white men like Marshall Stearns, André Hodeir, Nat Hentoff, Henry Pleasants, and Ross Russell. But the movement toward cultural awareness forced black writers to assume more responsibility for a critique of the music and its social implications. It forced them to listen to the music of the people in a new fashion. Ellison led the way with his essay in *Antioch Review* on the blues idiom in Richard Wright; and in a more polemical tone, Baraka's essay "Black Music, White Critic" confronted the question of white dominance in Afro-American musical criticism. Ultimately, writers as diverse as James Baldwin and Albert Murray became united in the idea that the music and the dance that accompanied it were the ultimate expressions of the African presence in America.

In his own manner, Kimberly Benston covers most of what I

have sketched here. *Baraka: The Renegade and the Mask* sets a very high standard for literary scholarship in this field. Watching Mr. Benston build this study has been a significant educational experience for me. I have learned a great deal, not only about Baraka, but about human will.

Larry Neal

Williamstown, Massachusetts
April 7, 1976

Preface

Imamu Amiri Baraka is one of the foremost American artists of our century. Better known to the general public as LeRoi Jones, he is also more often thought of as a "black militant" than as a creative writer. Unfortunately, the tendency to view him primarily as a politician and only incidentally as an artist also prevails among literary critics. The overwhelming majority of scholarly articles concerning Baraka's creations elucidate little or nothing of the aesthetic dimension of his work. Many of his critics might object that they are not interested in such standards and might cite Baraka's own statements rejecting "art for art's sake." Yet such a position confuses aesthetic investigation with aestheticism and actually verges on disrespect for the artist.

By substituting polemic and dogma for critical "negative capability," scholars have tended to ignore the subtle processes by which Baraka has given form to his perception of the Afro-American experience. Consequently, a need exists for a definition of Baraka's vision more exact than any provided to date. No single critical discussion of an author as accomplished and complex as Baraka can touch upon every aspect of his efforts. Yet, in light of his eminent position within the Afro-American literary tradition, some comprehensive and careful investigation of his work seems appropriate. The goal of this study, therefore, is to treat Baraka as the serious artist he is; to develop a meaningful conception of his vision and its evolution; and to examine his attempts to embody a canon of values and beliefs in formally effective fictions.

Baraka's career has shown the work of an artist self-consciously shaping his material, changing the forms available to him, and ultimately fashioning new ones. His early autobiographical novel, *The System of Dante's Hell*, provides insight into the genesis of this artistic quest. In the beginning of *The System of Dante's Hell* there is a most striking image:

> You've done everything you
> despised. Flowers fall off trees, wind
> under low branches shoves them into
> quick chill of the river, the high
> leaves disappear over stone fences.

The use of falling leaves as a metaphor for human destiny is certainly a literary cliché, yet Baraka's lines are exquisitely appropriate to his condition: the young black man faced with an awesome choice. Burdened with the guilt of past failures, the speaker implicitly asks himself whether he will be passive and hence ruined by the swirling forces around him, or will assert a claim to his fate and enter a realm beyond lethal confines. The image is suggestively ambiguous, inviting speculation as to how the leaf attains the right position from which to fall.

This process of self-determination, for the black man, is made gradually more profound, more exact and meaningful, by the attempt to discover individual fate in communal action. Baraka's works investigate the relationship between personal and collective conduct. They seek to integrate the one and the many into subtle and touching harmony. We shall find that the active journey from lonely individuation to fulfilling communality is the fundamental progress of Baraka's work: the salvation of his own soul and that of his people are inextricable.

Before attempting to re-create this journey critically, I would like to comment on one particular aspect of Baraka's transformation. This is his change of name from LeRoi Jones to Imamu Amiri Baraka. There are three essential aspects of this metamorphosis, each of which is indicated by one of the three new names. First, there is the self-determining creation of identity, an accomplishment of the vatic *Imamu*, or Mohammedan poet/priest. Second, there is a transcending of the slave past symbolized by the "slave-name" Jones, the revolt of an *Amiri*, or warrior/leader. And last is the religious conversion from Western Christian to non-Western Muslim, the gift of the *Baraka*, or blessing. These are, at least, the visible features of Baraka's name change. They are the main elements of Baraka's biography relevant to a study of his art,* particularly to one focused upon the least personal form, the drama. Yet given the intensity of his visionary quest, we cannot help but ask, with Baraka himself, the unanswerable question: what face lies between the songful renegade and the artful mask?

> Tough I am a man
> who is loud
> on the birth
> of his ways. Publicly redefining
> each change in my soul, as if I had predicted
> them,
> and profited, biblically, even tho
> their chanting weight,
> erased familiarity
> from my face.
> A question I think,
> an answer; whatever sits
> counting the minutes
> till you die.
>
> When they say, "It is Roi
> who is dead?" I wonder
> who will they mean?
>
> [from "The Liar," in *The Deay Lecturer*]

Acknowledgments

The debts incurred in writing this study are many. The Schomburg Center for Research in Black Studies helped me to procure Baraka's more obscure works, as did also Mr. Larry Neal. The officers of the Yale College Dean's Office (particularly Dean Marnesba Hill) kindly provided monetary aid that enabled me to travel to Detroit in Nobember 1973 to see Concept East's fine

* An excellent reference for biographical material on Baraka is Theodore R. Hudson's *From LeRoi Jones to Amiri Baraka.*

production of *Slave Ship.* I also received moral support from Charles T. Davis and Michael O'Loughlin of Yale University and Cynthia Smith of Wesleyan College, who expressed continuing interest in my efforts. In addition, Stephen Henderson of Howard University, and Ellen Graham and Barbara Folsom, both of the Yale University Press, made many helpful suggestions for improvement of the manuscript in its final stages.

I owe a great debt of gratitude to three people in particular. First, Larry Neal has been an inspiration to me in many ways. As a teacher, he has offered insights that have deepened my appreciation of Afro-American art and, particularly, of Imamu Baraka's work. And as an artist he has been an exemplar of the continuing strength of Afro-American culture.

Second, my mother, Alice Benston, has been an invaluable critic and mentor since the inception of this project. She has passed on to me a love of drama and taught me nearly all I know about the theatre. Countless hours of discussion with her have been instrumental in clarifying my thoughts about Baraka. Her confidence in me has been a profound compliment; her example of intellectual integrity, with that of my father, has been my basic guide.

Finally, my wife, Susan, has encouraged and aided me through the toughest and most enjoyable moments of writing this book. Her contributions to my efforts—from particular suggestions to constant warm companionship and affection—have been immeasurable.

Note on the Text

There are many unorthodox spellings, contractions, word-usages, and typographical arrangements in Baraka's work, especially in his poetry. While no claim of perfection can be made, the reader should rest assured that every quotation of Baraka in the text has been assiduously checked and rechecked. Because of Baraka's frequent use of ellipses in his writing, the form "[. . .]" has been adopted where omissions have been made from the quoted text, and the form ". . ." has been maintained where Baraka uses it himself.

I have employed one other typographical convention that may need brief explanation. Single quotation marks have been used to denote paraphrase, cliché, and popular proverb, as distinguished from direct quotation (for which the standard double quotation marks are used).

One final note. The question of what to call Baraka at each stage of my discussion has perplexed me for some time. Finally, it seemed to me that, although certain works were written by LeRoi Jones and others by Imamu Amiri Baraka, the alternation between these two appellations throughout the book would be at best tedious and probably somewhat confusing. Therefore, I have chosen to call Baraka "LeRoi Jones" only in chapter 1, which recounts his spiritual conversion from Jones to Imamu Amiri Baraka. Once this tale is told, Jones becomes Baraka for the remainder of the book.

Part 1

Backgrounds to the Drama: The System of Baraka's Cosmos

1 Baraka's Choice of Cultures: From Hell to Home

Imamu Amiri Baraka (LeRoi Jones) is an impressive and fascinating literary figure. Impressive, because of the range, volume, and often stunning quality of his writings. Fascinating, because he embodies all the essential impulses of both modern (post-Romantic) and contemporary black art. His work is a brilliant manifestation of both the despair of the modern West and the raw exultation of emerging civilizations. Because it has stood at the cusp, or crossroad, of these two disparate cultures, Baraka's art affords a unique opportunity to glimpse the intricate relationship—the cross-fertilizations and irremediable conflicts—between them.

Euro-American and Afro-American societies have a common problem: alienation. Modern man's goal is to *come home,* to be at home in the world. The growth of nationalism in the past century-and-a-half attests to a broad concern with this collective, archetypical desire for wholeness and security. On the other hand, the concurrent intensity of self-scrutiny indicates that the organic unity of individual and community has been lost. Baraka's career encompasses both these aspects of modern experience.

The reference point of this study is Baraka's drama, the most public and widely known form of his work. Yet no part of his corpus exists in isolation from the others: his criticism, theoretical essays, poetry, prose, and plays are interconnected facets of a basic temperament. The aim of this chapter is to explore the general influences upon Baraka's sensibility—and his sensibility itself should emerge gradually as his ideas and art forms are studied in the following chapters.

Baraka is well versed in the European, American, and Afro-American literary traditions. He borrows freely from authors as different as Hegel, Eliot, Hughes, Toomer, O'Neill, Genêt, and

Karenga, often placing diverse influences side by side. These specific references will be noted where appropriate in our investigations of particular works. The end product of each piece, however, is always unmistakably Baraka's own, organized around a central perception or purpose which inevitably transcends all other considerations.

What is of concern here is Baraka's movement from the avant-garde of the white, Euro-American tradition to the vanguard of black revolutionary art. The following analysis traces the pattern of conversion which Baraka's evolution manifests: first, a somewhat telescoped view of modern poetry's spiritual plight is given, indicating the tradition in which Baraka's career began and from which he sought redemption; next, Baraka's autobiographical novel, *The System of Dante's Hell*, which presents in literary terms the need and the way of salvation, is explicated (page references will be to the Grove Press edition); and the last section examines the Afro-American tradition in which salvation may finally be attained.

I

The alienation of man has its roots in the homelessness of man.

—Martin Heidegger

"Who am I?" asks Stendhal's Lucien Leuwen. "The truth is, I don't know what I am and I would give a lot if anyone would enlighten me." A common enough inquiry, to be sure. Yet in the modern world the search for identity takes on a new urgency and becomes the poet's primary theme. "What is the truth for me?" wonders Kierkegaard: the words are full of ethical purpose, but the concern behind them is self-regarding, the accent of wonder invariably falling upon the isolate "me" rather than upon the "truth" which that self supposedly seeks. The modern poet, like Kierkegaard, journeys to the interior but seldom returns. He assumes (as did Kierkegaard) that even if that "truth" were discovered it would be too private to be communicated to common men. Modern poets are, to paraphrase Stendhal, unhappy men at war with the whole of society and with themselves. They are "étrangers" to all accepted attitudes and, accordingly, alien in their own lands. They are homeless.

An impressive variety of modern writers begin with the feeling, or fear, of being (as Kafka put it) "a stranger, a man who isn't wanted and is in everybody's way." Exile is, so to speak, their common state; they abandon Dublin for Paris, Boston for London, Iowa for Rome, and even Newark for Greenwich Village, as a reproach to others and as a justification to themselves. These physical pilgrimages are indicative of the real obsession, the search for self. The modern writer seeks a nebulous inner 'freedom,' which is also exile, by will and by compulsion. Modern literature is thus, above all, a 'quest' literature, but the movement of the poet's journey is not outward and intellectual (as with Odysseus) or upward and spiritual (as with Dante); rather, it is inward and demonic. It is a descent into the darkness of modern lostness: like Joyce's chaotic, whirling Tumolt, the modern poet's descent is that of the "self exiled in upon his ego." The self-exiled poet must encounter all the dragons of his inner life—alienation, abandonment, isolation, and despair. And, having entered with Childe Roland "the ominous tract which, all agree, hides the Dark Tower," he rarely finds that fixed core of Being, that identity for which he risked all. "The Pilgrim Way," as Auden said, "has led to the Abyss."

Redemption was occasionally possible in early examples of this inner search: Kierkegaard, at least, posits a leap of faith out of the paradox of "inwardness" and its attendant awareness of smallness and human frailty; Rilke's Orphic meditations created the poetic field necessary for self-renewal and even *Wandlung* (self-transformation);[1] Stephen Dedalus returns "home" to his peculiar version of the eternal feminine. And in the years between the two world wars, the artist's public engagement and utility were major themes of Mann, Spender, Shaw, and others affected by the Depression, rising nationalism, the spread of socialist thinking, and other political and historical pressures.

But after World War II the quest to the self's interior was again energetically undertaken. Only now, after the massive horrors of the war, the failure of the liberal ideology of Progress, and the nearly complete divestiture of received systems, beliefs, and language, the contemporary poet is thrown into a spiritual void. The descent for him is more terrible than before, in that he has neither the myth-structure of Orpheus to support a self-regenerating ascent (as did Mallarmé and Rilke), nor the dogmatic, religious cornices from which to look beyond the bolgia (as did Eliot and Yeats). His is now the raw, unaccommodated descent of the ego into itself. And so the artist withdraws, like Dostoevsky's underground man of sensibility, the "very sensitive mouse" who in its dirty, stinking underworld immerses itself in a state of cold, malignant, perpetual rancor. The sense of loss, the inner rage at the paucity of what has been left to the living, creates the defense mechanisms of absurd humor and irony. This is particularly the case with the new drama (commonly known as the "Theatre of the Absurd"), in which meaning is relocated from traditional metaphysical categories toward a complex of emotions such as dread, guilt, and confusion. Conventional formulations give way to nameless and vague "currents within the spirit" [2] as the means for articulating these feelings. In the midst of this "universal Angst" (Lowell), life holds no continuity; no values are fixed and final. The ego's inner sanctum, once a haven for the Romantic Imagination, opens to an "Abyss" of solitariness.

The path taken toward this contemporary solitude is slightly different for the American writer. Individualism is nothing new, of course, in American life and art. One remembers Thoreau's civil disobedience, Emerson's stress on self-reliance, and especially Walt Whitman's ecstatic celebrations of what the self sees and becomes as it traverses the cycles of birth, death, and resurrection. Yet for all these exponents of traditional individualism the discovery of one's identity was also a discovery of fellow creatures, their songs of self a mode of asserting the collective dream. The American poet once traveled the "open road," anticipating an unencumbered new life as he explored the potentialities of virgin territory. His visionary song was future-oriented and optimistic, with its forward-moving, glad discovery of distances and the amplitude of a new time. But now the American road leads the poet, not to an edenic home of imaginative transcendence and communal reverie, but to the inner spaces of lonely self-examination:

> For all these wan roads
> I am pushed to follow, are
> my own conceit. A simple muttering
> elegance, slipped in my head
> pressed on my soul, is my heart's
> worth.
>
> [LeRoi Jones, from "I Substitute for the Dead Lecturer"]

It is clear that the new American poets are wary of commitment to any sort of 'otherness.' By and large they are disengaged. They have moved from the liberal sentiments and political optimism of the prewar years to a recognition of the ambiguities and the possibly irremediable nature of man's moral condition. They deny that man, in the ideal center of his mind, is a prelapsarian innocent who is coerced into evil by circumstances and institutions that can be changed by collective action. Allen Ginsberg's *Howl* sets the tone of their concern, with its keen sense of satire and pathos, of the conflict between man's ideals and his actions, between his creative life and imminent death, between his being and the encroachment of the material nonlife around him. This awareness disposes the poet to meditation, lament, and the despairing feeling that "a silence of motives / empties the day of meaning" (LeRoi Jones, "Footnote to a Pretentious Book"), not to action.

The contemporary poet's relentless retreat into the self leads him to several insoluble contradictions, or existential antinomies, which turn upon a moral duplicity involving the feelings of both guilt and victimization. He is a *tragic* figure—despite the lengthy arguments denying the possibility of such a creature in the modern world (for example, those of Joseph Wood Krutch, in *The Modern Temper*, and George Steiner, in *The Death of Tragedy*). His tragic pattern is not precisely that of the heroic individual set against external forces; rather, his agon is the private struggle of the self against itself. Guilt has become internal and personal, and in his self-enclosed and isolated world he is his own victim. There is often the desire to reform, to raze the 'sick' world and make a new one 'whole,' to find liberation in communal change.

Yet in a world where friendship is a delusion and love always disintegrates before one's eyes, where one cannot forget oneself even for a minute, where confidences have dubious motives, there can be no communion. Change can only occur by an individual act *against* society, and so ultimately against other people. Where the poet speaks for human desire as a general ideal he knows only of personal fulfillment. Desire had included the joy of life with others, the life of friendship, community, and love; but fulfillment is redefined as a getting away from others. Conflict then indeed becomes internal, desire pitted against and betraying desire. This agony is that of unsatisfied desire for a wholeness that never loses its appeal and mystery (whether God be dead or not), a desire for mystery in which the human being can feel enclosed. Instead, the human being is enclosed in himself, surrounded by his desire to break out and be embraced by something or someone which he cannot map or control, and yet which recognizes him. "Though I never cease to desire, I never hope," wrote Proust, and so might the poet of the young LeRoi Jones's generation.

What happens to this desiring self without hope? Blake asserted that "he who desires but acts not breeds a pestilence," and he seems proven right by the contemporary poet whose tortured psyche is wrapt in a sickness unto death. The sense of being utterly alone, of being unraveled, impotent, and alien, leads in time to a despair beyond initial agony. The world appears illusory and fictitious and individual behavior is perceived as equally 'absurd.' And past the comic pain of absurdity lies a more terrible emptiness. The self, left alone long enough, exercises its "muttering elegance" only as a last, desperate entertainment to consciousness: "sometimes I feel I have to express myself [. . .] to ease the horrible boredom" (LeRoi Jones, "Vice").

Some men are bored because they have no vision of life beyond what passes them; others have a vision of something beyond or beneath the appearances but have grown tired of waiting for the Godot that never reveals itself. This lassitude is akin to despair, and if it is not acutally an agony, it is only because even agony usually becomes weary and listless. The ensuing passivity is the last and most horrible stage of the descent within—an abandonment to an indifference and immobility which court the voiding Muse of silence:

> Emotion. Words.
> Waste. No clear delight.
> No light under my fingers. The room, The
> walls silent & deadly. Not
> music.
> [LeRoi Jones, from "The Death of Nick Charles"]

> And silence
> which proves / but
> a referent
> to my disorder.
> [LeRoi Jones, from "The End of Man Is His Beauty"]

The individual is so isolated in a permanently meaningless world that even connections within the personality break down, and the mind is released into a state of silence and terror. In the total condition of reality's deceptions and illusions, only death and anguish seem certain: "they give birth astride of a grave, the light gleams an instant, and it's night once more" (*Waiting For Godot*). In the face of such a 'reality' the once hopeful journey inward arrives not at the inspiring dream of human liberation but at the nightmare of an ineradicable destructive instinct, and ultimately at the death-wish:

> Stand there
> counting deaths. My own, is what I wanted
> you to say, Roi, you will die soon.
> [LeRoi Jones, from "This Is the Clearing I Once Spoke Of"]

For the contemporary writer, the moral incommensurability of the self and the life offered to it by the world has become an article of faith. Even when the idea of reviving the self and moving past nihilism is attractive (as it was for Camus, for example), the opposition between hope and reality flings him back into the void. This opposition is expounded with dialectical and aesthetic skill, but its outcome returns upon the artist's moral isolation. "There is a goal, but no way," as Kafka said; "what we call way is only wavering." Nevertheless, in the experience of LeRoi Jones the self-negating feeling of isolation brought him sharply upon the dialectical junctures of his own moral and existential duplicities where decision *must* be reached. Was the inferno of this tradition and the poet's fate of self-immolation his destiny? Or was there a hidden way, a forgotten road leading up, out of the self entirely, toward some promised but neglected homeland? The awesome question could only be confronted in the dark of the Abyss, in the literal Bottom of young LeRoi's hell.

II

YOU LOVE THESE DEMONS AND WILL NOT ABANDON THEM

—*The System of Dante's Hell*, p. 59

The words blast fear into the soul of LeRoi Jones—the fear of utter and irredeemable failure. The message strikes with a terror resembling that of its prototype, the inscription on the Hell-Gate of Dante's *Inferno*: "Abandon all hope, ye who enter here." The nascent poet, like the damned of the *Inferno*, is faced with the nature and significance of Hell, of sin in its horrible fulfillment.[3] The way of damnation cannot be missed by him who travels it. It is the acceptance of "these demons" and the refusal of all that is salvation. It is the ultimate estrangement from wisdom, passion, love, blackness—all those general and local attributes that would make his self whole.

Yet Jones is not fully damned; the frightening sentence is not a final proclamation but a taunt at the hero's *will*, a kind of warning. The drama of his torment, like the crisis of Dante lost in the dark wood, is Pauline: "I see the good, but do not do it." The fear that afflicts him is that of the lost, not the damned. His "way" is not necessarily toward one fixed, timeless bolgia. It is, in fact, the way of the Prodigal, and his narrative thus implicitly includes the dual possibilities of alienation and return: "Go away & try to come back. Try to return here. Or wherever is softest, most beautiful. Go away, panderer. Liar. But come back, to it." (p. 37).

The twin impulses of deceitful escape from and hopeful return to the true roots of identity stem from a "split down the center [. . .] of the black man unfocused on blackness" (p. 153) and lend the narrative a curious double focus. Indeed, *The System of Dante's Hell*'s whole autobiographical attempt is built upon the fundamental paradox of death and resurrection that enables each scene to be viewed and judged from the author's complete perspective. It is the paradox of an organic unity between observer and observed which, for the experiential time of the story (as opposed to the later, peaceful time of retrospective vision) is yet "the *torture* of being the unseen object, and, the constantly observed subject" (p. 153—my emphasis). In LeRoi's hell, life looks like death and death like life. Near the novel's beginning he asks for any gesture to prove his existence: "All I want is to move" (p. 19). Yet when he is first able to posit a series of definite (albeit petty) actions, the assertion is ironically negated by the acknowledgment that lifeless agents inspire him: "I am myself after all. The dead are what move me. The various dead" (p. 59).

Technically, Jones elaborates the formal equivalent of this double focus: a series of multiple inner reflections to reinforce the larger patterns of affirmation-negation, outside-inside, despair-hope, death-resurrection. Thus, for example, when near the climax of his purest sexual experience, an initiation into love with a southern black whore, he momentarily thinks of his confrontation with homosexuality in Chicago, and the two attempts at "flesh to flesh" communion fuse imaginatively at the crucial moment: "To be pushed under a quilt, and call it love. [. . .] A real thing in the world. See my shadow. My reflection. I'm here alive. Touch me. Please. Please, touch me" (pp. 138–39). Awareness of fundamental antithesis also manifests itself through antithetical images—the bright sun rising into blackness, the word *tenderness* used only to describe a vicious rape ("Circle 9: Bolgia 1"), the childhood friend from the flaming ghetto "hole" parenthetically named "beautiful praxiteles" (p. 76). Throughout the novel (as in many other works), Jones is a master of dramatic and grandiose images that create an effect of enlargement and tenseness.

The tension and dualities peculiar to the hero in the early stages of the novel seem to depend upon two principles. First, he is incapable of true contrition for his transgressions. He is clearly capable of some regret in varying degrees for a variety of physical and mental sins, but he cannot divorce himself from the sum of his sinfulness by a profound and total act of recommitment. In some degree he still wills and loves his sins (which we shall soon delineate). But tangent to that continuing passion is the second principle of his condition, namely, that he is incapable of doubting the propriety of his punishment and of his agony. A continual wash of guilt suffuses the descriptions of his early years; he accepts the harshness of his experience, even as he clings to the habits that bring him pain.

Condemnation to this hell confers upon him a form of self-knowledge that leads to self-loathing since it is helpless to alter his moral being. Not only the anguish but also the pattern of evil within himself seems inescapable. He must exist between the clashes of pride and ineffectual remorse, desire for goodness and knowledge of debasement, complacency and disgust ("I am myself. Insert the word disgust. A verb"—p. 15). Repetition, knotted syntax, labored intricacies, and complex introversion make the language a perfect indication or mimesis of this general estrangement of the self from the self, the self lost from its home:

> The way this is going. Who? Go back. Turn. The door will swing open into sun. Into Autumn. Into the cold. Into loud arguments at night with the door open. Small children die. I kill everything . . . I can. This is This. I am left only with my small words . . . against the day. Against you. Against. My self. [p. 45]

Who are the "Demons" who set LeRoi Jones against himself and keep him from his needed con-version, his *turning* back to the complexities of roots ("into sun . . . into the cold")? On a simplistic level, they are the cavalcade of white, Western poets and thinkers to whom the young poet was irresistibly drawn, the "various dead" who "move" him: "I said my name was Stephen Dedalus. And I read Proust and mathematics and loved Eliot for his tears. Towers, like Yeats [. . .] The Isle of the Dead" (p. 58; elsewhere, Pound, Cummings, Williams, and finally, Dante—

"Dante, me," p. 126—are also listed in this anatomy of "the Dead"). What afflicts him particularly, or actively, is the 'curse' of this "demon" tradition's own dichotomy: the intellect dreaming its dream of absolute freedom, and the soul knowing its terrible bondage.

The mind—seemingly self-sufficient, intelligent, skeptical, ironical, splendidly trained for the great game of pretending that the world it can describe in sterile sobriety is the only and ultimate reality—is yet incapable of understanding the inner reality of the soul or the expressive totality of one's identity. The spiritual evolution the poet seeks must be accomplished in the interior of the *complete* individual, not in the interior of the intelligence alone. A constant theme of *The System of Dante's Hell* is that the mind, when severed from emotional and physical passion, is in fact inimical to the complete fulfillment of man. Neither syllogistic thoughts nor deep analytical solutions exist when switch-blades flash or when the "loud arguments" of black people's underground night life speak their language and their truths.

Thus, having satiated himself with the texts of an alien tradition, the hero finds that "I am left only with my small words." He feels at every moment the pathos of language's "elegant" attraction and frustrating insufficiency. There is constantly the unwillingness to release his mind from the physical contact of words, which are conceived not only as the means but also very strongly as the materials of expression. Rhythm and sound provide a sense of the body, and the novel is full of pride and despair at the sensuous character of his vision ("Your world / has sunk in space, immersed in romance, like whatever in / my head / fastens dreams upon my speech"—p. 55).

Although words, and the perceptions expressed through words, are sensuous, the employment of language is found to be incapable of acting upon the thing perceived. When he was a child, "bigboys" on his block would let him share their street-corner jiving because his mind was quick and his words sharp. He would "win dozens constantly"; but the nuances of his art were unrecognized and therefore unvalued and useless:

> The surface appreciated, and I, sometimes frustrated because the whole idea didn't get in . . . only the profanity. [p. 78]

The analogy of this early annoyance to the greater frustrations of his maturing intellect is more than implicit. The Euro-American tradition is hellish not so much because it values mind over soul (though Jones often feels it does) but because it is completely foreign to the life of these streets and it has led him away from them into the tortured privacy of his own mind. Throughout the novel it is the streets and their dark inhabitants who "flow" and "move," not the poet; he observes them and their secrets but finds organized perception powerless against his own paralysis. The knowledge gained from the demon influences (his poetic 'masters' in both a traditional and a sinister sense) offers him only a morality of cowardice. Protected from the ghetto's 'seething cauldron,' he cowers in the shelter of "our language scared at the shadows of our crimes" (p. 70).

The solitary mind, at play with itself as it fastens phantoms to words and fashions immoral shields with language, is decadent above all in its lack of passion, its refusal to act. Ineffective, incapable of moving past his sorrow, the solipsistic hero becomes bitter and sullen, withdrawing into a self-observing stupor while the ghetto is enflaming others: "He sat and was sad at his sitting. The day grew around him like a beast" (p. 20). If the pure mind has pejorative connotations to Jones, it is precisely because of this separatist tendency, this unwillingness to be "in the world." Not only in *The System of Dante's Hell*, but throughout his writings the urge for action gives Jones's ideas the peculiar quality of being not simply ideas, but outlines of *gestures* calling for a succession of external movements. It is what makes his vision demand so imperiously to be acted out, to be made into a physical object belonging to the real world.

As early as *The System of Dante's Hell*, we find Jones rejecting any proposition that cannot be directly translated into a force, an act, or a series of acts; hence, as a matter of principle, he gives preference to the possibility of a dramatic and emphatic gesture over the elusiveness of implied meaning. For mere, as it were "unfleshed," ideas serve to evade if not betray decisions. Thus it is proper and not surprising that the theme of prostituting one's soul for the spoils of the Western intellectual and artistic traditions should be enacted literally as drama in *The System of Dante's Hell.* The eighth ditch—the bolgia of the fraudulent counselors—"is drama" (pp. 79–91).

Here, in a "tent among tents," a "smooth-faced" black youth, called 46, is confronted by his "foil," 64. Of 46, 64 says: "Your earth is round & sits outside the world. You have millions of words to read." Despite his accumulated "knowledge," 46 is "puzzled" by 64's definitions and asks him, "Who are you really?" "The Street!" 64 proclaims, not without dignity. "Things around you . . . I am a maelstrom of definitions." As 64 unbuttons his shirt and rises to approach 46's bunk, the befuddled youngster sits, "suckling my thots," enquiring further of 64 how he might do something significant: "What is it I shd talk about now? What shd I be thinking up?" 64 ignores the plea for mental stimulation; his mood is that of some dark certainty, not malaise. He tells 46 accusatorially, "I understand your gestures," but 46 can respond only by admitting his aversion to those streets which 64 embodies. As 46 lies inert on his bunk, playing a game of cultural dozens with his older rival, 64 advances toward him. Soon 64 is sprawled on top of 46, the latter methodically "reading a book" in placid ignorance of 64's motives. When 64 begins to assault 46 sexually, the youth is momentarily startled: "What? What're you trying to do?" But immediately this rape becomes seduction, as 64 offers his "victim" a very special kind of recompense:

> *64:* I Got. Abstract Expressionism blues. Existentialism blues. I Got. [. . .] Yeah, the po-E-try blues. And then there's little things like "The Modern Jazz Blues." [. . .] Talkin bout blues. There's a bunch. [. . .] Blues, comeon, like yr beautiful self.

Soon 46 "begins to move with the other" selling what he least values (body) for shards of the mental artifacts he prizes.[4] "What does that make you think?" taunts 64 when they finish. 46 actually reflects very little, however; soon, he is openly 'struttin his stuff' for more of 64's peculiar compensation:

> *46:* What other blues do you have, Herman? How many others?

64: (*Screaming with laughter*) Oh, yes, yes, yes. I got all kinds, baby. Yes, indeed, as you will soon see. All kinds. Ooooh, thass elegant. [. . .]

46: But what kinds, Herman. What kinds?

64: Oooh, baby, just keep throwin it up like that. Just keep throwin it up.

The final image of this drama of false counsel is of a mad rush for 46's corporeal, substantive "elegance" by a throng of hip men. These, like 64 (Herman), are named—only 46 remains nameless, without identity. Just as he allowed Herman to define them both, so he remains a hollow, questioning voice, trading the body he ignores for the "blues" of a foreign heritage. Incapable of action, 46 suffers the indignity of having his "gestures" chosen for him. He is not merely the "unseen" but the totally *acted upon* "object."

The drama of Jones's eighth ditch, following the guiding principle of Dante's *Inferno*, inflicts punishment upon 46 that is the same as his sin, a punishment that is in fact a perpetuation of the sin. The schism between body and mind is a violence to both, and 46 embodies the rigidity of a personality condemned to repeat endlessly the gestures of perverse desires. 46 achieves not self-awareness but self-estrangement; every step he takes toward consciousness is paid for with a step toward debasing solitude, so that the fullness of the "knowledge" he seeks corresponds only to the emptiness of isolation. European civilization is depicted in the eighth ditch as a self-contemplating madness, the intellect as a ridiculous if not evil ornament—the mind turning in a vacuum.

The identification of young Jones with 46 need not be greatly elaborated. Both reach a nadir of moral isolation—they are lost souls: "Violence to my body. To my mind. Closed in. To begin at the limit. Work in to the core. Center. At which there is—nothing" (p. 71). The alienation from black culture is the main reason for the Prodigal's irregular wanderings, his literal *error*—one might say 'his head is out to lunch.' But just as he cannot heed the voices that call for a return to roots, so he cannot endure for long his direct gaze into the abysmal emptiness of his lostness. He recoils from the final plunge into his voided interiority. What prevents his damnation is a belief in the abstract principle of change which generates a continual, although submerged, hope for salvation. The hideous eighth ditch spectacle is yet "a foetus drama," and the piteous 46 is the "foetus." The play's "Narrator" glosses the action with hopeful words: "Everything *must* make sense, must *mean* something some way. Whatever lie we fashion. . . . Some blank gesture towards light." The avowed aesthetic that underlies Jones's writing of *The System of Dante's Hell* reinforces this positive implication of moral process: "I don't recognize myself 10 seconds later. Who writes this will never read it" (p. 59). Indeed, the novel's drama of self-consciousness, a dynamism of rigidity and change, can last only as long as it stays 'open,' as long as hope for a "gesture toward light" remains.

This hope depends upon a psychic flexibility, a disposition to see the wretched self honestly while not ruling out the possibility of peripeteia, of self-renewal. Memory works to keep the painful details of experience alive in the hero's changing consciousness; but also memory is a vehicle of revelation. It periodically recalls to the hero images of the black-owned streets and The Life's pulsating rhythms; it reawakens his deepest need, the hunger for communion: "[I had] an actual longing for men that brooded in each finger of my memory" (p. 125). But with memory alone he can merely love phantoms. An agent of the mind, it turns up crucial items from the past and makes him see, but it cannot move him as if he were in communion. Thanks to hope and memory, he remains "alive to mystery" (p. 124), but he can experience the feeling of mysterious presence only by immersing himself in the "wordless energies" of The Bottom—"where the colored lived" (p. 121).

The last chapter of *The System of Dante's Hell* finds Jones in the circle of The Heretics, "the deepest part of Hell" (p. 7). It is set in the environs of some backwoods Louisiana Air Force (or "error farce," as Jones called it elsewhere) base. The literal story is about a leave from the base spent in the red-light district with an Air Force buddy—a "Virgil" to Jones's "Dante"—who points the way toward the wildest juke joint (p. 126). Although the evening is meant to bring quick, lascivious pleasure to the feckless duo, it leads to a bizarre, shattering, but ultimately redemptive experience for the black poet in khakis.

Heresy, Jones tells us, is a sin "against one's own sources" (p. 7). Thus, just as the descent to The Bottom begins, the existential purpose of his journey (which is morally "higher" than, but literally submerged beneath, the search for lewd fun) is hinted at. He steps off the bus, like a dead soul from Charon's bark, and finds himself suddenly confronted with the culture he had forgotten:

> A culture of violence and foodsmells. There, for me. Again. And it stood strange when I thot finally how much irony. [p. 124]

Worlds of possibility, raw but alive, open before him by the force of involuntary memory. After the foppish "elegance" of college had come the jolt of army life, and now "Everything I learned stacked up and the bones of love shattered in my face.[. . .] The books meant nothing. My idea was to be loved" (p. 124). He feels himself awakening to the "mystery" of the strange black world he had left and never really been a part of; the need for love naturally accompanies intimations of renewal.

Yet love remains for him an "idea," a construct of pure reason. Though not borrowed from someone else's concepts or "books," this "idea" has little to do with moral or even passionate desire. And while he opens himself to the smells and spectacles of the teeming black Bottom, he maintains an emotional distance from its life and responds with fear and arrogant judgment. This world seems to him an utter chaos. He is more sensitive to its dangers than its delights, more afraid of what appears an "abandon of suffering" than happy at its celebrations. He even seems offended by the way "drunk niggers" and "coons" engage unabatedly in their heated activities while in his presence (though *he* is, of course, the intruder): "Each dead nigger stinking his same suffering thru us" (p. 125). He is, above all, alienated from what he calls their "heritage of hysteria and madness," a phrase which indicates just how much white culture—what Jones will later call the "insane asylum of the West" [5]—has turned his head around.

Yet Jones's initial alienation from The Life does not stem from condescension or even simple disgust. He is genuinely moved—to the point of revulsion—by the agony of the black lives he thinks he understands. His assessment is that of the sensitive but painfully ignorant voyeur who judges by foreign, inexperienced, and therefore inapplicable standards. Jones speaks of "their frightening lives" but he is still, at a deeper, more instinctive level of perception, aware that he is "running in terror" (p. 7) from his own horrible life: "Frightened of myself, of the night's talk, and not of them. Of myself" (p. 127). What he will confront in The Bottom, among the mass of black faces, is his own naked, unaccommodated self. By finding them he shall find himself: in this last ditch, the paths of the self-searching poet and the black Prodigal join. In the story of this experience the entire life of the hero is reevaluated: all the idealisms and all the failures.

Following the pattern of Dante's travels from Hell to Paradise, Jones's journey to The Bottom, both physically and thematically, traces the form of a gyre or spiral.[6] After his first descent, he twice starts to leave The Bottom, returns twice, and finally departs a third time, ascending the hill leading to the Air Force base. Between each descent and each attempted escape Jones repeats a specific pattern: (1) some form of self-negation which makes of his psyche a tabula rasa enabling him to (2) raise crucial questions about his life, followed by (3) some positive step toward self-definition. With its motif of recurrence within progress, this spiraling motion is a perfect representation of the directional force of the hero's forward movement. If we follow Jones down (or, more accurately, *up*) this spiral, we shall come to the goal of this fateful *ascesis.*

Once in The Bottom, Jones and his guide find themselves two prostitutes to accompany them to "The Joint." Jones feels completely separate from this "sudden midnight world"; an "imitation white boy" (p. 128), he is startled and paranoid:

> And when I spoke someone wd turn and stare, or laugh, and point me out.[. . .] the whole place had turned a little to look. And the girls ate it all up, laughing as loud as their vanity permitted.[. . .] putting us all down. [p. 128]

He is soon transfixed by the mysterious fury of the dance floor:

> They stunk. They screamed. They moved hard against each other. They pushed. And wiggled to keep the music on. . . . All that screaming came together with the smells and the music, the people bumped their asses and squeezed their eyes shut. [p. 129]

Here is the black man's threshing floor, where the wheat and the chaff, the spit and the grit, of The Life are separated, where the agony and the joy of daily existence is exorcised and celebrated, where apparent absurdity is distilled by collective expression into a throbbing black essence. Jones, awed and frightened, is led onto the floor by his whore, Peaches:

> The dancing like a rite no one knew, or had use for outside their secret lives. The flesh they felt when they moved, or I felt all their flesh and was happy and drunk and looked at the black faces knowing all the world thot they were my own [. . .] I danced. And my history was there, had passed no further. Where it all ended, here, the light white talking jig, died in the arms of some sentry of Africa. [. . .] I was nobody now, mama. Nobody. Another secret nigger. No one the white world wanted or would look at. [pp. 129–30]

This exquisite passage is the novel's most precise expression of the knowledge gained by the suffering and struggling Prodigal. Jones has entered the hidden, mystical, and magical territory of black life, experiencing its sacred rituals of celebration, the "rite" of the 'blood.' Here is the physical, emotional, 'down-front' dynamism of black life: an ecstasy of "wordless energies." It is an image far removed from the respectable, "civilized" constructs of the white culture Jones feels he has emulated, for this uninhibited dancing is a crucible of violence, impulse, and visceral gestures of passion. Here is the style of what Jones later called the "freedman" segment of the Afro-American population, the bad-mouthing, signifying, preening, black-as-the-tar-bucket 'bad niggers' (see chapter 3 below for a discussion of this concept). Here the "white *talking* jig" gives way to the purely expressive and functional ceremony of the black dance; the latter's straight-ahead, direct insistence upon commitment to life negates any need for abstract reflection upon it. And in the dance, black people do not merely celebrate black life—they *are* black life.

The passionate intensity of this musical rite is epitomized in the "screams," the gutteral grunts which punctuate the night of black festivity. Before he had been taken up by the dance, Jones took these screams as signs of pure suffering: "Yelling as not to hear the sad breathing world" (p. 128). But they are not fitful, anguished cries flung against the hell of experience. As Jones elaborates in *Blues People*, a sociological-aesthetic investigation of black music, the scream is itself a highly sophisticated form of experience. The scream, in its various forms, such as field holler, street yell, gospel shout, or simply as sheer vocal outpouring of emotion, carries all the expressive depth of Afro-American existence.[7] It is the very incarnation of the black ethos:

> You've got to feel
> Just—you got, got to—
> I've got to feel, give it to me.
> You got to, let me.
> Uh—uh, uh—let me. Let me have it.
>
> Uh, uh—let me—
> Ahhhhhh, I've got to. Tell me—
> I—I've got to—feel it.
>
> [James Brown, "Let Yourself Go"] [8]

Jones now knows, with the kind of stark recognition brought about only by sudden illumination, that he can be "happy" pressed against black flesh like his own—as the man says, "You've got to feel." This is, in Mel Watkins's excellent phrase, "an *ethos* of immediacy." [9] It is also an *ethos* of the *act,* of gestures that create present meanings and self-creating attitudes. As James Brown, master of the "*ethos* of immediacy," said: "I am an actor that is now. . . . Everyday is history for me." [10]

In the ritualistic drama of the dance, this ethos provides an exquisite *kairotic* event, an instant in which the structure of personal experience and racial history converge. On the dance floor, tradition is evoked which extends back through slavery to African roots. LeRoi Jones, "half-white," brooding poet from Newark, and Peaches, fat, screechy whore from The Bottom, are only time-bound, trivial instances of a larger and ultimate reality: the black commonality of African heritage. "And my history was there [. . .] in the arms of some sentry of Africa." The natural black soul is redeemed here by historical right (and rite) in this dance of apocalyptic energy. We find in this scene the poetic rendering of a major thesis put forth in *Blues People*—that in the African tradition, "*Expression* issued from life, and was *beauty*." [11] So the expressive black ethos is a timeless, pan-African phenomenon susceptible of presentation in a juke-joint 'nigger' party as much as in tribal ceremony.

The underground world where LeRoi finds his "secret" life is a rich darkness in which energetic black life maintains itself beneath the oblivious "mainstream" society. This 'lower' life has its own history, values, and power. Jones's discovery that he could become "another secret nigger. No one the white world wanted or would look at" is very close to the perception gained by the protagonist of Ralph Ellison's *Invisible Man*: the recognition of *invisibility* to the white world. *Invisible Man*'s hero comes to this realization largely through the experience of a similar underground world as personified by the Protean character Rinehart; Ellison's description of this insight provides an excellent gloss to Jones's passage: "The world in which we lived was without boundaries. A vast, seething, hot world of fluidity. . . . You could actually make yourself anew." [12]

With all boundaries down, freedom to "make [himself] anew" surges over Jones. And so he strikes out against those who would force his identity into an alien mold and destroys the very concept of personality in their eyes—"I was nobody now, mama. *Nobody*." It recalls the "nothing" which he had earlier found at "the core," but that world has now been turned topsy-turvy. He is "nothing" to the white world because he has, momentarily at least, thrown off the habits of white styles and concerns and bathed himself in blackness.

But it takes little insight to see why Jones does not find an end to self-search on the pulsating dance floor. His assertion is shrouded in uncertainty and posturing: "all the world *thot* they were my own," but did *he*? His discovery is less a triumphant declaration than a taunt to the white and neo-white societies that still influence him (the very repetition of "white" and "white world" throughout the passage, in addition to the final address to "mama," points to this weakness). Amidst the dance's chaos, Jones seems to intuit the danger of selfhood without delineation, the horror of complete shapelessness which, as Tony Tanner has eloquently shown, made Ellison's hero turn away from Rinehart's world of pure fluidity.[13] Salvation and happiness may be attained once one is beyond the controlling forces of white culture. Yet the leap past all confines also brings the dread of uncharted space. The desire to deny all shaping definitions is therefore muted by the need to discover a new, coherent mode of being. Jones faces this fear immediately upon leaving the dance floor; he looks for his "brother" companion but sees "only the shape of black men [. . .] I wanted to panic" (p. 130). He pushes Peaches away and runs again in terror, "out of, I hoped, Bottom, towards what I thot was light" (pp. 131–32). He has been shaken enough to ask himself essential questions for the first time: "What was it? Why was this going on? Who was involved?" (p. 132). But even while undergoing this catechism, he wanders as aimlessly as ever, trying to retrieve his army cap from Peaches so that he can return to the Air Force base.

Ironically, he must go back to the center of Bottom with Peaches—against his will—because he knows that a black soldier caught out of uniform is put into the stockade. With Peaches as his new Virgil, he descends once again, this time into the Cotton Club, a dark haunt "at the outskirts of Bottom" (p. 133). He is drunk and distraught; memories of childhood shames assault him. He feels more and more the weight of guilt, of wanting to be "some separate suffering self" (p. 134). His physical and mental selves are moving in opposite directions: while one is deteriorating into drunken weakness, the other is seeing his existential dilemma with increasing clarity. "Locked in a lightless shaft," he feels himself struggling with the Prodigal's dilemma, lost in "the old wood" (p. 134). He imagines himself sprawled on the ground, beaten, verbally abused, and, most painfully, shocked with the question he has refused to face: "Eyes of the damned uncomprehending. Who it was. [. . .] Drunk punk. Get up. *Where's your home?*" (p. 134—my emphasis).

The Prodigal knows he is lost, and now other questions—"The world? Literate? [. . .] Can you read? Who is T. S. Eliot? So what?"—break in upon him, wave after wave of hidden or forgotten sin crashing down with accumulated fury. He knows he must sever himself from Eliot's world and find another; an old command from football practice comes back to him, taking on a remarkable new significance: "Break, Roi, break" (p. 134). As James Brown would say, "Let yourself go." Jones cannot "break," for he has no strength of will; first he must begin to exorcise his sin, by seeing it plainly, without abstract obfuscation. He must see that it profits him to know moral truth only if he is able to will it, and he can will it only after he has plumbed the depths enough to recognize his failure for what it is:

> Willful sin. [. . .] What you want. What you are now. Liar. All sins, against your God. Your own flesh. [. . .] I was sad because I fell. From where it was I'd come to. My silence. The streets I used for books. All come in. Lost. Burned. [pp. 136–37]

The power of his recognition is magnified by the simple way it gathers up and intensifies all the feelings of earlier self-condemnations. His former moods reappear, sharpened by the pressure of imminent and momentous decision.[14] Here is the deep spiritual cleansing of a man who is overcome by a sense of despair in the agony of his returning self-knowledge and his realization that the struggle for salvation requires self-rending confession:

> I was crying now. . . . I'm beautiful Stephen Dedalus. A mind, here where there is only steel. Nothing else. . . . My soul is white, pure white, and soars. Is the God himself. [p. 140]

He had pretended to accept himself, his errant past, his miserable present, but he could not sustain the lie. The awareness of moral responsibility, the intolerable knowledge of being himself, is implacably revealed in its torment for all the misguided hysteria of former deceptions. This self-deprecation is, in fact, the ultimate Narcissus gesture that is an integral feature of the quest for identity: the self-examination in which the beholder abolishes himself in order to go "beyond." [15] The judgment upon the transgressing self becomes an instrument of self-transformation, and the personality yields to its refinement. Yet, seeking one last evasion of black selfhood, he leaves Peaches again.

Out in Bottom, in the still, blackest predawn hour, LeRoi walks the deserted streets "not knowing where I was or was headed for" (p. 141). The dirt roads, broken-down shanties, barren shacks all return his stares blankly: they will not reveal to him their secrets again without his asking. And in the utter solitude and silence of his being, lost and desirous of home, he touches for the first time something real amidst the chaos in himself: "The place was so still, so black and full of violence. I felt myself." Not "I *knew* myself," or some other echo of Cartesian duality. "I felt myself"—wounded, hurt, but somehow (body and soul) sentiently alive: "you've got to *feel.*"

The hellish and frenzied mood which earlier characterized his quest has now turned somewhat mellow. He is coaxed forward by some vague expectation, by renewed hope. It is the mood of Dante's Antepurgatory, where souls are preparing for the ordeals to come. Helpless, nostalgic, yearning for a solid anchor to the world of "real flesh," Jones moves with the cautious and faltering step of a child learning to walk. The similarity to Dante's Antepurgatory is explicitly and dramatically drawn when Jones encounters "someone kneeling under one of the houses [. . .] kneeling in the dark" (pp. 141–42). This figure—so much like Dante's Belacqua, who assumes a crouched, or fetal, position while awaiting entrance to Purgatory—is a pathetic, grotesque man made of a "dripping smile and yellow soggy skin full of red freckles" (p. 142). He first asks, then begs, Jones to commit fellatio with him, and the hero is struck dumb by the sheer bestiality of the pleading creature ("I was backing away like from the hyena cage. [. . .] Baboons?—p. 142).

As Jones moves away, the man screams at him louder and louder—the farther Jones runs the more horrible is the creature's howl: "his scream was like some animal's, some hurt ugly thing dying alone" (p. 142). The gibes, the hunched position, the mad animalism merely conceal the pathos of a soul without hope as it withdraws into its own anguished loneliness (his hopelessness is perhaps more reminiscent of Beckett's tramps, who have resigned themselves to eternal and purposeless waiting, than of Dante's lethargic Belacqua).[16] This haunting scene serves as an exquisitely appropriate reminder to Jones that, while he has begun to find himself in quiet solitude, he can be redeemed only through some type of communion, not in the bitter and frustrated isolation where the scream indeed proclaims an endless despair.

Though he tries to find an escape from The Bottom, he is driven back to Peaches. Coming upon a dying black soldier, he realizes he might be caught, framed, and thrown in jail "30 days for nigger killing" (p. 144). On the surface his sense of need is relatively paltry, but he seeks Peaches *willfully* nonetheless. Soon they are together in bed, Peaches telling the near-impotent youth: "I still got to teach you" (p. 146). He has sought learning before, but he has received only the apparent end-in-itself of Western *morphosis.* What he needs is an education in the root sense of "leading away from"; he must be shown the path from a sterile to a fertile tradition, and this requires a transforming experience: a *meta*-morphosis.

Finally, relaxed with Peaches after the night's 'lesson,' feeling morning sun streaming through the window, and breathing good "daytime smells" (p. 147), Jones learns that the truly fundamental experiences of his people are not so much known as perceived. He learns that the body's senses and rhythms are frequently more adequate means of communication than are carefully arranged words. Eloquent clutching of black hands, visceral participation in a human communion: these are as crucial to The Life as Mother Wit and a fast rap. Jones is now given insight into a mystery that reveals rather than elucidates its secret:

> And I felt myself smiling, and it seemed that things had come to an order. Peaches sitting on the edge of the bed [. . .] eating the melon in both hands. [. . .] It seemed settled. [. . .] I

> thought of black men sitting on their beds this saturday of my life listening to their wives' soft talk. And felt the world grow together as I hadn't known it. [. . .] A real world, of flesh, of smells, of soft black harmonies and color. [. . .] "Now you get dressed, and go get me some tomatoes . . . so we can eat." And it was good. [pp. 147–48]

An unmistakable certitude and peacefulness have replaced the painful ambivalence of the past. A new life and a new understanding have arisen from the embers of the old—Jones has returned to where he began, his home in blackness. He has achieved the Prodigal's early desire for a "Vita Nuova. To begin. There. Where it all ends" (p. 29). This regeneration earns him the edenic pastoral and Genesis-like tone of assurance; luxuriant vegetation and inexhaustible leisure for love are possible because virtue and clear vision have wedded sensuousness and desire. Jones has plotted the path of self-search, fully aware that this achievement would have been inauthentic without the tremendous *ascesis* which led, tortuously, to it. Now, through communion with Peaches, he gains the blessing of a black communality: "The day was bright and people walked by me smiling. And waved 'Hey' (a greeting) and they all knew I was Peaches' man" (p. 149).

Through his experience with Peaches, Jones has found he need not be alone. He has discovered that home "in the world" does exist for him in the enthralling mystery of a black presence. This pastorally sanctified revelation has been at one and the same time a paradox in light of his sinful past, a pattern for the immediate present, and a wondrous promise of the foreseeable future. Yet Jones soon finds he cannot fully realize the resolution of the paradox or the power of the pattern or the total glory of the promise. His ecstasy is short-lived: it carries the weight of reality and change within it. The pastoral state of communion remains for him a happiness of an 'as if' world, where the mind has reached out for a virtual image of the redeemed self and consecrated it for its desires.

Jones seems to recognize with Proust that "the only true paradise is the paradise we have lost." This formula would be one-sided and deficient if we did not add that, for Jones, the paradise he has lost is also paradise regained. Hereafter, Jones's spiritual quest is specially conditioned by his having already breathed this air: in truth, that is its beautiful and moving quality. He has come to feel perched on a summit of communion, not exactly a communion controlled by him, but a communion belonging to him, enclosed within him. It is this feeling that he salvages from his experience in The Bottom. As strangely as he came, so must he leave:

> Something touched me. "That color which cowardice brought out in me." Fire burns around the tombs. Closed from the earth. A despair came down. Alien grace. [. . .] Beautiful unknowns. And my marriage a heavy iron to this tomb. "Show us your countenance." Your light. [. . .] Introitus. That word came in. And the yellow light burning in my rooms. To come to see the world, and yet lose it. And find sweet grace alone. [pp. 149–50]

This passage is one of the most revealing in all of Jones's corpus, and it provides the key to a final appraisal of *The System of Dante's Hell.* These delicate, careful lines—so precisely poised between renunciation of The Bottom and understanding of its significance in his regeneration—can be grasped only in relation to that portion of Dante's *Inferno* which they purposefully echo. Jones evokes here the scene of *Inferno* 9, in which Dante's approach to the city of Dis and Virgil's description of the arch-heretics are set forth: through direct quotation ("That color, etc." is a translation of the opening line of Dante's Canto)[17] and borrowing of specific details (the fire-encased tombs are the receptacles of Dante's arch-heretics as described in *Inf.* 9: 118–31), Jones re-creates the atmosphere of suspense and crisis which characterizes Dante's canto.

Yet Jones has brought Dante in only to stand him on his head. Whereas for Dante heresy is the only sin that is an error of the intellect as opposed to an aberration of the will,[18] for Jones heresy is the most *willful* of all transgressions. Coming hard upon the description of pastoral reverie, this passage seems to say of Jones's perverted, weak will: *et in Arcadia ego.* Lest he grow complacent in the arms of Peaches, Jones openly attacks himself with the sin of heresy, calling upon his pilgrim's strength to continue the quest for a perfectly refined desire, to 'keep on keepin on' until an absolute black communality has been achieved through fully conscious, willful effort.

The repetition of "grace," the invocation of the Mass's "Introitus," the imitation of the Psalmist's attitude toward the severity and loneliness of the quest for salvation (" 'Show us your countenance.' Your light" is a paraphrase of *Psalms*, 4:6)—these linguistic nuances suggest the religious dimension of Jones's evolution. Black life teaches a communion with the world through an exalted consciousness of its fundamental energy (as embodied in the juke-joint dance) and peculiar rhythms (as felt throughout The Bottom). Yet Jones knows that the deterioration and degeneration of the old man, and the reconstruction of the new man, take place all the time as a kind of dialectic. In the world where Jones seeks his salvation there is both the realization of educative epiphanies (the dance, the encounter with the kneeling creature, life with Peaches, etc.) and the acknowledgment of a gradual, on-going *process* of Becoming. Jones has traversed his inner hell to reach, not paradise, but the realm of *purgatorial* movement. His is the domain of flux, change, progression: the domain from which hope is not excluded and which is not yet the realm of beatitude. It is not the modern 'purgatory' of a Joyce or Beckett, which is actually a hell, a purgatory without progress. The action of Jones's spiritual strivings, now that he has discovered the "Introitus" to a black-oriented religiosity, is the action of a "foetus drama," a continual purgatorial enactment of changes toward an ever 'blacker' self.

It is thus highly appropriate that the last scene of *The System of Dante's Hell* is a dream-ritual sequence that takes place in a "cave," the archetypical setting of the purgatorial struggle for self-knowledge. He reads aloud from a book as Negroes dance to music and his reading:

> The negroes danced around my body and spilled whisky on my clothes. I woke up 2 days later, with white men, screaming for God to help me. [p. 152]

In this last exorcistic ritual, Jones's Orphic being is subjected to the mythic *sparmagós,* or dismemberment, upon its emergence from hell. He is fractured yet he is one, and through his ordeal he guarantees the possibility of later assuming the Orphic role of shaman, the singer-prophet capable of establishing harmony and unity out of the shattered fragments of black civilization. The descent to The Bottom is not, finally, a descent to hell but a triumphant return to life. As with Dante, "fondo a tutto l'universo" ("the *bottom* of all the universe"—*Inf.* 32: 8; my emphasis) is the way through to Purgatory, where the final ascent to one's God begins. For LeRoi Jones—soon to be reborn as Imamu Amiri Baraka—the discovery of a home away from the 'hell' of the self fixated upon Western culture brings with it the recognition that black people carry their home *and* their God within their collective soul: "They have no God save who they are. Their black selves" (p. 122).

III

We are unfair, and unfair.
We are black magicians, black art
s we make in black labs of the heart.

The fair are
fair, and death
ly white.

The day will not save them
and we own
the night.

—LeRoi Jones, from "State/meant"

LeRoi Jones's journey from the hell of an alien tradition to home in blackness was not carried out in a historical vacuum. His search for identity, while intensely personal, coincided with the dramatic changes in Afro-American sensibility which have been variously described as the Black Power, black consciousness, or Neo-Black movement. By whatever appellation, there did occur in the 1960s a profound process of revaluation, redefinition, and regrouping, primarily among young black intellectuals and artists, which has irrevocably affected the shape of Afro-American culture. The history of this movement can scarcely be written, for it is still in process, and its more lasting results have perhaps not even been glimpsed.[19] Yet it is possible to delineate the most salient features of the new movement, those which affected LeRoi Jones most deeply and which he himself has helped to create.

There is a simple but striking similarity between Jones's self-inquiry and the question of cultural identity that has haunted the Afro-American writer since Phyllis Wheatley's awkward search for literary ancestors in the late eighteenth century. For, like Jones, the Afro-American writer in general has been plagued by an acute psychological dilemma, a confusing association with two conflicting cultures. The descendants of (African) "aliens" brought to a strange (American) world, Afro-Americans have found themselves in the paradoxical situation of strangers moored to a foreign land. W. E. B. DuBois defined this problem most succinctly over three-quarters of a century ago as the crisis of "double consciousness":

> It is a peculiar sensation, this double consciousness . . . One ever feels his two-ness—an American, a Negro—two souls, two thoughts, two unreconciled strivings: two warring ideals in one dark body, whose dogged strength alone keeps it from being torn asunder.[20]

Two basic cultural theories have offered radically different solutions to the "two-ness" of black/American life. On the one hand, there is the pro-integrationist or "assimilationist" school of thought, which accepts the American-ness of the black man as incontrovertible. Proponents of this view argue that black Americans will realize their total rights only by becoming fully participating members of the American mainstream, and that the alternative to assimilation is the suicide of exclusion. On the other hand, there is the anti-integrationist or "nationalist" viewpoint, which maintains that assimilation means merely the suicide of decolorization, an eradication of cultural identity through the adoption of white manners and values. The nationalists insist that the semicolonial status of black America has allowed it to develop an autonomous life-style which could not survive the assimilation process, and that it is upon this autonomy that the strength of any struggle for power must depend. Moreover, the nationalist theory holds that integration is a mirage as fanciful as the American Dream, a chimerical notion based on the erroneous assumption of an American homogeneity. Finally, the nationalists assert that only through willful separation—the logical extension of what America has given the black man for over three centuries—can the necessary political, economic, and cultural resources be gathered for the ultimate liberation of the race.

Harold Cruse, a veteran nationalist among the new wave, has taken great care to show that the assimilationist-nationalist debate is not at all new; that its roots can be traced to antebellum arguments between such men as Frederick Douglass and Martin R. Delany; and that this debate will continue as long as the black man's essential status of "semi-dependence" (Cruse's term) is unchanged.[21] Nationalism has enjoyed brief bursts of popularity since its debate with assimilationism began, particularly in the form of Marcus Garvey's "Back to Africa" movement of the late teens and early twenties, and the more economics-oriented concerns of post-World War II Harlem, emblemized by the slogan "Buy Black."

In the 1960s, however, nationalism took on an unprecedented attraction and vitality. Many historical, political, and even psychological factors are recognizable in this rejuvenation: the growth toward black pride initiated by the civil rights movement; the rise of liberated African countries; the Cuban Revolution; the fate of Robert F. Williams and his Monroe Movement; violence against civil rights activists in Birmingham, Mississippi, Chicago, and elsewhere; the assassination of Medgar Evers; the influence and assassination of Malcolm X; increasing racial polarization, particularly in the northern cities; Stokely Carmichael's dramatic call for "Black Power" in 1966; the assassination of Dr. Martin Luther King, Jr. But these events reflected the development of nationalism as much as they contributed to its rise, and the matrix of influences out of which the movement has grown is probably too complex to describe. My purpose is not, in any case, to record the history of the new nationalism but rather to understand how this ideology has motivated and functioned for black artists such as LeRoi Jones. It is convenient to this discussion, therefore, that the psychology, strategy, background, style, and indeed the very character of the new nationalism should have been embodied in one man, El-Hajj Malik El-Shabazz: Malcolm X.

Whether his supposed topic was Africa, self-defense, codes for living, or particular current events, Malcolm's underlying and persistent theme was black identity. He believed that no cultural or political advance was meaningful, or even possible, unless it followed upon an unshakable pride in oneself and in the race. Although well versed in particular political issues, Malcolm lent the greater portion of his eloquence to inculcation of a consciousness of the black *self*—its alternative roles and gut aspirations—in the minds of his black listeners. He felt that the root of any self-appraisal leading toward self-esteem must lie in a sense of one's context or place in the large sweep of affairs, and this entailed a fundamental grasp of history:

> The number one thing that makes us differ from other people is our lack of knowledge concerning the past. . . . the only difference between them and us, they know something about the past, and in knowing about the past, they know something about themselves, they have an identity.[22]

Without a knowledge of history the black man has no idea of his cultural origins and strengths. Without a past, he could own and deserve only the damnable present, its sufferings and injustices willed as an eternal hell. Yet the reclamation of history can only result from a dialectic of personal and cultural identities. The black man must control the vehicle of historical knowledge to possess a meaningful and useful history, and this requires a proper use of language. You are what you are *named,* Malcolm taught; unless you control your name you have only that identity and that history which your namer chooses to give you. Malcolm *Little* was in some measure the slave his given name signified; contrarily, Cassius Clay, reborn Muhammad Ali, asserts the dignity of his whole race by crying out "What's my name, what's my name!"

The concern with naming, which Ralph Ellison believes is the hidden essence of the American experience[23] and which certainly plays a dominant role in the black oral tradition, reaches a new intensity with the rise of "black consciousness." Following the preachings of Elijah Muhammad, Malcolm argued that the "so-called Negro" can only have the history of a "Negro"—the limiting and debasing legacy of slavery. Thus:

> The worst trick of all is when he names us Negro and calls us Negro. . . . One of the main reasons we are called Negro is so we won't know who we really are. . . . As long as you call yourself a Negro, nothing is yours. . . . You can't lay claim to any name, any type of name, that will identify you as something that you should be.

The "negro" has no language, no history, no culture, no land, no home—no identity: "the man doesn't exist." Yet know yourself as the *black* man and you gain back your history, retrieve a claim to African origin, find a homeland (if but as a form of spiritual association), and control your destiny.

History, culture, language, homeland, identity—taken together these comprised for Malcolm the intricate organism of black selfhood, an indissoluble whole in which each element reflects the others in their mutual dependence. This ideological unity is the natural counterpart to the black nation's own form of collective survival, a mode of communality in which individual fulfillment is realized only through creative identification with the group. The nationalists' avowed hatred of whites must be seen in relation to this unifying impulse. The Manichaean equation of white with evil and black with righteousness serves the *ideological* function of organizing individual experience (discrimination/oppression) into a generalized response to existing conditions and a common form of action.[24]

Herein lies the powerful appeal of The Nation of Islam, for it locates the dignity of the Afro-American in a coherent and totally accepted framework of values. The Black Muslim eschatology, mythology, and religious regulation orient its adherents to a love of self as black through a specific definition of what "black" is and is not. Malcolm sought to integrate the religious code and mythology of The Nation of Islam with an awareness of secular history and traditional black cultures. His vision of liberation thus fused all the particular aspects of nationalism: religiosity, vindication through mythologizing and allegorizing, separatism, historicity, African heritage, and affirmation of Afro-American life-styles. Malcolm made it much easier for black thinkers to speak rigorously of a homogeneous yet infinitely varied black ethos, to sustain a vision that utilized and synthesized the possibilities of James Brown and John Coltrane, W. E. B. DuBois and Frederick Douglass, street jive and ideological abstractions.

The appeal of Malcolm's concept of black liberation is clearly understood when contrasted with that of his generation's great prophet of assimilation, Dr. Martin Luther King, Jr. Dr. King brought the black liberation movement to the steps of the Capitol; yet the apparent inability of the King-led civil-rights marchers to proceed beyond this symbolic gesture made them appear hollow and impotent in the face of American reality. Dr. King's accomplishments were legion, but his singular failure is a key to black nationalism's dramatic upsurge. His movement was born and raised in the South among an essentially rural people. His black followers had a strong (and conservative) feeling for the land and for traditional black institutions such as the church. The Reverend's formality and high station ennobled him in his adherents' eyes; his rhetoric, with its pastoral reverie and Christian typology, spoke to their own vision of peaceful coexistence with what surrounded them.

When he sought to disseminate this vision in the teeming and violent ghettos of the North he met with much superficial respect but little concrete progress. The northern black's life was more uprooted, fast-paced and turbulent than that of his southern brother. As Stephen Henderson points out, Dr. King's abstract formulae of "universal love were difficult to believe after a day with the Man, or after a night with the blues." [25] Dr. King himself articulated the pathos of his situation and foresaw the impasse at which his philosophy of nonviolent brotherhood would arrive: "How could I make a speech that would be militant enough to keep my people aroused to positive action and yet moderate enough to keep this fervor within controllable and Christian bounds?" [26] The tragic fact is that by the mid-1960s Dr. King's language could not "arouse" ghettoized blacks up North as it had moved whites and southern blacks. Only the sermons of more uncompromisingly "militant" preachers (especially Reverend Albert B. Cleage, Jr. and Minister Malcolm X) spoke effectively to the festering dreams of the northern urban black masses.

Malcolm's appeal was to the most downtrodden, 'low'-life class of urban blacks. His career of hustling, drug addiction, and street-wise survival (which preceded his conversion to Islam) was one his audience could readily understand and in many cases identify with. Seen in light of this life-style, the contrast between Malcolm and Dr. King takes on a peculiar significance with great implications. What Dr. King could not speak to as Malcolm did was the fundamental *chaos* of violent, urban, ghetto life. The situation of the northern brother has evolved into an experience of astounding complexity and variety—witness the typical thoroughfare with its currency exchanges, liquor stores, funeral parlors, store-front churches, bars, pimps, charlatans, preachers, orators, etc., a virtual tempest of competing pursuits swirling about the black pilgrim in dark-yet-loud colors.

This chaos is not, however, a mere disorder or overwhelming confusion that relentlessly tears apart those within it. Perhaps it is because such chaos could be seen only in its frightening aspect by those of Dr. King's persuasion that his approach failed to impress the people who have lived so long in chaos's presence. Malcolm knew instinctively and by experience that this chaos concealed an approach to life, an adaptability in the face of abuse and painful dues-paying that created something beautiful amidst and despite the enveloping misery—the will and character to survive. This chaos was akin to the music of Malcolm's time, epitomized by the 'life-in-death' lyricism of John Coltrane, which the fearful took to be cacophony. Malcolm went into the bars, prisons, slums, and streets to preach his message; he spoke to the whores, pimps, and hustlers as well as to others. He sought to change their lives, but he did so with respect. He addressed the innate power, elegance, and dignity of his people and talked directly of transcending their superficial and oft-imposed depravity.

If the influence of Malcolm X among ghetto blacks was considerable, among young black artists it has been of mythic proportions. Countless poems, plays, and stories have elegized his leadership, reflected his intense commitment, repeated his philosophy, and interpreted his legendary achievement.[27] What is important to realize is that for these artists Malcolm X is not merely a man and heroic martyr. More exactly, he is the symbolic representative of the nationalistic themes and approach to life's chaos which he avowed. The new artists refer to Malcolm so often because his name immediately evokes (and invokes) the principles of the black nation they seek to build. Yet use of Malcolm's name and memory are relatively minor weapons in the poetic arsenal of the black revolutionary writers. More prevalent, more noteworthy, and indeed more revolutionary, is the remarkable creative ferment which the young nationalistic artists have initiated, a development of aesthetic consciousness stylistically, thematically, and spiritually akin to Malcolm's contribution.

The revolution in the arts—what Larry Neal first called the Black Arts Movement—has been analogous to the political movement's quest for freedom in its search for freer, innovative forms. If liberation for the black man is predicated upon control of his "name," then meaningful black writing can exist only in a truly black language. The aesthetic experimentation of the Black Arts Movement takes its theoretical lead from new analyses of black music (see chapter 3, below). Afro-American writers have always been affected by their musical counterparts. Black music, from blues and Louis Armstrong to bebop and Charlie Parker, has always been the most vital of black mediums, and poets such as James Weldon Johnson and Langston Hughes have been directly inspired by musical forms. What the Black Arts Movement's theorists and poets added to the traditional respect for black music was an awareness of the revolutionary spirit inherent in this music's evolution. Black music could now be seen as an attitude as well as a style, its revolutionary character considered the result of a distinctly non-Western and, specifically, black mode of expression. Freshly inspired by the sounds of Coltrane, Rollins, Ayler, and others, the new writers seek a lexicon as vivifying and authentically black as the musical vocabulary. The poets of the Black Arts Movement infuse their work with the syntax of "ordinary" black people, a rich and complex language "as changeable as Blacks who left the South." [28] In particular, traditional oral (especially street) forms such as the chant, the toast, scatting, dozens, and the unwritten dictionary of off-the-wall jive, are utilized by the poets. Like certain of their literary ancestors (particularly Hughes, Sterling Brown, and Jean Toomer), they push their language in what Don L. Lee calls "the direction of actual music." [29] And indeed their poetry, with its polyrhythmic texture, short lines, delayed rhymes, and mimetic techniques (bebop/scat/scream/preach/chant), is meant to be read aloud, performed with improvisational and antiphonal flair characteristic of the typical musician/audience jam session.[30]

Just as black music has an unmistakable personality, so too does a true black language: these forms can be said to fuse into a general expression of black identity. While the Euro-American tradition which LeRoi Jones abandoned has increasingly lost faith in its language, the Black Arts Movement has elevated the black word (nommo) to a magical status. For the black writer the word, born in the street and consecrated in the musical affirmation of the poets, does not signify a concept abstracted from private experience, but magically conjures up real things, real feelings—it becomes an incantatory formula. Mastering the words that stand for the elements of his world, each black poet transforms them into something unmistakably his own (Sonia Sanchez plays in a different key than Etheridge Knight), but this transformation does not deny further uses of them to other 'singers of the same.' The impulse is that of the self fully engaged in the act of creating a structure which makes for the possibility of further creation: an infinite series of poetic spaces ("*Space* is what we are fighting for" [31]—LeRoi Jones), each to be the locale, the occasion, and the means to the creative, self-assertive, self-discovering act of that mass of Afro-Americans who would be drawn into them.

The value system which the Black Arts Movement makes is thus open, a guide to a way *toward* life as well as a way *of* life for the individual artist:

> A poet must & would
> give truth substance & form
> Truth needs a second career
> SO CRACK THE OTHER SIDE
> Black Poet
> that it be felt
> that it be looked at
> & into . . .[32]

The poem is a titanic act of adoption; the poet is an Adamic creator, giving everything he hears and sees and feels its rightful name. His office is to make everything a beautiful and useful part of the black nation: the sense of community is revealed as he discovers, and then yields to, his infinite sense of himself as a kind of black priest, a singer-prophet "leaving songs of praise . . . a love supremely unafraid . . . black bright, and binding / ear to sight unseen" (Ebon, "Legacy: In Memory of Trane"). The "love supreme" for black people is thus a primal sense of creativity to which the poet must return. Most important, it is a source within the poet, the deepest aspect of himself as authentic person. Returning to his natal root, he returns to himself as lover-creator, returns home to the source of life's rhythm.

Thus discovering and confirming his relationship to the world, the poet discovers the possibility that the nominally antipoetic can be made into poetry itself. Inversions of mainstream attitudes and language (from the 'goodness' of *badness* to Maulana Karenga's nation-emblem "US") are insisted upon as never before. The new art is proudly "Black Art," for "poems are bullshit unless they are / teeth or trees or [. . .] / Assassin poems" (LeRoi Jones, "Black Art"). The poets' irony, sarcasm, and anger by turns elucidate "the enigmas of our Neon Diaspora" (David Henderson).

He gives the black world a new meaning—transforming it by alienating it from the enveloping culture and the crude, harsh, antipoetic reality which characterizes the mainstream. Doing so, he intensifies his sense of himself as strong, autonomous, and creative —*T*ogether/*C*ollected/*B*lack. He wishes to create persons like himself—in effect, to save them from the antipoetic world to which the demands of daily survival commit them:

> There are fights in the streets with the cops
> and a brother is wounded and jailed. His wife screams curses
> at life, the time, the motion, god, all beauty, and her wounded
> self. Would that that self would disappear and she grow more
> beautiful
> Would that we would
> all become what the dream of reality insists we can become.
> [LeRoi Jones, from "Sisters in the Fog")

The Black Arts Movement, like Malcolm X, seeks to harness the chaos of black life as a revolutionary force. Music, dance, and religiosity especially are key aspects of black culture's energy and are therefore central themes of the writers. Moreover, the nationalist artists have gathered for themselves a specific cluster of symbols, myths, and heroes which best exemplify the principles and practice of this energy. Just as Dr. King's philosophy is less immediately attractive than Malcolm's, so Uncle Remus gives place to John Henry, Simple moves aside for the Signifying Monkey, and heretofore cautious canons of propriety make room for the elegance of bad, foul-talking owners of the street.

Yet the primary impulse of the new movement transcends any need for a hierarchy of icons, heroes, or myths. What it desires most is the integration of *all* cultural, political, and spiritual qualities that have dignified and strengthened the Afro-American throughout his history. If history truly functions as the Black Arts Movement's "unitary myth,"[33] then a meaningful black history must encompass the significance of Trickster John and Shine, Bessie Smith and Charlie Parker, Alain Locke and Richard Wright, Denmark Vesey and Nat Turner—Lumumba, DuBois, Stokely, Garvey, Elijah Muhammad, and Fanon; it must speak of Malcolm

X and Martin Luther King and in the idioms of funky rhythm and cosmic abstraction; it must retain the memory of the blues and bebop, voodoo and Islam, Africa and Watts; it must house Ishmael Reed's "fez-wearing mulatto in a pin-striped suit" (*Mumbo Jumbo*) and the hipper reality of Bobby Blue Bland shouting African-rooted blues in a dashiki and konk-o-lee do-rag. The young artists preach the joy and necessity of being "beautifully and incontrovertibly black" (Mari Evans); but they know this also means "don't say goodbye to the pork-pie hat" (Larry Neal).

Though in the avant-garde of the Euro-American tradition traces of 'morality' may be kicked over to demonstrate self-will, the black artist sees his ultimate duty as the reconciliation of ethics and aesthetics. Whether or not his goal is as programatic as Karenga's Kawaida value system, he strives to attain for his people the first and central aim of Kawaida—unity (umoja). The most articulate spokesman for a unified sensibility has been LeRoi Jones:

> Fanon [said], "the concept of nation and culture are inseparable. If you talk about nation you talk about culture." [. . .] It is a creation of some sensibility. It issues out of some value system. The largest sensibility we deal with now is the National sensibility. *To free the nation is at the same time to free the culture ie, the way of life of . . .*[34]

Among artists and critics, the effort to describe a viable black culture has led to formulations of a "black aesthetic." Whatever the particular nuances of each theorist's case, the "black aesthetic" discussion represents not only a desire to locate those traits which constitute a definite black style, but also an attempt to define the ways in which black artists can best employ their style in the people's interests. Led especially by Addison Gayle, Jr., and Hoyt W. Fuller, proponents of a "black aesthetic" argue that the final assessment of the work must be in terms of its *affective* quality, its ability to be *utile* as well as *dulce*:

> The question . . . is not how beautiful is a melody, a play, a poem, or a novel, but how much more beautiful has the poem, melody, play, or novel made the life of a single black man?[35]

The individual's creativity is celebrated insofar as it serves the group. For the black artist there can be no achievement outside the collective aspiration of his audience, and his audience must be black.

Finally, the will toward communality goes beyond the insistence that the artist create for an exclusively black audience. In some sense that audience, that nation of black souls, must also create the black artist. They must each, as the finest act of umoja, sustain the other: "in this writing black people are not only the poets and the audience, they are the poems." [36] The new black writers may see men such as Malcolm X as exemplars, but their true hero is the black community itself. Every work produced by the Black Arts Movement is thus a microcosmic cell of the black nation it envisions, each poem a shadow of tomorrow's reality:

> We want a black poem. And a
> Black World.
> Let the world be a Black Poem
> And Let All Black People Speak This Poem
> Silently
>
> or LOUD
>
> [LeRoi Jones, from "Black Art"]

IV

The poor have become our creators. The black. The thoroughly/ ignorant.
Let the combination of morality/ and inhumanity/ begin.

—LeRoi Jones, "Short Speech to My Friends"

LeRoi Jones is commonly thought to be the founder or father of the revolution in black art. The truth is that while Jones was still toiling in the wasteland of America's 'mainstream' avant-garde, several black innovators were already sowing the seeds that later sprouted as the Black Arts Movement. Such figures as Askia Muhammad Touré (formerly Roland Snellings), Daniel H. Watts, Bobb Hamilton, and Hoyt Fuller were actively working toward a nationalist aesthetic in the early 1960s. Political journals such as *Freedomways*, *Liberator*, and *Black America*, and small literary magazines including *Umbra*, *Soul Book*, *The Journal of Black Poetry*, *Black Dialogue*, and *Negro Digest* (now called *Black World*) were publishing straightforwardly "revolutionary" articles, poems, and theoretical manifestos several years in advance of Jones's full entry into black letters. While Malcolm X was making speeches and dozens of other black artists were formally working toward a black aesthetic, Jones was editing "beat" poetry magazines in Greenwich Village (*Floating Bear* and *Yugen*) and working primarily with white writers such as Charles Olson and Robert Creeley.

William C. Fischer has shown with great tact that the elements of a unified black sensibility were latent in the earliest of Jones's work.[37] Blues motifs, communal values, racially edged irony, and distinctively black rhetoric can be found in many early poems and essays. Yet there is no doubt that Jones underwent a radical reorientation of spiritual purpose such as that experienced by the protagonist of *The System of Dante's Hell*, the outward manifestations of which were divorce from his white Village associates (including his former wife, Hettie Cohen) and the move uptown to Harlem. His year of crossroads, as for so many others, was 1965. Though the particular persuasions of Touré, A. B. Spellman, Max Stanford, and some few others may have added impetùs to Jones's change, the death of Malcolm X was clearly the preeminent influence upon him.[38] His impassioned "Poem for Black Hearts" implored himself as well as others to realize the dead prophet's dream:

> For all of him, and all of yourself, look up,
> black man, quit stuttering and shuffling, look up,
> black man, quit whining and stooping, for all
>   of him,
> For Great Malcolm a prince of the earth, let
> nothing in us rest [. . .]
>   let us never breathe a pure
> breath if
> we fail, and white men call us faggots till the
>   end of
> the earth.

Nineteen-sixty-five also saw the intensification of Jones's leadership in the Black Arts Theatre and School, the first well-known performing organization with a nationalist outlook. Jones himself later called his participation in the Black Arts Theatre the "true move to Home and light." [39] Though occasionally attacked for his previous associations with white writers, he was by this time recognized as the most versatile practitioner of the Black Arts. Since then, most black artists have acknowledged him as the vanguard representative of their efforts, the most visible if not the central protagonist in the movement. As Theodore Hudson assessed Jones's stature in his study *From LeRoi Jones to Amiri Baraka*: "according to existing principles of black literary authority, LeRoi Jones is considered to be the supreme writer." [40]

LeRoi Jones once remarked that Dante's *Inferno* was an "imitation" of an Arabic text and cited it as an archetypical Western "shadow" of nature.[41] If this is true, then Jones's own exorcistic *The System of Dante's Hell* can be described as the shadow of a shadow, twice removed from the natural world. In the effort to step out of the cave of shadows where *The System of Dante's Hell* left him, and into the world of natural blackness, LeRoi Jones went through many changes. It was Imamu Amiri Baraka who wrote:

> I love you black people
> because I love my
> Self.
> And you are that self, thrown big
> against the heavens.
>
> [from *In Our Terribleness*]

2 Black Nationalism and Art: Being in the World

In 1963 Imamu Baraka wrote an essay entitled "Brief Reflections on Two Hot Shots." [1] It is a bitter and impassioned condemnation of James Baldwin and Peter Abrahams (the South African writer), an explicit rejection of their "individualism" and privately cultivated sensibilities. The essay is interesting as documentation of the major change of both theoretical and practical orientation that took place among black writers and intellectuals in the early 1960s. An early manifestation of the burgeoning nationalistic trend in black political thought, it is also one of the first well-articulated statements of the aesthetic principles that were to guide the arts of the new movement generally and, what is more crucial to this study, the work of Imamu Baraka in particular:

> It is deadly simple. A writer must have a point of view, or he cannot be a good writer. He must be standing somewhere in the world, or else he is not one of *us,* and his commentary then is of little value. But even air is warmed by the sun. How can a man escape?

We need to read nothing else of Baraka's to know that, for him, no isolation of artist from society, of the aesthetic realm from the realm of morality and utility can be at all tenable. Nor can he tolerate an Idealist notion of aesthetic pleasure, since "disinterested satisfaction"—or contemplation of art untempered by immediate, moral concern—is "hedonistic" and valueless:

> Individuality is not merely the cross one select number willfully bears among the broken heads and lives of the oppressed. We need not call to each other through the flames if we have nothing to say, or are merely diminishing the

> history of the world with descriptions of it that will show we are intelligent. Intelligence is only valuable when it is contained naturally in the matter we present as a result of the act (of writing . . . or feeling). A writer is committed to what is real not to the sanctity of his FEELINGS.

Obsessed by the notion of individualism and individual antagonisms, Baldwin and Abrahams forever explore the 'inner world' of their characters but neglect what alone in man is strong: his ability to take sides and to find solidarity in common action. Only the jolt of choice, action, can put an end to the "pestilence" of desire. Only in action, Baraka argues, can we find some clear necessity, if not rationality.

Art, like the artist, is of and in the world. To ignore this basic truth is, in a world of political conflict, to be ineffectual as an artist and to emasculate art itself. For Baraka, then, engagement is necessary not only for social, political, and moral reasons; it is the very lifeblood of artistic endeavor:

> If Abrahams and Baldwin were turned white [. . .] there would be no more noise from them. Not because they consciously desire that, but because then they could be sensitive in peace. Their color is the only obstruction I can see to this state they seek, and I see no reason they should be denied it for so paltry a thing as heavy pigmentation. Somebody turn them! And then perhaps the rest of us can get down to the work at hand. Cutting throats!

The sardonic tone leading with precise rhetorical rhythm to a violent exclamation is symptomatic of much of Baraka's dramatic theory and of the drama itself. But what is particularly noteworthy in this passage is Baraka's confession that as an artist, no less than as a political or simply human being, he cannot maintain the pulse of his sensibility "in peace." To be is to be *in the world;* to create is to show, with a poet's language, the facts in the "consciousness epic" which contains all that is "happening." In a major document of his artistic purpose, "The Revolutionary Theatre" [2] (1964), Baraka again presents these ideas distinctly and clearly: "we will talk about the world, and the preciseness with which we are able to summon the world will be our art. Art is method. And art, 'like any ashtray or senator,' remains in the world. Wittgenstein said ethics and aesthetics are one. I believe this."

Baraka's theory of art and aesthetics, then, are utilitarian and moved by a particular political and moral orientation toward the world. It comes as no surprise that these views should have a direct influence in formulating a theory of drama, and especially in determining a type of content which the drama should employ. The "revolutionary theatre" is a political theatre, a "weapon" against what is "unnatural" and "mad"; as one might expect, its impulse is violent, its vision apocalyptic:

> What we show must cause the blood to rush, so that pre-revolutionary temperaments will be bathed in this blood, and it will cause their deepest souls to move, and they will find themselves tensed and clenched, even ready to die, at what the soul has been taught. We will scream and cry, murder, run through the streets in agony, if it means some soul will be moved, moved to actual life understanding of what the world is, and what it ought to be. We are preaching virtue and feeling, and a natural sense of the self in the world. All men live in the world, and the world ought to be a place for them to live.

The sense of engagement, of moral urgency this statement conveys runs like fire throughout Baraka's plays. This passion for "causing the blood to rush" seems to carry with it the justification for Baraka's devotion to art. But the very writing of plays, the very fact of a play, also runs counter to the need for immediate, raw action which the drama itself calls for, and Baraka has been acutely aware of this problem at every stage of his work. In an early poem (dated July 1960), we already find Baraka caught between a lyrical sensibility given to contemplation and undisturbed observation, and an acute, often consuming desire for action:

> I think he knew
> all this would happen, that

when I dropped the book
the sky would have already
moved, turned black, and
wet grey air
would mark the windows.
                                                That
there are fools
who hang close
to their original
thought. Elementals
of motion (Not, again,
that garden) but some
slightness
of feeling
they think is sweet
and long to die
inside.
            Think
about it! As even
this, now, a turning
away. (I mean I think
I know now
what a poem
is) A
turning away . . .
from what it was/had moved us
us . . .
      A
madness.
            Looking at the sea. And some
white fast boat.

[from "Betancourt"] [3]

Seven years later, in a story from the collection entitled *Tales*, which together gather fragments of purpose and energy amid an essential, spiritless, decadent, and blighted wasteland, the opposition of stagnating thought and meaningful experience is as vividly actualized: "to keep from thinking, which is evil. Sky does not think. Nor trees. To stand at the edge of that feeling because I couldn't use it. Instead I'd be in Alabama *with the fire*" (from "No

Body No Place";[4] my emphasis). In his drama, Baraka's concern about the relative values of knowledge, creation, expression, and action often lead to attacks upon the cumbersome nuances of words, the useless, even monstrous productions of art, and also the very activity of creation:

> *Nasafi.* It is evil to pursue creation even into the lost spaces of the universe. What you bring back will be of no benefit to man. Remember the old myths, brother. The forbidden fruit of madness.
>
> *Tanzil.* Yes. Tho we turn earth into gold, and cause the sun's rays to turn our engines. What you call thought is the projection of anti-humanity. The compassionless abstractions, the opposites. The mirror image of creation, turned and distorted, given power, by the forces of good, tho these forces breed hell itself.
>
> *Nasafi.* Yacoub. You are working at what task now?
>
> *Yacoub.* I told you. Thought. The creation of new energy. Yes. New energy, and new beings [. . .] Yes, brother. I have created time. Now I will create a being in love with time. A being for whom time will be goodness and strength.
>
> *Tanzil.* This is animal sense. This is magic against humanity, Yacoub.
>
> [from *A Black Mass*] [5]

Baraka can never really escape the paradox of the revolutionary playwright's desire to "break the chain of ignorance" (from *The Baptism*) and the political activist's disdain for the trappings of complex thought and art. We have already seen that for Baraka it is not enough to describe the peculiar, inward value of art; it must be further established that art has a functional value. There are three major classes of people who might question the value of art in this sense: the puritan (to whom art is immoral), the philistine (to whom art is useless), and the proletarian (to whom art is a cruel waste).[6] Baraka obviously has closest affinities with the latter: art is not necessarily immoral or useless; it only becomes so if it is misdirected, if it serves no end but undisturbed, "disinterested," and "hedonistic" satisfaction.

The same principle holds true for Reason's formulations, as we see in the passage already quoted from "Brief Reflections on Two Hot Shots": "intelligence is only valuable when it is contained *naturally* in the matter we present as a result of the act (of writing . . . of feeling)." I emphasize here the word *naturally,* for it becomes abundantly clear once one has studied Baraka's entire corpus, that it is not art, creation, expression, and thought in themselves which he finds repugnant; he is neither a puritan nor a philistine. What is problematic are the contexts, or more exactly the forms, in which the given ideological content is to be discovered and then, in turn, conveyed. Accordingly, there is in Baraka's essays an increasing attempt to discover the nexus at which the concept of Black Power finds its proper cultural form and a vigorous insistence that such a meeting place exists and must be recognized. It is only in light of this endeavor to unify political and cultural content and form that many and diverse passages from his drama (such as that quoted above from *A Black Mass*) are properly understood.

II

The unification of political ideology and cultural expression is not a new problem in Afro-American aesthetics. The "Negro Renaissance" of the 1920s, in a radical departure from the standards of past black writers, saw the emergence of the so-called "New Negro" (Alain Locke's phrase) who demanded recognition, not in relation to the standard of an alien tradition, but as the heir and representative of a separate, dynamic culture with a distinctive history and canon of values. The black writer, intent on inculcating a fresh sense of identity and heritage, turned to Africa as a source of inspiration. The search for roots expressed itself in emotional, exotic, even sentimental tones; Countee Cullen's poem "Heritage" reveals the idealization and mythic impulse that informed this return to Africa:

> What is Africa to me:
> Copper sun or scarlet sea,

Jungle star or jungle track,
Strong bronze men, or regal black
Women from whose loins I sprang
When the birds of Eden sang? . . .
What is Africa to me?[7]

Yet, as C. W. E. Bigsby points out,[8] this call to Africa was as much a turning from as a turning toward: in embracing the 'dark continent' the black artist abandoned America; in his emotionalism and exoticism lay an implicit rejection of Western rationalism and propriety; in idealizing the African past, he transposed the edenic myth from the new to the old world; in yearning for this prelapsarian time, he protested the damnable present:

So long,
So far away
Is Africa.
Not even memories alive
Save those that history books create,
Save those that songs
Beat back into the blood . . .
Subdued and time-lost
Are the drums . . .[9]

This artistic development, somewhat naïvely enthusiastic, manifested itself politically in the "Back to Africa" movement of Marcus Garvey and his followers. As Harold Cruse says,[10] the philosophy of the Garveyites was the first clear and overt articulation of "Negro Nationalism" that engendered a significant following. Yet this philosophy never fully came to terms with the relation between African-oriented nationalism and African-inspired art. Baraka himself has observed that the Garvey movement was important as a *stage* in the development of Afro-American nationalist thought.[11] A coherent aesthetic, based on clear harmonization of political theory and artistic inclination, was in no way an achievement of the great Renaissance of the 1920s.

There are several basic reasons for this failure which shed light upon the Black Arts Movement's own achievement. First of all, the Renaissance was in great part limited to a few metropolitan centers, particularly Harlem, and therefore became subject to a peculiar kind of urban provincialism. Only that which met the thematic and ideological standards of New York's entertainment-hungry marketplace could expect great attention. By contrast, the Black Arts Movement encompasses every major city (Philadelphia, Detroit, Chicago, San Francisco, and Los Angeles were in fact 'ahead' of New York in the early stages of the movement) and, increasingly, much of the South. Secondly, the very idea of a "new" Negro implied a negative view of the immediate past and contributed to the Renaissance's inability to develop a historical consciousness of Afro-American identity.[12]

But perhaps most problematically, the Renaissance's efforts were not addressed to those who could share their militant intent. While the "New Negro" spoke eloquently of "race-building" and "shared experience," the audience he sought to convince was the white literary establishment. The attempt to popularize Negro culture was made in the rhetoric of traditional Anglo-Saxon American values. Self-assertion was announced in terms of 'self-reliance' and 'self-help,' and the hopeful reward was to become "a collaborator and participant in American civilization" (Alain Locke). The Negro artist, patronized by whites such as Carl Van Vechten and Max Eastman, tended to write much of Negro circumstances and habits but not of Negro life-style or identity. The Harlem Renaissance proclaimed a new Negro pride, but the assertion was usually made in supplicatory and borrowed terms.

The Negritude movement of the 1930s was an important sequel to the Harlem Renaissance in the development of a Pan-African black consciousness. Led by the French-African poets Léopold Sédar Senghor, Aimé Cesaire (who coined the word *negritude*), and Léon G. Damas (whose volume *Pigments* sounded the poetic manifesto of the movement in 1938), the Negritude writers voiced their fresh awareness of racial pride in language evocative of Africa's regality, sensuality, and nascent possibility. The Negritude artists were greatly influenced by the Harlem Renaissance's major figures, men such as Locke, DuBois, Hughes, Claude McKay, Jean Toomer, and Sterling Brown. Though the Euro-African poets went beyond their American predecessors in heralding black beauty, power, and even nationhood, they were also concerned with harmonizing certain elements of Western and African cultures. As African exiles writing in European languages, they yearned to find meaning and identity in Africa but were subject to that same "double focus" DuBois had recognized in Negro Americans. Like the Afro-American, the Negritude writer had begun the journey but had yet to reach home.

Since that time, every major black writer has had to address the problem of the relation between aesthetic and political theories. Richard Wright (at one point in his career) felt that Marxism was the ideal starting point from which the Negro writer could maximize his social consciousness and realize his 'responsibility' as a writer. His attitude toward nationalism was, however, more reserved: "Negro writers must accept the nationalist implications of their lives, not in order to encourage them, but in order to change and transcend them. . . . For purposes of creative expression it means that the Negro writer must realize within the area of his own *personal* experience those impulses which, when prefigured in terms of broad social movements, constitute the stuff of nationalism" [13] (my emphasis).

Several black artists have rejected this problem as specious and counterproductive, chief among them Ralph Ellison, Lorraine Hansberry, and (until quite recently) James Baldwin. Ellison, for example, sees his primary role as a writer to be in his individual exploration, understanding, and depiction of the essential humanity of the Negro, for "art is a celebration of life even when life extends into death and . . . the sociological conditions which have made for so much misery in Negro life are not necessarily the only factors which make for the values which I feel endure and shall endure." [14] Many academically prominent black critics and scholars—Saunders Redding, W. Edward Farrison, Darwin T. Turner, and others—also rejected the problem of nationalism, demanding, rather, that the values of Negro fiction be examined without regard to political ideology.

It is in reaction to the belief that the job of ethnic renewal lies in autonomous artistic fulfillment rather than racial separatism or political revolution (a belief clearly latent even in Wright's work) that the young black intellectuals and artists of the 1960s made a rejuvenated attempt to establish a black aesthetic that would account for matters of politics as well as of art. The aesthetic discussions of the Black Arts Movement, led principally by Imamu Baraka, are an echo of those of the Harlem Renaissance and Negritude eras; but in tones more assertive and magniloquent than previously imaginable, these discussions unified social and artistic ideology into one coherent black aesthetic theory.

Our interest lies with the development of one man's aesthetic concepts—those of Imamu Baraka; what is true for him will not be perfectly mirrored in the writings of other major contemporary theorists (Hoyt Fuller, Maulana Karenga, Julius Lester, Ed Bullins, W. Keorapetse Kgositsile, Askia Muhammad Touré, and others). Yet, as we have stressed throughout, Baraka's work, in fact, should be regarded not merely as representative but as actually inspirational to the core of theoretical inquiry in the Black Arts Movement. The following explication of Baraka's attitudes toward the relation between politics and culture is meant primarily to serve as a model against which similar beliefs embodied in his poetry and plays may be studied and understood; however, the example Baraka's theory presents may be taken as a paradigm of the complex "black aesthetic" which the Black Arts Movement has produced.

On March 14, 1962, Baraka gave an address before the American Society for African Culture entitled "The Myth of a 'Negro Literature.' "[15] It is a fascinating essay; for, on the one hand, it presents a view of the black writer's role that Baraka's later works would seem to repudiate and, on the other, it reveals the boldly etched outline of several key concepts which those late works fleshed out in full form. It opens by bluntly attacking the shortcomings of the Afro-American literary tradition, characterizing the lineage from Phyllis Wheatley to Charles Chesnutt straight on to the "present generation" as one of "agonizing mediocrity," and placing the blame for this lack of distinction on the predominance of middle-class writers and their bourgeois attitudes. To be a writer in this tradition "was to be 'cultivated' . . . to be a 'quality' black man. It had nothing to do with the investigation of the human soul. It was, and is, a *social* preoccupation rather than an *aesthetic* one" (my emphasis).

Baraka thus attacks black writers for treating their role with disrespect by adhering to spiritually debilitating literary models (those of the "American mainstream") in order to attain the status such imitation afforded. To achieve "high art" the writer must be true to basic *aesthetic* principles; his work must "reflect the experiences of the human being, the emotional predicament of the man, as he exists, in the defined world of his being. It must be produced from the legitimate emotional responses of the soul in the world . . . It can never be produced by appropriating the withered emotional responses of some strictly social idea of humanity . . . It must issue from *real* categories of human activity, *truthful* accounts of human life, and not fancied accounts of the attainment of cultural privilege by some willingly preposterous apologists for one social 'order' or another."

Baraka's early emphasis on the writer's response to "the defined world of his being," in light of what has already been noticed in his writings, is no surprise. What is, perhaps, at first glance quite astonishing is his insistence that fine art must be free from slavish attachment to a social order or, implicitly, to political ideology. It is clear from these statements that for Baraka art has a definite and profound aesthetic justification, and that its role cannot be defined by principles wholly external to the laws of its own internal logic. Yet this aesthetic justification does lie in "the legitimate emotional resources of the soul *in the world*" (my emphasis), and for the Afro-American writer this means the emotional history and life of the black American. Why have past black authors failed to produce "high art"? Because they have willfully separated Negro life (i.e. "as an emotional experience") from their own Negro art.

> Where is the Negro-ness of a literature written in imitation of the meanest of social intelligences to be found in American culture, i.e., the white middle class? How can it even begin to express the emotional predicament of black Western man? Such a literature, even if its 'characters' are black, takes on the

> emotional barrenness of its model, and the blackness of the characters is like the blackness of Al Jolson, an unconvincing device. It is like using black checkers instead of white. They are still checkers.

The call, then, which Baraka is here issuing, is for discovery of the legitimate cultural tradition of the black man, its peculiar quality of "Negro-ness." This Negro-ness, Baraka continues, expresses itself in popular traditions of music, religion, and folklore that reflect "Africanisms"; yet (and this qualification must be kept solidly in mind in dealing with subsequent essays and the late drama), "It is not an African art American Negroes are responsible for, but an American one." The black writer must recognize the peculiar position of his place in society, and determine his function and modus vivendi accordingly: "the paradox of the Negro experience in America is that it is a separate experience, but inseparable from the complete fabric of American life. . . . Thus, the Negro writer . . . should [utilize] the entire spectrum of American experience from the point of view of the emotional history of the black man in this country: as its victim and its chronicler."

Here is the earliest evidence of the concept of *victim* which plays so dominant a role in the evolution of Baraka's drama. But, further, Baraka is beginning to establish the position of the black writer with respect to the enveloping American environment as that of omniscient outsider, a "no man's land completely invisible to white America, but so essentially part of it as to stain its whole being an ominous gray." To be meaningful and effective, Negro literature must "disengage itself from the weak, heinous elements of the culture that spawned it, and use its very existence as evidence of a more profound America."

There are really two impulses, then, in this early essay on black literature. To establish a literary community that can match the vigor of such other black media as blues and jazz, black writers must recognize their isolation from the American mainstream, cultivate this isolation, and, as members of the most knowledgeable social group in or out of this mainstream, create works which affirm the value of separation and condemn the decadence, hypocrisy, and violence of American artistic and social institutions. Herein lies the logic behind Baraka's criticism of "protest literature" which occurs early in the essay: by existing as a social object within an order understood and controlled by the dominant group, the protest writer "never moved into the position where he could propose his own symbols, erect his own personal myths, as any great literature must." Alongside this principle of knowledgeable isolation, which could eventually lead to the development of autonomous symbols and modes of expression for black authors, is set the idea that the black writer and his culture *are American,* are indeed more fully, more richly American than the oppressive majority. The Afro-American is, in fact, depicted here as the *quintessential* American.[16]

As Baraka's thought and aesthetic ideas evolved and matured through the 1960s, the first of these principles was enlarged and the second was completely transformed. Increasingly, as the concern for nationalism became more dominant, Baraka conceived of black culture and Black Power as necessarily fused concepts. The idea of "Negro-ness" was converted, under the influence of political thought, into the concept of "black consciousness." In an essay significantly entitled "The Legacy of Malcolm X, and the Coming of the Black Nation" (1965),[17] Baraka exhorts his people to respond to the "National Consciousness" that is the root of black culture. The consciousness is at once "national" and "cultural," and its creations will be the expression of "The National Genius."

Culture (which Baraka graphically depicts by his "Axis of Culture")[18] is the center around which the main forms and orders of art, politics, and religion gather and proliferate. As he had said in 1962, the strength and growth of black culture rest in the understanding and cultivation of separation from the white man; but now, the early suggestion of redemption of the American experience by black wisdom has been completely obliterated. In its place has risen the concept of the "autonomous Black Nation," based on the unification of Black Consciousness. This unified sensibility involves nothing less than total coordination of all categories of experience which emanate from the central spirit, or race *Geist*, of Black culture:

> Art, Religion, and Politics are impressive vectors of a culture. Art describes a culture. Black artists must have an image of what the Black sensibility is in this land. Religion elevates a culture. The Black Man must aspire to Blackness. God is man idealized. The Black man must idealize himself as Black. [. . .] The Black man must seek a Black politics, an ordering of the world that is beneficial to his culture, to his interiorization and judgment of the world. This is strength. And we are hordes.

For Baraka, black people are hereafter simultaneously and interconnectedly a race, a culture, and a nation. The black artist's role is not merely to elucidate and celebrate the emotional history of the Afro-American psyche but "to aid in the destruction of America as he knows it." [19] Baraka's writings become increasingly simple and lucid in asserting this double role for the artist; he echoes the words of Malcolm X and Frantz Fanon in insisting that "the purpose of our writing is to create a nation." [20] As black culture and Black Power are to join as a total reflection of black humanity and its spiritual aspirations, the aesthetic creed for the Black Arts Movement can be in great part reduced to simple aphorisms: "black art—the re-creation of our lives, as black . . . to inspire, educate, delight and move black people";[21] or "the 'Good' and 'Beautiful' [must be] synonymous";[22] or yet more succinctly, "enlighten by delightin." [23] This last phrase is no doubt a deliberately jivin' "seed-store feed-store" transcription of the Horatian dictum "dulce et utile"; the didactic thrust of the latter is certainly as dominant in Baraka's version of this utilitarian-moral aesthetic. By 1969 the conceptual unification of art and politics has hardened into the uncompromising position that "art without Nationalism is not Black." [24]

Were "enlighten by delightin" the only aesthetic precept to emerge from Baraka's views of culture and politics, his work—critical and creative—might seem less vital and certainly would be less complex. There is, in fact, something much more profound occurring beneath the surface of this rhetoric. Even the most casual perusal of Baraka's essays from 1965 to the present reveals an increased concentration on nationalism as the ideological mecca to which the collective consciousness of all black people must travel in its quest for power and freedom. This development produces in Baraka all of the key features traditionally associated with trenchant radicalism: a deep estrangement from the existing order, an insistence upon values incompatible with those embodied in actual institutions, a refusal to entertain projects of compromise, a mood of impatience, suspicion, and even at times exasperation, an embittered class or race consciousness reaching the point of hatred,[25] a determination to destroy and to create, and a belief that both destruction and creation can be readily achieved.

What Baraka desires, therefore, is nothing short of a complete restructuring of the Western world, and this depends equally upon political power and cultural liberation:

> Black Power movements not grounded in Black culture cannot move beyond the boundaries of Western thought. The paramount value of Western thought is the security and expansion of Western culture. Black Power is inimical to Western culture as it has manifested itself within black and colored majority areas anywhere on this planet. Western culture is and has been destructive to Colored all over the world. No movement shaped or contained by Western culture will ever benefit Black people. Black power must be the actual force and beauty and wisdom of Blackness . . . reordering the world.[26]

Black people must know themselves as separate not only to discover and deepen their own emotional history but to escape the depravity and ruination of decayed "Western" modes of art and life as well.[27] The Revolutionary Theatre must therefore be ultimately anti-Western;[28] and all manifestations of black culture must strive to realize "the post white, or post american form." [29] Baraka's aesthetic is thus also a visionary-exploratory manifesto, a call for "humanization" of form by imagination and "Spirit":

> The Art is The National Spirit. That manifestation of it. Black Art must be the Nationalist's vision given more form and

> feeling, as a razor to cut away what is not central to National Liberation. To show that which is. As a humanistic expression Black Art is a raiser, as a spiritual expression it is itself raised. And these are the poles, out of which we create, to raise, or as raised.[30]

This emphasis on the Black or National Spirit cannot be overemphasized. Baraka is, as we have already noted, concerned with maintaining a status and justification for art based on internal necessity, not mere political expediency. There is no political achievement without cultural achievement, for it is only in their simultaneous representation that Black Consciousness, or the very soul of the Black Nation, finds itself *in the world.* The desire for new symbols, myths, and forms expressed in "The Myth of a 'Negro Literature' " takes on a particularly challenging and urgent tone when placed in the context of radical nationalism. The abandonment of decayed "Western" forms and the creation of newer, spiritually vital expressions places the artist in the very forefront of revolutionary activity; indeed, he must, in his effort to realize the Spirit of Black Consciousness, become God: "the Black Artist is a creator. The Creator. He must become as the creative function of the universe." [31]

III

Imamu Baraka's dramatic works, as his evolving aesthetic viewpoint suggests, are conditioned by a moral and didactic urge which takes the shape of a particular vision. He is motivated by the same impulse of other artists who have similarly sought to achieve conversion of others through their works (for example, Augustine, Milton, Blake), and is faced with the same essential task: to organize effectively the materials of a rhetorical, didactic structure into the form of a new, whole aesthetic structure. Whatever Baraka's aesthetics, he cannot avoid the history of the world that surrounds him (including the history of the theatre); he must belong, as Lucien Goldmann would say, "reflexively" [32] to the mental structure of the enveloping civilization. Thus it must be emphasized that, however sure Baraka is of achieving a new, "post-Western form," he cannot, in fact, wholly create any such entity; he can only discover the peculiar materials and their ideal configuration through which his ideological and poetic presuppositions are best realized. Specifically, he can discover two things: (1) the roots of black experience and "Spirit"; and (2) a dramatic form to convey the lessons and essence of these roots.

Baraka, as we have seen, developed in the 1960s a particular vision of black culture and history that would realize fulfillment in the creation of the Black Nation and reification by a unified Black Consciousness. But, as Northrop Frye has repeatedly stressed,[33] literary substance or "shape" does not proceed simply from a view of life, or from life itself; it comes from tradition, and so ultimately from myth. Baraka is quite alive to the necessity of orienting his vision of the future to the symbolic power of the past; statements such as the following permeate his discussions of unifying sociopolitical and cultural movements: "A culturally aware black politics would use all the symbols of the culture, all the keys and images out of the black past, out of the black present, to gather the people to it, and energize itself with their strivings at conscious blackness . . . Black Power must mean a black people with a past clear back to the beginning of the planet, channeling the roaring energies of black to revive black power. . . . Our actual renaissance." [34]

This call for the resurrection of racial symbols and forms of consciousness coetaneous with the race itself indicates that Baraka's ultimate objective is nothing less than discovery and re-creation of a national myth. Only in the mythic can the visionary poet realize the aspirations which his imaginative impulses produce; this is especially true for Imamu Baraka. The path of Baraka's literary career, and specifically in the dramatic works, describes a curve which moves indomitably toward the mythic. It is a major problem of this study, then, to plot this curve as it develops through various dramatic forms which are themselves the apparatuses created to put forth various aspects and phases of mythic content. Of major interest will be not only what this form and content ultimately become, but how the development and final achievement of Baraka's drama realize and diverge from the aesthetic and visionary ideas that motivated the attempt. Something more than simply knowledge of Baraka's own art may be, perhaps, arrived at; we can hope to reach some understanding, first, of the creative process that informs the work of poets with similar problems, and second, of the particular issues that confront most contemporary Afro-American writers as artists.

Our task demands a foundational analysis of the directions the mythic impulses of a moral and visionary artist such as Imamu Baraka are likely to take. Of paramount importance is the dialectical quality of myth that derives from the primordial discrepancy between the world of brute facts, by which man's immediate reality is circumscribed, and the world beyond the actual, to which man continually aspires. This dialectic divides the universe into two counterposed realms, a heaven and a hell, such as those found in the *New Testament* and Novalis's *Hymns to the Night.* In the myth that Baraka develops, of course, these two states are marked off by the separation of white decadence from black humanism, the Black Nation from America, the Black Spirit from the white devil. The language he employs to indicate these fundamental oppositions is not merely that of political rhetoric; it is the simple and more deeply understood logos of the vatic urge:

Be somebody Beautiful
Be Black and Open
Reach for God
And succeed
in your life world heaven
will scream at you
to enter, enter Black Man
bathe in Blackness

Energies exploding
Black World Renewed
Sparks! Stars! Eyes!
Huge Holocausts of Heaven
Burning down the white man's world
Holy Ashes!!!

Let the rains melt them into rivers.
And the new people naked bathe themselves

And look upon the life to come as the heaven
we
seek
Sonni Weusi Akbar

[from "The Calling Together"] [35]

As "The Calling Together" (1967) suggests, the contrast between 'is' and 'ought' which the dialectic of myth projects, leads to a rigorous dichotomy between that which is natural and that which is inimical to a harmonious existence and fulfilling destiny for man. That which is black is most *natural:* this is one primary element we can expect to discover in the development of myth in Baraka's work. The dualism of man's seemingly limited power to realize his hopes and his unlimited vision is reconciled in myth by the central mythic ideals (for example, in Christianity, the Incarnation and the Resurrection); whatever they may be, the power of these ideals (at least in Western mythologies) stems from assimilation of natural to human forms. This humanizing of nature is the basic force of civilization, which is what Baraka really means when he speaks of Black Culture.

Baraka's concept of culture, then, which is the nexus of all expressions of Black Consciousness, is one major ingredient of the myth he strives to realize. And then, too, black art, which is the creative root of Black Culture, is seen as the key to the attainment of the spiritual goals of the Black Nation:

> To create for the universe reflect blackness and the universe will listen. You must begin with black to begin with the human raising his head above what exists. What exists is dead. It is slow to your eye to fall. But look up one day and it will be gone, and you must not go with it.
>
> To create for everything is spiritart. Black Art is the first step pointing our heaven.[36]

If Black Culture is one major element of Baraka's central myth, another is prophecy. The controlling idea of Baraka's prophetic utterances is the emancipation of black people; they are myth-oriented projections of the final achievement of liberation, to which the heaven-bound art of Black Culture points. If the revolutionary theatre is to be a prophetic theatre in this manner, it must "take dreams and give them a reality. It must isolate the ritual and historical cycles of reality . . . it must be food for all those who need food, and daring propaganda for the beauty of the Human Mind. . . . It must be a theatre of World Spirit. Where the spirit can be shown to be the most competent force in the world." [37] It is interesting to see the precise role the imagination plays in making this drama speak not only of the existent and possible but, further, of the "probable improbabilities" [38] which mythic content deploys:

> What is called the imagination (from image, magi, magic, magician, etc.) is a practical vector from the soul. It stores all data, and can be called on to solve our 'problems.' The imagination is the projection of ourselves past our sense of ourselves as 'things.' Imagination (Image) is all possibility, because from the image, the initial circumscribed energy, and use (idea) is possible. And so begins that image's use in the world. Possibility is what moves us.[39]

Not unlike Blake, who also developed a unique mythology from archetypical elements to combat the oppressiveness of what surrounded him, Baraka calls here for the use of creative faculties aligned with the spiritual extension of the black man's sensibility to move the soul past materiality and make the "theatre of World Spirit" into an unbounded reality. As with Blake, the language of apocalypse permeates Baraka's work ("The Calling Together" is exemplary), and the idea of apocalypse is central to his mythic constructs. In order to effect the transformation from the world-that-is to that which should be, the complete synthesis of the spiritual and the human must be achieved in a natural form. Thus it will be the playwright's duty to write "plays of human occasion" wherein "the humans we will show [embrace] spiritism." [40] To motivate Black Consciousness toward absolute "spiritism," black art must "let the black beauty glow through, whether attained or desired what we are and what we all *can* be. Stress evolution, what the world can be in strong and beautiful hands."[41] Eventually, there must be plays to show "how we triumphed."[42]

The mythic content that heralds this triumph must be presented in a form appropriate to it. The following statement summarizes the intent toward which Baraka's mythic impulse is directed and raises the concomitant problem of form, which is so central to our study of the development of Baraka's drama:

> The separation, the hunting, for fresh natural experience, is the approach to the self, but further, is the key to the move past the self, as if to become part of the forces of nature, the creative 'urge' which is Godliness. Black people are strong for the reasons they are strong. Despite what you think exists we, black people, are the spiritual people, yes, caught here among sinister materialists. The end of one epic is the chaos (anti-form) preceding (as different families, races come around in different guises, through the centuries) the new.[43]

Separated from white Western culture, the black man seeks resurrection of his root identity in order to transcend personal fixations upon that fresh sense of self and achieve integration with a natural order of Spirit. This achievement rests upon complete transformation of the materials the black man has inherited from his oppressor into new and vital forms of expression and being. It should be emphasized that the statement just quoted does not describe the actual myth these new forms will presumably enclose; but these words do explicitly indicate Baraka's inclination and need to mythologize.

Just what effects can we expect this tendency to have on Baraka's dramatic form? A short discussion of the nature of alternative methods of literary design will help us greatly in answering this crucial question. Of course, every poet (in the largest sense) has a private mythology, his own choice and organization of symbols. His "mythology," in this sense, is a selective cross-section of his life and perceptions, and the manner in which this cross-section is presented determines the literary shape of the poet's work. However, as Northrop Frye has demonstrated with great care, a poet, whatever his private vision, may work within the poles of *mimesis*—fidelity to verisimilitude and descriptive accuracy—and *mythos*—the use of stories free from requirements of probability and mimetic credibility.

In between these poles of literary design lies the whole area of romance, the tendency to "displace" myth from the godlike and impossible toward the human and plausible, and to contrast realism by "conventionalizing content in an idealized direction." [44] The closer the poet's thematic concerns (or vision) move him to the fictional modes most clearly associated with *mimesis,* the more his work will take on the attributes of an *ironic* structure. If his vision necessitates a move toward the fictional modes associated with *mythos,* his work will begin to approximate a mythic structure. Irony, Frye tells us, "begins in realism and dispassionate observation." [45] In its most trenchant form, it approaches a point of extreme "realism" or representative likeness to life. But, as it does so, it "moves steadily toward myth, and dim outlines of sacrificial rituals and dying gods begin to reappear in it." [46] This reappearance of myth within the extreme examples of ironic structure is found in the best of twentieth-century "ironic" authors: Joyce, Kafka, Beckett, Ellison. As the movement from ironic to mythic modes of fiction progresses, we find a parallel stylistic development from extreme realism to the most abstract and conventionalized expressions.

Frye's categories of literary structure provide us with a perfect model for the study of Baraka's development of dramatic form. We have seen how Baraka's aesthetic theory has evolved from a concern with "standing somewhere in the world" and belief that "a writer is committed to what is real not to the sanctity of his FEELINGS" to the messianic propagation of a National Myth of Black Consciousness as a prophet/priest of the black race *Geist.* The constant in this changing sensibility is engagement, the desire to unify the political and the cultural in the larger effort to achieve freedom. One can see at once what pressures these different aesthetic viewpoints will bring to bear upon problems of form. One can expect works of the early period to be more realistic, more concerned with rooting out what Baraka perceives to be current problems facing the black man and depicting them and their proposed solutions in a relatively plausible fashion. One can expect them to be *in the world*—that is, in the world as we commonly understand it. But insofar as Baraka will be attentive to projecting solutions, or commenting upon the given reality of black-white relationships, we will likely find allegorical frameworks surrounding realistic designs, and even, perhaps, the "dim outlines" of mythic and/or ritualistic conventions. As we move to works of later stages, we can anticipate these mythic elements becoming more dominant in the formal structures and the desire to maintain the artifice of plausibility less severe.

Since every work of literature has a thematic as well as a fictional aspect, a change in the nature of theme and characters accompanying change in form is a certainty. Most prominently, the role of the hero, as Baraka's idea of the black man is transmuted from black-man-as-victim to black-man-as-god will alter with the dramatic context. Frye's analysis of literature begins with the observation that "fictions may be classified by the hero's power of action" [47] ranging from mythic, wherein the divine hero has powers superior in kind to other men and his environment, to the ironic, wherein the hero is inferior in power (and intelligence, or at least in knowledge) to ourselves. As Baraka's dramatic form changes to accommodate his movement from an ironic to a mythic sensibility, we can expect the black heroes of his drama to change accordingly. And as these heroes change from victims to something approaching gods—the former isolated from society and its oppressive powers, the latter integrated into the ideal society of the national myth—we can further expect a general shift from generic plots resembling or approaching the tragic to those more nearly comic.

I have already noted that realism involves a mimesis of ordinary experience while the mythic requires a contrasting tendency toward abstraction and conventionalization. As the poet attempts to give imaginative coherence to the lifelike and common, the language he employs becomes consciously simplified and relatively free of explicit connections with mythic patterns. This has been a major thrust of poetic diction since Wordsworth's plea for "a simple produce of the common day," and the dramatists in the "naturalist" tradition have also sought a more lifelike speech. For example, in Strindberg's naturalist manifesto "The Author's Preface to 'Miss Julie,' " the playwright asserts of his construction of dialogue: "I have, to a certain degree, broken with tradition by not making catechists out of my characters . . . I have avoided the symmetrical, mathematical construction commonly used by the French in their dialogue. Instead I have had my characters use their brains only intermittently as people do *in real life* where, during a conversation, one cog in a person's brain may find itself, more or less by chance, geared into another cog" (my emphasis).

As long as the writer is concerned with divorcing his language from the inorganic allusions which are the stuff of literary "tradition," he will more likely appear to record accurately the gearing of one cog of thought into another. But when the mythologizing tendencies are stronger, the fanciful and abstract imagery appropriate to the mythical subject emerges and more refined patterns of language prevail. If Baraka's drama does indeed evolve formally from ironic to mythic structures, from the exploration of the actual to the projection of the ideal, then the language employed in the drama should equally change from a mimetic to a more stylized type.

Thus, we can expect certain thematic, generic, and linguistic changes to occur as Baraka's drama develops in search of a new, "post-Western" form to accommodate his particular conception of the black experience. Imamu's black nationalist-inspired mythology is the fundamental starting point of his plays; it defines the place "in the world" from which his "point of view" is determined. There is, however, a complementary element of his "black aesthetic" which has an equally profound effect upon the drama's evolution: black music as the epitome of black ethos. An analysis of this subject—crucial to any fruitful investigation of Baraka's art—will facilitate a comprehensive understanding of his aesthetic vision.

3 Music as Black Aesthetic: African Energy and Historicity

Imamu Baraka's cultural ideology has evolved from a general sense of malignancy in the Western world to a sharply focused black nationalism. In turn, his concern to develop a formal aesthetic has moved from criticism of the 'mainstream' Afro-American writer and of fragmentation among black art forms to assertion of a unified black ethos. There is in this complex and not precisely linear evolution a crucial constant: *black music* has long represented for Baraka the model and in some ways even the means for attaining the desired Afro-American cultural independence. As with many others in the Afro-American literary tradition, Baraka finds in black music the essence of black experience. For him, the "black aesthetic" is preeminently a musical one, and his theoretical reflections upon this subject provide a profound insight into the basic object of his art.

I

Baraka's belief that music is central to Afro-American life is not at all new, yet his understanding of what constitutes *truly* black music and its history is strikingly different from that of his predecessors. To grasp the impact and implication of Baraka's music-oriented aesthetic, one must be aware of the traditional intellectual tune on which he riffs his new notes. Some historical perspective on the Afro-American writer's conceptions of his community's music is therefore imperative to my examination of Baraka's theory.

Afro-American writers have generally asserted that the musician affects black people more immediately than any preacher, politician, or ideologue. Whether his expressive vehicle be gospels, blues, jazz, rhythm and blues, or soul, the black musician transforms the daily agony of his audience's experience into bearable and even meaningful form. The old call-and-response pattern of African songs and American field hollers informs the symbiotic relationship between the improvising musician and his jiving audience. The musician thus acts as a spiritual leader to the people, a quasi-Orphic priest whose descent to the underground grit of experience teaches and reaffirms the fundamental principles of black survival. Whether by Ellington-like elegance or soul shouts à la James Brown, the black musician makes sense of the chaos of The Life in terms of a distinctively black style. The identification of the poet with the musician in Afro-American literature is, therefore, quite natural. The black poet, from Langston Hughes to Sonia Sanchez, has looked to the musician for strength, vatic inspiration, and the source of pure joy and spirit.

In terms of specific influence, black poets have consistently employed tonal, rhythmic, and structural effects first utilized by black musicians. The language of black poetry is in great measure a product of various oral modes, of which music is the most important.[1] Thematic uses of music by the poets, however, have changed greatly over time. The Harlem Renaissance saw the first widespread discussion of black music as a distinctive cultural contribution. Langston Hughes especially opened his art to the verbal riches of blues, gospels, jazz-lyrics, and other musical forms. Moreover, music served Hughes as a symbol for black creativity in the face of oppressive conditions. Yet there is little idea in Hughes's work, or (with the notable though relatively uninfluential exception of Jean Toomer's *Cane*) in the efforts of other Renaissance writers, of music as a rebellious and vitalizing element of Afro-American life, organically related to Afro-American history.[2] To the Harlem Renaissance artist, music was a formal resource and an uplifting (albeit 'exotic') entertainment but not a manifestation of the most serious cultural experience.

With the work of Ralph Ellison and James Baldwin, music takes on a far greater thematic role in Afro-American literature. The nameless protagonist of Ellison's *Invisible Man*, whose search for identity underlies every major scene, finds that this quest is dependent upon discovery of his people's folk origins. The primary metaphor for this folk tradition is the blues (as exemplified by the character Trueblood), and Ellison's hero ultimately learns to recognize his personal complexity by accepting and emulating the blues pattern established by Trueblood early in the novel. In several of Baldwin's works (particularly "Sonny's Blues," *Blues for Mister Charlie*, and *Another Country*) black music also functions as a motif expressing a complete mode of life.

In contrast to Ellison's Trueblood, however, Baldwin's musician illustrates the despair of isolation rather than the possibility of reintegration with the community by way of personal expression. As Sherley Anne Williams perceptively notes, Baldwin's musicians are more typical twentieth-century artist-heroes: "the embodiments of alienation and estrangement . . . they are also commentaries upon the brutal, emasculating, feared—and fearing—land from which they are so estranged." [3] Yet, as Williams goes on to show, Baldwin's use of music is at one with his vision of the black experience and is particularly the vehicle for his exploration of historically conditioned sufferings. Baldwin, like Ellison, finds in music all the thematic details necessary to create an image of black life; with their fiction, the black musician attains the status of exemplary black soul.

The Black Arts Movement writers build upon Hughes's, Ellison's, and Baldwin's efforts to incorporate black music into an Afro-American ethos. As already noted, music has become not only the model but the actual goal of black poetry. The new writers seek to go beyond hypostatization of music as the perfect metaphor for black life; rather, they have collapsed the distinctions between musical and other black expressions to such an extent that black music is seen as black life itself, pressed into its purest essence. The black musician is deemed heroic not because he best exemplifies the possibilities of self in relation to the group (as with Ellison) but because he represents the black nation at its most powerful and expressive pitch.

Henry Dumas's remarkable story "Will the Circle Be Unbroken?" [4] may be taken as a mythical rendering of this new sensibility. The story tells of the legendary saxophone player, Probe, and his "afro-horn," which is "the newest axe to cut the deadwood of the world." He is playing at the Sound Barrier Club to an all-black audience that is shaped into a womblike and pulsating "circle" by his music. Probe's afro-horn breaks all walls of consciousness, and only those within the circle are immune to its vibrating "motives." But to some, the notion of deadly musical frequencies seems too wild to be true. Three whites, led by a hipster who "blew" with Probe years back, gain access to the Sound Club against the protestations of the black doorman, who warns them, "We cannot allow non-Brothers because of the danger with extensions." Soon, Probe's descent to "motives" gets deeper, and, "Samson"-like among "white pillars," he stretches his newborn spirit against the alien walls of white consciousness. "He moved to the edge of the circle, rested his sax, and lifted his axe . . ."

> Inside the center of the gyrations is an atom stripped of time, black. The gathering of the hunters, deeper. Coming, laced in the energy of the sun. He is blowing. [. . .] Under the single voices is the child of a woman, black. They are building back the wall, crumbling under the disturbance.

The "new philosophy," carried by the sound waves of the afro-horn, kills the three intruders who, in fact, submit to the music's greater energy. The horn, in turn, penetrates the womb-circle of the black collective and helps to conceive the black child, the fresh promise of liberated Afro-consciousness.

In "Will the Circle Be Unbroken?" music has become both a damning judgment of the nonblack consciousness and the medium of a redemptive apocalypse in which the physical and spiritual aspects of black being are fused. The musician has taken on an evangelical and revolutionary role, and his message (the music's explosive vibrations) and the black audience join in giving birth to the black nation. Music is all that black life was, is, and ever shall be:

> Listen to the sound of my horn, my people.
> This rhythm of years long past.

Listen to the sound of my horn, I say;
Music and I . . . have come at last!
[Henry Dumas, "Listen to the Sound of My Horn"]

Dumas's story indicates that the Black Arts Movement's conception of black music makes possible a music-oriented black aesthetic consonant with black nationalist cultural ideology. On the one hand, Maulana Karenga speaks of "the rhythmic reality of a permanent revolution";[5] on the other, James Stewart asserts that "music comes closest to being" and blazes the revolutionary path away from the West toward "definite black values."[6] Clearly, what music teaches and what revolutionary ideology preaches are fundamentally alike. In the late 1960s, this equation received widespread recognition among black theorists. But it was Imamu Baraka who first (and best) formulated the relation between a black music aesthetic and a black revolutionary ethic.

Baraka's writings on black music are well-represented by two volumes, *Blues People* (1963) and *Black Music* (1967). *Black Music* is a sheaf of essays and liner notes about avant-garde jazz of the 1960s. *Blues People*, the better known of the two, is a theoretical/historical treatise dealing with black music from its African origins to the "new wave" jazz discussed extensively in *Black Music*. The earlier work, because of its unifying historical interpretation and self-conscious theorizing, provides the basic text for our analysis of Baraka's music aesthetic. The ideas proposed in *Blues People* underlie the more specific investigations collected in *Black Music*.

Baraka's music criticism is not primarily concerned with 'music appreciation' or questions of style, formal innovation, or individual method—although he often examines these at great length. Rather, he seeks to demonstrate that black music "is essentially the expression of an attitude, or a collection of attitudes, about the world"; it is "only secondarily an attitude about the way music is made."[7] The "attitude" (or approach to reality) that lies at the root of black music imbues this art form with a specific "social and cultural intent." The musician's notes are merely 'musical' insofar as they are susceptible to technical analysis. More crucially, these notes emanate from a "body of socio-cultural philosophy" and convey a precise emotional response to life. Thus, a meaningful history of black music would be a description of a historically valid black "attitude" (ethos):

> The African cultures, the retention of some parts of these cultures in America, and the *weight* of the stepculture produced the American Negro. A new race. I want to use music as my persistent reference just because the development and transmutation of African music to American Negro music [. . .] represents to me this whole process in microcosm. [pp. 7–8]

These two essential motives of Baraka's music criticism—to understand black music's basic "attitude" and to explain the historical character of that attitude—indicate that Baraka admires this music for more than its originality or durability. For in his people's songs, Baraka discerns a viable philosophy of life that is rooted in the spiritually pure time and place of Africa. Looked at each in its turn, these two motives reveal the essence of Baraka's black music aesthetic.

II

When Africans were brought to America as slaves their physical powers were harnessed for the profit of others. This was not a suddenly new experience; Africans had long been enslaved by other Africans, particularly in West Africa. In Baraka's view, the original element introduced by American slavery was only tangential to its economic consequences, for the fundamental opposition in America between white and black was not physical but philosophical: "to be brought to a country, a culture, a society, that was, and is, in terms of purely philosophical correlatives, the complete antithesis of one's own version of man's life on earth—that is the cruelest aspect of this particular enslavement" (p. 1). The clash of world-views between master and slave was beyond either party's control—both had inherited their cultures as inevitably as their skin colors. And this unalterable contradiction is the root of

America's tragic conflict between the descendants of African slaves and the descendants of Western masters:

> There was no communication between master and slave on any strictly human level, but only the relation one might have to a piece of property. [. . .] It was this essential condition of nonhumanity that characterized the African slave's lot in this country of his captivity, a country which was later and ironically to become *his land* also. [p. 3]

Who, then, was the Western slave-master? What characterized his cultural identity, his way of looking at the world? Baraka frames the answers to these questions in very simple and uncompromising terms. Modern Western man is the creation of the Renaissance and its 'humanistic' ideology. Whereas the life of pre-Renaissance man centered upon worship of God and was organized in nearly all facets by the Church's strict authority, his post-Renaissance scion 'liberated' secular activity from the prison of religious concern. Alongside (and ultimately replacing) the traditional metaphysical beliefs was the worship of the human mind and, concomitantly, the mind's absolute emancipation from the vigilance of moral judgment. The myth of 'Progress' gradually supplanted the old theological inhibitions; man came to feel "life itself was of value—and could be made *perfect*" (p. 5). The searching mind and the restless imagination were declared sacrosanct. No longer held in check by a commonly accepted ethic, post-Renaissance man acts on the assumption that everything that can be known is also worth knowing. Wherever he sees the chance of a new departure, he will take it because an a priori sense of what *ought* to be known doesn't exist for him. This new man—Faust, the individual, in the Western mythology; Yacoub, the insatiably inquisitive "new critic" [8] (a wildly haruspicating rather than signifying monkey), in the Black Muslim mythology—hides behind the role of 'objective' or 'neutral' observer of Nature and finally of himself, the scientist/merchant whose products are designed to improve man's material lot, not his soul.

Post-Renaissance man thus adopted a view that had hitherto been regarded as a satanic temptation—that his reason was the guarantee of a preestablished harmony between himself and the God of Creation: *cogito ergo sum.* But the greatest invention of this Faustian researcher was the spiritual hell of a world without meaning for the soul, a world ruthlessly examined by the detached intellect and exploited by the acquisitive material instincts but confusedly suffered by the useless passions. Modern man is still paying back the debt overdue the devil. Or, as the harsh Black Muslim legend says of Yacoub's descendants, Western men are a race of evil magicians about to perish in the grips of machines unleashed by the 'magic' formulae of ratio; a horde of "cave-dwellers" sheltering themselves from the creations of their overproductive minds.

In *Blues People* Baraka does not dwell upon the character of Western man quite so metaphorically. Here he is interested principally in the way this sensibility determined the modern Western aesthetic. If post-Renaissance man is a secular individual whose actions are severed from preestablished religious codes, then art no longer has any specific *use* for him:

> "Serious" Western music, except for early religious music, has been strictly an "art" music. [. . .] "Serious music" (a term that could only have extra-religious meaning in the West) has never been an integral part of the Westerner's life; no art has been since the Renaissance. [p. 29]

The art-work could now be appreciated only for nonfunctional, "aesthetic" attributes—beauty of line, proportion, clarity, etc. Since the soul was of little or no value in life, pure expression came to have little value in art. Western man worships the artistic *artifact*—the poem, painting, building—as opposed to the creative and expressive process that presumably shaped the particular work. The Western aesthetic is thus basically static: regularity triumphs over emotive dissonance, statement over implication, artifact over improvisational expression.

In opposition to the post-Renaissance Western aesthetic, Baraka sets a very different conception of the non-Western, African cultural dynamic. Whereas Western man witnessed the gradual fragmentation of society and compartmentalization of life's enterprises, the African viewed life as a network of activities unified by the ruling purpose of religious devotion. The white slave-master subverted most concerns to the pursuit of commercial success; the African believed in "complex concepts of predetermination and the subservience of the human being to a complex of gods" (p. 6). Thus the Western distinction between art and life, as well as the removal of art from the store of 'useful' avocations, never occurred in African culture. Rather, art maintained its functional role in the "complex" activity of religious service:

> It was, and is, inconceivable in the African culture to make a separation between music, dancing, song, the artifact, and a man's life or his worship of his gods. [p. 29]

Art was thus no less important than the places or tasks it embellished. Beauty, emotion, intention, and meaning were a synthetic whole: "*Expression* issued from life, and *was* beauty" (p. 29). Thus the concrete art object was no more valuable than the manner of creation and presentation, nor did it signify any better than a fleeting yet direct response to a particular situation. The African aesthetic placed the natural quality of expression above all other possible categories.

There are several ways in which this contrast between Western and African Weltanschauungen can be formulated. In a highly metaphorical sense, it may be thought of as the distinction between language, which delimits the territory of its referents, and music, which like reality itself, proceeds relatively without contour. For Western man, life has rigorously projected and detached from itself its own opposite, something which might be loosely termed consciousness, reflection, or thought. Once detached from life, the feeling or consciousness of life, by filtering through the mind, tends to 'cool off,' to clarify and idealize itself; from the particular, changeable, ephemeral state it was, it will eventually crystallize into a general, abstract idea. Having risen through logical abstraction to its own second power, having become reflective thought, the consciousness of life tends to confine life within fixed borders, to channel it between chosen banks, to pour it into stiff, definitive molds: the conventions, mores, traditions, and laws of society.

What traps men within those frozen forms, without their even so much as surmising that a dark, furious ocean may stir beneath them, is language. Even feelings, when expressed in linguistic codes, tend to become the prisoners of words, which fix them, isolate them, and thereby make them typical. As Bergson noted in his *Essay on the Immediate Data of Consciousness*: "Words, as soon as they are formed, would turn, of course, against the sensation which gave them birth, and having been invented to testify that sensation is unstable, they would impose their own stability on it." Thus, to a culture dependent upon words as tools of analysis, language immobilizes feelings, arrests them into the stable condition of artifacts.

Baraka argues that there is no such dualism in African culture; that no world of solidified forms or system of constructions is allowed to dam up and compress that dark turmoil of life which flows restlessly through each moment's renewal. Baraka stresses the fact that Africans "used drums for communication" and that meaning in African languages "can be changed simply by altering the *pitch* of a word" (p. 26). He suggests that for the African the highest form of expression takes its most salient features from music, and implies further that the most precise mode of communication is music itself. African music is functional not only in being an indispensable part of worship but also because the essential lessons of African society were taught through various types of dance, drumming, and song.

Two qualities of this music explain how it operates so integrally in the African's life: first, its basic form is the "antiphonal singing technique" (similar to that employed in Christian liturgy), which allows for a fluid relationship between the conventional theme supplied by the leader (tradition) and the response of the community (expression); the second vital aspect of African music is clearly related to the first: improvisation, which (unlike Christian chant, with its fixed texts) equates the process of response with the final creation. Hence life and the feeling of life were fused in the African musical idioms.

We may recognize this discrimination between language and music as another form of the cultural dichotomy explored in *The*

System of Dante's Hell. Perhaps closer to the particular theoretical concerns of *Blues People* is Baraka's analysis of the ways of expressing that are intrinsic to Western and African cultures. William Fischer, in his excellent commentary on *Blues People*, notes that Baraka's distinction between Western and African-based styles is founded upon an analogy to language itself:

> the black writer, in order to capture the quality and feeling of process . . . [must] place the emphasis on what I would call *predicate* forms . . . and not on the nounal forms that tend in themselves to impede forward motion . . . European-American culture tends generally to favor the noun. Its writers ordinarily cultivate the object-image.[9]

Fischer points out that in a chapter of *Blues People* entitled "Swing—From Verb to Noun," Baraka charts the progress (or, more truthfully, the degeneration) of Afro-American jazz of the 1930s from its basic improvisational impulse to the static re-creation of black motifs by white practitioners such as Benny Goodman. Baraka's discussion of the word *swing* illuminates this general contrast:

> *Swing,* the verb, meant a simple reaction to the music (and as it developed in verb usage, a way of reacting to anything in life). As it was formalized, and the term and the music taken further out of context, *swing* became a noun that meant a commercial popular music in cheap imitation of a kind of Afro-American music. [pp. 212–13]

The important subject-matter of *Blues People*, then, is this opposition between the changing, ever-becoming activity fundamental to African aesthetics and the formalistic impulse of Western art. The survival of the African process in Afro-American music is, in fact, of greater concern than the styles, schools, and creators of that music, for these latter elements are merely the *artifacts* produced by the African sensibility. The real theme of *Blues People* is the same as that of his overtly theoretical essay, "Hunting Is Not Those Heads on the Wall":

> I speak of the *verb process,* the doing, the coming into being, the at-the-time-of. Which is why we think there is particular

> value in live music, contemplating the artifact as it arrives, listening to it emerge. *There* it is. And *There.*
>
> But even this is after the fact. Music, the most valuable of artifacts [. . .] is still not the activity that makes itself possible. Music is what is left after what? *That* is important.[10]

To locate the "what" of which the sounds of black music are merely traces—this is the true goal of *Blues People.*

The emphasis upon expression and functionality in the African aesthetic had a profound effect upon the cultural life of the black slave. Uprooted from every possession, the African perforce suffered the loss of those cultural forms which depended upon tangible *things:* "The artifact was, like any other material manifestation of pure African culture, doomed" (p. 16). But (ironically, perhaps, in light of the slave-master's attempted denial of African humanity) this threatened the preservation of the essential African character very little: "Only religion (and magic) and the arts were not completely submerged by Euro-American concepts. Music, dance, religion, do not have *artifacts* as their end products, so they were saved" (p. 16). Denied the means of reproducing the material features of his culture, the African captive was left to cultivate the aesthetic/metaphysic "complex" which, in fact, constituted his people's ultimate value-system. Thus the master subjected the slave only on a physical level; the *system* of African culture continued to exist, though the master was, of course, blind to its presence. Moreover, confrontation between Westerner and African was waged covertly from their first encounter and continued as the slave evolved into the Afro-American:

> The African's belief in the supernatural was carried over into the life of the American slave. The retort to the Western derision of the African's "fear" of the supernatural is simply that the white man conducts his life without thought to the gods. If the former idea seemed "childish" to the master, the latter idea seemed extremely dangerous to the slave. So one man becomes a child, and the other a fool. [p. 9]

Before the Civil War and Emancipation, any conflict between African and Western world-views was obfuscated by the brute reality of slavery. But when the black slave was set free in America, this latent opposition surfaced as the Afro-American's choice between assimilation and adaptation. Assimilation was not a meaningful cultural option for the slave, except in the religious sphere where Christianity proffered an escape into 'eternal life' in return for a movement away from African tradition in the 'here-and-now.' Emancipation seemed to offer the Negro a far greater opportunity to join the white mainstream than did the Christian church: now he could seek full "citizenship." The crucial result of Emancipation, Baraka observes, was the creation of a "meta-society" among Negroes, "one whose members strove to emulate exactly the white society" (p. 54). The freed black slaves thus divided into two disparate factions: the "freedmen"—those who maintained their separate identity and Africanisms; and the "citizens"—those who sought to shirk whatever customs seemed 'too Negroid' and thereby gain entry into the dominant culture. Stated in terms more germane to Baraka's study of black music, the Western *and* the African aesthetics appeared equally available to the freed slave: the conflict between them took the form of a schism in the *black* community itself.

This nationalist version of DuBois's "double consciousness" pits the African-oriented freedman against the seeker of pure American citizenship. Naturally, Baraka sees the former's course as superior, for the latter's belief that citizenship can be fully attained is 'delusory': "There was always a border beyond which the Negro could not go, whether musically or socially. [. . .] The Negro could not ever become white and that was his strength" (p. 80). The drama of the freedman-citizen conflict is played out most excitingly in black music, for here the choice between aesthetic approaches takes immediate and striking effect. No matter how well he mastered the white, Euro-American way of "being in the world," the ex-slave was clearly and ultimately just that: a black, former African. At the point of this realization, the Afro-American "had to make use of other resources, whether African, subcultural, or hermetic. And it was this boundary, this no man's land, that provided the logic and beauty of his music" (p. 80).

Baraka describes the historical relationship between Afro-American music and its polar influences of African and Western cultures in several ways. One obvious question he poses is whether music played a major role in the Afro-American's religious life as it had for the African. Baraka points out that the middle-class Negro "citizen" molded his ceremonial devotions to the patterns established by white Christian churches. Hymns expressing the longing for Jordan supplanted songs and chants about Africa; dancing, shouting, and "spirit possession" were exorcised as much as possible in favor of the more austere and 'proper' Protestant music. But for most Afro-Americans, black musical forms and religion have been inextricable. Not only in the many 'heathenish' cults but in Afro-Christianity as well, African elements were imported into the music that accompanied devotion. Because the music's lyric content was obviously dictated by the beliefs of the particular cult or church, the African-based dimension of Afro-American religious music has been wholly stylistic: emotional intensity, dancing, and ritual performance have long been essential aspects of black religion. Again, we recognize in them essential qualities of the African aesthetic. Indeed, Baraka perceives that the bases of both Afro-American religion and Afro-American music coincide with that of African culture: spirituality and expressiveness.

Although crucial components of the African aesthetic survived in the music of Afro-American religion, it was the Negro's secular music which maintained Africanisms in their purest condition. Like the role of music in religion, the development of this secular black music has been an intricate phenomenon reflecting the tensions of the assimilation-adaptation alternative. Baraka is careful to note that this music is, in its many forms, a product not of the African *or* the Westerner but of that complex figure, the Afro-American: "But what I am most anxious about here is the American Negro. When did he emerge? Out of what strange incunabula did the peculiar heritage and attitudes of the American Negro arise?" (p. xi).

Baraka does not answer these questions by selecting a date or specific event with which to designate the birth of the American

Negro. Nor does he go to great lengths in determining the "strange incunabula" from which the Negro's character may have arisen. This does not merely reflect a suspicion of facile paradigms or an awareness of the overwhelming mass of data that one must evaluate before approaching the problem in such a manner. His concern demands a wholly different historiography; for what interests him is the Afro-American as a type of consciousness, a *way of expression:*

> When America became important enough to the African to be passed on [. . .] to the young, those renditions were in some kind of Afro-American language. And finally, when a man looked up in some anonymous field and shouted, "Oh Ahm tired a dis mess, / Oh, yes, Ahm so tired a dis mess," you can be sure he was an American. [p. xii]

The Afro-American's "language," especially his musical language, is neither purely African nor purely American; nor is it a simple synthesis of these two ingredients. The truest form of Afro-American musical expression is still African in sensibility. Influences from the Euro-American mainstream have been entirely formal—specific melodies, types of popular song, etc. The Afro-American musician has borrowed these elements only to *adapt* them to the inherent black style, thereby "broadening and extending" the older expressions. The Negro idiom has thus been an amalgam of traditional Africanisms (for example, polyphony, sharp accents, rhythmic syncopation, and harmonic variation) and some Euro-American conventions. Since Baraka's concern is with the retention of the African element, he interprets the evolution of this idiom as the struggle of African expressiveness to assert itself in ever-changing musical forms.

Thus, at every stage of his investigation, he esteems in black music the qualities indicative of Africanesque emotiveness: the shout, holler, or "scream"; roughness; atonality; improvisation; communal modes. Against these he sets the diametrically opposed values of 'white' music that often found their way into jazz—softness or "legitimacy" of tone; fixed arrangements the musician could simply learn by rote; commitment to a generally sweet "artifact-like" beauty. Baraka illustrates the difference between these styles, not only by contrasting contemporary white and black practitioners of the same jazz instrument (for instance, Louis Armstrong's strident, brassy, dramatic sound versus Bix Beiderbecke's learned, "intellectual," reflective tone), but also by noting how these interests conflicted (Miles Davis) or blended (Duke Ellington) in the work of a given black musician. The basic standard he employs to measure the validity of each phase and performer of black music is that of functionality. By "functionality," however, Baraka does not mean exercise along with other outward activity ("no Negro music had had a [mechanical] 'function' since the work song"—p. 200), but rather the "emotional and aesthetic" utility the music offered its black listeners. Clearly, then, Baraka's "history" of black music is an attempt to praise the African in Afro-American music at the expense of the American, to define black music in terms of an African ethos subsumed in an American form.

Baraka proposes that the African essence, while present at every stage of black music's development, crystallizes at very special moments in forms that may be called "roots." The archetypical root form is the *blues,* the first native American musical expression. Baraka takes great pains to show that the blues was an extension of African music's basic elements: the shout and its three-line structure, the call-and-response pattern, dissonant accents, etc. The bluesman is the very model of the "freedman" Afro-American: clearly ostracized from white society, he was in addition considered by the emerging Negro middle class as the representative 'backslider' heathen whose loudness and 'vulgarity' are the very traits of the devil. Thus blues music is "roots" not only in a musical but, even more significantly, in an emotional sense:

> Blues as an autonomous music had been in a sense inviolable. There was no clear way into it, *i.e.,* its production, not its appreciation, except as concomitant with what seems to me to be the peculiar social, cultural, economic, and emotional experience of a black man in America. [. . .] It was as if these materials were secret and obscure, and blues a kind of ethno-historic rite as basic as blood. [pp. 147–48]

If the "secret" ritual impulse of the blues finds its source in African spirit, the blues themselves reflect the more complicated experience of the Negro. Although the basic blues pattern of call-and-response is a communal form, the blues has really been the expression of the individual. As with their African ancestors, blues singers created from "natural inclination" rather than from formal training. But their songs dealt with personal exploits, not the community's. Whereas the subject-matter of African songs concerned the gods, nature, general qualities of earthly life and religious expectations, the blues spoke of love and love-loss, sex, travel, and other private experiences. Baraka delivers his explanation of this discrepancy with trenchant clarity:

> this intensely personal nature of blues-singing is also the result of what can be called the Negro's "American experience," [. . .] [it] is a manifestation of the whole Western concept of man's life, and it is a development that could only be found in an American black man's music. [p. 66]

The blues, even as "roots," is thus a mixed blessing to Baraka. On one hand, it is the ritual link between the African and Afro-American sensibilities in black music; on the other hand, it developed an area of private expression nonexistent in African culture. Insofar as the blues' 'individuality' manifested the Negro's autonomous status in America, it underscored the viable path of adaptation for the black ex-slave—a characteristic that allowed the blues to take on aspects of white mainstream music only to mold them into a shape consonant with the separate, "secret" African traditions. Yet individuality could also degenerate into the facile 'style' of the artisan, with its accompanying tendency toward professionalism and formalism. This, Baraka argues, is precisely what took place in the "classic blues," which became popular at a time when the Negro began to feel he might become a member of the dominant society. One might say that the frank sexuality and harshness of classic blues were its ties to the *blues* as roots, while its slickness, entertainment-consciousness, and 'universal' themes constituted the *classic* or commonly acceptable element of this music.

Blues as roots—African expressiveness embedded within a

native Afro-American context—did not die with the increasingly sterile derivatives of the classic blues. Instead it went "underground" along with the freedman who did not partake of the assimilationist dream. One of its strongest forms was Rhythm and Blues, which went beyond merely preserving the autonomy of original blues. Rhythm and Blues, a product of the new chaos of urban life, lent a greater importance to the shouting, screaming, and other intensely emotional vocal effects characteristic of Africanesque collective expression than had the older, "primitive" blues. Moreover, with its insistent 'vulgarity' and uncompromising commitment to the reality of chaotic existence, Rhythm and Blues began to make separation from white canons a conscious value. Blues roots were now employed to make a dramatic cultural statement: they became *functional* in the total life of those "blues people" who were emotionally attached to its "blood rite."

Rhythm and Blues is the link from blues as roots to the second great moment of black music—*bebop*. By returning to the rhythmic orientation of earliest Afro-American (and, indeed, of African) music, and by making unprecedented harmonic variations available to the improvising musician, bebop introduced a whole new lexicon to black music comparable only to the original blues improvising. Not only were the functions of several instruments revolutionized, but the nature of the musical group was also reformed considerably to conform to the collective thrust of the new music. Bebop set out to restate the "basic blues impulse" in black music. Yet Baraka designates it as "roots" because it also initiated a true advance, and this was again more a matter of cultural than of specifically musical statement. The boppers "sought to erect a meta-culture as isolated as their grandparents', but issuing from the evolved sensibility of a modern urban black American who had by now achieved a fluency with the socio-cultural symbols of Western thinking" (p. 201). At first, this "fluency" allowed for well-crafted gestures of defiance and nonconformity, a simple "emotional analogy to the three hundred years of unintentional nonconformity his color constantly reaffirmed." Soon, however, this dissent developed into a startling revolution of black consciousness:

> By the fifties [. . .] alienation was seen by many Negro musicians not only as valuable, in the face of whatever ugliness the emptiness of the "general" culture served to emphasize, but as necessary. [p. 219]

The black musician's embrace of alienation involved a significantly split reaction to earlier Negro roots: it inculcated a sense that "roots" both existed and were valuable, but it took issue with certain conventional sentiments of these roots—"White is then not 'right', as the old blues had it, but a liability, since the culture of white precludes the possession of the Negro 'soul' " (p. 219). Bebop, then, is roots for Baraka because it began the Afro-American's march away from America toward a purer African "soul."

Finally, Baraka, writing in the early and mid-1960s, felt that the contemporary "new wave" jazz of Coltrane, Rollins, Taylor, Coleman, and others represented a third, and yet more valuable, form of roots. Again, this is not merely because this music, taking up where the boppers left off, developed even greater harmonic and rhythmic methods, or because the new musicians' aching lyricism recalled the old blues cry. The avant-garde jazz (like the new musicians themselves) is perhaps the most communal of all black musics, for here the improvising individual and the improvising group create sounds interdependently.

Moreover, adoption and use of alien forms is no longer an acceptable action—in pieces such as Coltrane's renditions of Rodgers-Hammerstein tunes, these forms are employed only to be dissected, twisted, and finally destroyed, as the musician negates the fixed idea in favor of present expression. Baraka's desire (subliminally expressed throughout *Blues People*) to obliterate the American element of blues roots, to re-Africanize black musical expression, seems to him fulfilled by the new jazz. Full of the screaming, improvisational, natural emotiveness central to the African aesthetic, this music harks back to the Negro roots of blues and field hollers; but at the same time it leaps back beyond American origins to the pure tribal ur-root of the African collective: "New Black Music is this: Find the self, then kill it." [11]

III

Baraka's conception of Afro-American music, especially of the blues "root," has received vociferous criticism from a group of thinkers who regard the blues in quite another fashion. In contrast to Baraka's rigorous discrimination between African and American elements in the blues and in black music as a whole, this school holds the blues to be a distinctly American art form developed from a welter of complex and often contradictory experiences which, while directly associated with the Negro's life, have reference to a 'universal' meaning. The most articulate proponents of this view have been Ralph Ellison and Albert Murray, both of whom have long argued that the blues is primarily an artistic, and only secondarily a political, response to life:

> The blues ballad is a good example of what the blues are about. Almost always relating a story of frustration, it could hardly be described as a device for avoiding the unpleasant facts of Negro life in America. On the contrary, it is a very specific and highly effective vehicle, the obvious purpose of which is to make Negroes acknowledge the essentially tenuous nature of all human existence.[12]

Murray and Ellison assert that the blues, far from being an extension of African culture completely opposed to the enveloping white society, constitutes the very spirit of the American 'mainstream.' Murray labels theories based upon separating the Negro's experience from the basic fabric of American life "social science science fiction," and (possibly with Baraka in mind) he contends that those who

> insist that political powerlessness and economic exclusion can lead only to cultural deprivation . . . insinuate that [Negroes] are unassimilable. The blues idiom, however, represents the most comprehensive and the most profound assimilation. It is the product of a sensibility that is completely compatible with the *human* imperatives of modern times and American life.[13]

Murray's plea is for an understanding of the Negro and his music that accounts for the "arbitrary complexities" as well as the obvious features of the Afro-American experience. He excoriates, for example, the kind of attacks on the black middle class with which Baraka (following the lead of E. Franklin Frazier) enlivened *Blues People*, for being too sweeping and uselessly imprecise. Like Ellison, he thinks of the bluesman as a "harmonizer of chaos" rather than a purely 'expressive' ex-slave whose style confronts that of the post-Renaissance 'humanist.' Ellison, in his review of *Blues People*, presents this view in direct opposition to Baraka's:

> Jones attempts to impose an ideology upon this cultural complexity, and this might be useful if he knew enough of the related subjects to make it interesting. But his version of the blues lacks a sense of the excitement and surprise of men living in the world—of enslaved and politically weak men successfully imposing their values upon a powerful society through song and dance.[14]

Ellison and Murray's bluesman is the archetype, not of the reemerging African, but of the ever-various and decidedly mainstream "Omni-American."

The Baraka-Murray/Ellison controversy has many ramifications; to do justice to either side would be not only extremely difficult but even irrelevant to my purposes. What Ellison and Murray point to in their argument with Baraka is the emphatic polemical thrust of Baraka's theory and, specifically, its attempt to see black music as working (consciously or not) in the service of nationalist ideology. They are angry with what Charles Kiel more evenhandedly calls Baraka's " 'myth of the Negro past,' "[15] Yet, perhaps because they are intent upon fashioning their own blues ideologies, neither Kiel nor Ellison and Murray quite grasp the nature of Baraka's 'mythology.' They all hint at its purpose by describing it in relation to "history":

> his theory flounders before that complex of human motives which makes human history;[16]

> Jones is really writing about a complex sort of nativism or,

> more accurately, a musical revitalization movement. Negro music . . . has become progressively more "reactionary"—that is, more African in its essentials.[17]

Ellison, by introducing the idea of "history" as that which Baraka ignores, merely reveals his own ideological presupposition that what composes history is a blurry collage of "human motives." Kiel comes much closer to the truth in suggesting that Baraka's aim is to reveal the Afro-American's relentless repossession of Africanisms during the past several decades. What these critics fail to perceive is that Baraka's account of black music is neither blandly unhistorical nor simply "reactionary"; rather, it is deliberately dialectical and teleological, and its mythicizing of the African/Negro past is, in fact, the nucleus of an idealistic historicism which portrays the persistent growth of African Spirit.

Baraka's historical method—as this brief description of his mythology should imply—is at base Hegelian. Esther M. Jackson has shown that, although Baraka has never mentioned Hegel explicitly in his criticism, Hegelian ideas permeate his theoretical writings, particularly in the early phase to which *Blues People* belongs.[18] We may recall that his essay "The Revolutionary Theatre" was a blueprint for a theatre of process that would reveal "what the facts are in this consciousness epic": "This should be a theatre of World Spirit. Where the spirit can be shown to be the most competent force in the world." The plea for representation of "World Spirit" clearly indicates a neo-Hegelian desire for an art 'in tempo' with the march of 'inevitable' revolutionary progress. An early (pre-1963) poem, entitled "Hegel," reveals a preoccupation with Hegel easily frustrated by reality's obvious ('superficial') facts:

> I scream for help. And none comes, has ever
> come. No single redeeming hand
> has ever been offered [. . .]
> no single redeeming word, has come
> wringing out of flesh
> with the imperfect beautiful resolution
> that would release me from this heavy contract
> of emptiness.

Another poem written in the same pre-Black Arts Movement phase of Baraka's career, "History as Process," also makes it clear that the systematic movement toward "utopia" is what attracts him to Hegelian thought:

> The thing, There As Speed, is God, as mingling
> possibility. The force. As simple future [. . .]
> Bankrupt utopia sez tell me
> no utopias. I will not listen.

With the writing of *Blues People*, Baraka seems to have seen the "redeeming word [. . .] come wringing out of flesh," for his study of revitalized Africanisms in black music is founded upon a decidedly neo-Hegelian theory of "history as process."

Baraka's understanding of Hegel seems much like that of such late-nineteenth-century aestheticians as Edward Caird, Walter Pater, William Wallace, and Bernard Bosanquet. They believed that the directing principle of Hegel's thought was the search for unity, for an ideal of perception to which the differences and contradictions in experience might be reduced. In their view, Hegel felt that Descartes had constructed a false dualism between mind and matter, which in experience were not so easily distinguished. This dualism, or "polarity" as Wallace called it, had served the disintegration of the social as well as the intellectual structure. Hegel sought a secure, vivid sense of certainty in reality, which the distinctions between mind and matter, with their arbitrary definitions and their consequent distortion and division of experience, had destroyed. As Caird wrote, in a passage that would serve well to gloss the condition of LeRoi Jones in *The System of Dante's Hell*, "A longing had been awakened, as it were 'a thirst of Dives for a drop of fire . . . for a concentration of living intuition,' which might destroy the divisions of reflection, and reveal again the organic unity of the world." [19]

The mood of insecurity provoked a search for an alternative condition. Hegel formulated the concept of "Geist" to give expression to his sense of the unity underlying change. The longing for 'home,' the feeling of confusion, the resistance to the idea that the world is only a solitary prisoner's dream—a reading of Hegel can be made to satisfy all these. To gain the status of a substitute for the lost religious faith and the lost confidence in metaphysical argument, the Hegelian activity of looking at the physical world and observing the consciousness in operation over it assumed a very important purpose. It searched for the World-Will, for *Geist*, for the "logos or reasonable order" (Pater)—and this was only gained when particular, performed acts of knowledge were linked together to form an all-inclusive reality, or when, in each such act, the sense of expanding connection with the larger reason was felt.

The purpose of the activity of trying to see the object as it really existed was to gain contact through it with that source of life. When this is achieved, in Caird's words, "the multiplicity of forms, the endless series of appearances, will begin to take on ideal meaning, because we shall see in them the Protean masks of a Being which is never absolutely hidden, but in the perishing of one form and the coming into being of another is ever more fully revealing itself." [20] The principle of Geist, then, asserted an underlying life-giving force, however various the matter through which it was diffused.

This idealistic philosophy gave meaning not only to life's confusing "multiplicity of forms" but also to the strange variety of the past. All forms of knowledge and sense are seen as stages of Being which have always existed implicitly and unconsciously. The present has been the past; the succession in time of human ideas comprise an eternal 'now.' But further, whether regarded as present or past, the spirit of the system's dialectic is always moving onward from one determination of thought to another, impelled by an irresistible necessity from one idea to another until the cycle of human thought and existence is complete.

Clearly, these general abstractions of Hegel's system so conceived were applied by Baraka to the specific question of black music's history and development. Just as Hegel, in his *Aesthetik*, described the evolution of art forms as corresponding to the evolution of Mind or Spirit, so Baraka, in *Blues People*, portrays the evolution of black music as the unfolding of the African aesthetic. This African aesthetic is Baraka's life-giving principle, or Geist; and his 'history' of Afro-American musical forms is the history of the emergence of this Geist. Again and again, he describes the development from one type of jazz to another in dialectical terms, with the given Afro-American form provoking its Western-oriented antithesis, in turn producing a third, even more Africanesque idiom:

> What usually happened, as I have pointed out, was that finally too much exposure to the debilitating qualities of popular expression tended to lessen the emotional validity of the Afro-American forms; then more or less violent reactions to this over-exposure altered their overall shape, [. . .] And these reactions almost always caused valid changes in the forms themselves:

or again:

> Rhythm & blues, the urban contemporary expression of blues, was the source of the new popular revitalization: rock 'n' roll its product.

Baraka argues that this ceaseless shift from one controlling musical idea to another kept black music "vital," for without this constant process a given expression would harden into the fixity of an artifact. This hardening is precisely what occurred when black forms were imitated and "learned" rather than used as the basis of still fresher statement. Since the African Spirit always thrived with the underground freedman, it did (and continues to) evolve into purer and purer form. In effect, what Baraka calls "roots" will be continuously produced as ever-finer manifestations of the African Spirit—that constant (underlying) yet changing principle of black experience.

Thus Hegelian methodology allows Baraka to posit a cyclical return to an archetypical ideal while viewing the Afro-American's history as a progressive redemption of this ideal. Hegelian dialectic gives direction to his analysis of black music, enabling him to 'save the negative' in Afro-American history by incorporating it into his scheme of the positive, by making it a necessary element of the ultimate fulfillment of the African Spirit. Neo-Hegelianism permits Baraka to speak of the "redeeming hand" of African Spirit in the face of the 'reality' that seems to obfuscate its emergence.

Moreover, the Hegelian cure for 'home-sickness' involved the ideal synthesis of the self with the object it contemplates—an abstract analogy to Baraka's ideal of the improvising musician merging with his community into one perpetually evolving organism, developing in absolute coherence.

Baraka undertakes an optimistic search for African Spirit because it at once posits an end toward which the process of Afro-American life is tending, and at the same time insists that the present carries an important weight of meaning. It effects a reconciliation between the facts of constant and often violent change and the longing for security, for though each phase of black life and art is fleeting, it may carry in it the accumulated value of the whole expressive experience of Afro-America. The choice Baraka makes, though he often seems unaware or unconcerned with it, is for the general at the expense of the particular—hence Ellison and Murray's strong objection that he reduces individual characteristics to a state of blurred outline and confused identity. Yet, as the poem "Hegel" shows, Baraka is concerned to redeem the Afro-American past rather than simply to accept its awful contradictions; his concepts of African expression and its history in Afro-American form allow him this 'myth.'

IV

William Wallace, paraphrasing Hegel, saw art as the means whereby a creative relationship with the world may be established:

> To apprehend the truth . . . we want an organ of intelligence which shall unite in itself the conscious activity of free production with the unconscious instinct of natural creation. Such an organ is found in the aesthetic power of genius, in the Artist. The artistic product is the work of two intimately-conjoined principles: of the art (in the narrower sense) which can be taught and learned . . . and of that "poesy in Art", and the unconscious grace of genius which can neither be handed down nor acquired, but can only be inborn by free gift of nature.[21]

Imamu Baraka has written of black music in notably similar language:

> The *roots,* blues and bop, are emotion. The *technique,* the ideas, the way of handling the emotion. And this does not leave out the consideration that certainly there is pure intellect that can come out of the emotional experience and the rawest emotions that can proceed from the ideal apprehension of any hypothesis. The point is that such displacement must exist as instinct.[22]

The high status Baraka gives to music, like the glorification of art in vogue at the turn of the century, is no arbitrary or trendy posture. For Baraka music is the surest way of making contact with the uniform and coherent sequences of Afro-American life. When a black musician, à la Probe, penetrates as far as these, he comes into contact, through the process, with the ultimate reality, and is able to perceive what all Afro-Americans should desire—the African Spirit beneath apparent chaos.

Baraka sees all expression as a function of "two intimately-conjoined principles": the "root" feeling and its "technical" use. In the same section of *Black Music* as that quoted above, he says that by the term *technical* he means "more specifically being able to use what important ideas are contained in the residue of history or in the now-swell of living." He goes on to explain that *use* means "that some idea or system is employed but in order to reach or understand quite separate and/or dissimilar systems." Thus, if "technique" may be thought of as the determinant of form, and "roots" as the determinant of content in artistic expression, then historicism (which Baraka borrows from Hegel only to "reach a dissimilar system") and music should be seen as the "intimately conjoined" form and content of Baraka's aesthetic vision. In an essay subtitled "Black Aesthetic," Baraka wrote: "a way of feeling (or the description of the process of) is what an aesthetic wd be." [23] His theory of black music provides for both elements of such an aesthetic: the "way of feeling"—African expressiveness and style—and the "description of the process of" its ascension in Afro-American culture.

We may remember that in *The System of Dante's Hell* music, dance, the emotive scream, and the full weight of African antiquity joined on The Bottom dance floor to help propel LeRoi Jones from 'hell' to 'home.' It seems only right that Imamu Baraka should have later conceived these forces to be the aesthetic tools of his people's liberation:

> As Africans we want Africans free to contribute to world health and world vision. We have a "song" * (* Manifested historical energy) we want to play, it is communal and uplifting. It is filled with images of how we need to think in the future. [. . .] Life must be perfected. And the doing of that is itself an eternal process, but each level will point the way to even more dazzling possibilities. Utopia is an African's fuel, it is in motion, and combustible. It drives us to higher equations of purpose.[24]

4 Baraka's Poetry: The Vision in Verse

I *Preface To A Twenty Volume Suicide Note* and *The Dead Lecturer*

Imamu Baraka began his literary career in the late 1950s as a poet. Ensconced within the coterie of "beat" and bohemian dilettantes residing in Greenwich Village, Baraka (then LeRoi Jones) was immersed in the concerns and methodology common to the beats and the tradition from which they emerged. As publisher and coeditor (with his wife Hettie Cohen) of *Yugen*, one of the best "little" literary magazines of the 1960s, Baraka was intimately involved with the work of such poets as Allen Ginsberg, Gilbert Sorrentino, Gregory Corso, Jack Kerouac, Robert Creeley, and Charles Olson—all of whom had poems published in *Yugen* at one time or another. It is within and against the tradition these poets represent that Baraka's early poetry must be read and measured.

Surely the most essential aspect of the tradition of modern poetry into which Imamu Baraka stepped as a young, precocious black American over fifteen years ago is the exploration of self-awareness I mentioned in chapter 1, a process begun with the German Romantics Novalis and Hölderlin, the English Wordsworth, the American Edgar Allan Poe, and particularly with the French Baudelaire. Poetry itself, and thus the act and agent of the poetic process, became the object of extraordinary concern and, as Jacques Maritain said, "poetry was engaged more and more deeply, more and more irremediably, in a spiritual experience of its own." [1] The private life of the poet himself, especially under stress of psychological crisis, became a major theme. The poet was now an extraordinary person who lived in a higher and more imaginative order of experience than that of nature or the existing social structure. Even in the late Romantic tradition represented by Tennyson, Swinburne, Arnold, and Meredith, one finds the growing sense of an essential opposition between the human spirit and its environment, and can trace even in them the fear that nature might be unfriendly, that man might not be a free agent, that immortality and progress might be illusory, that the accounts of life might reveal a balance of suffering over happiness. As this "Neutralization of Nature" (I. A. Richards's phrase) proceeded, the poet increasingly created his own world. But this private universe was not illumined by the "inner light" of Milton's "paradise within," which is rejected as sentimental; rather, it was colored by vulnerability, self-torturing confession, and the proliferating imagery of doubt and failure which characterizes such works as Pound's "Mauberly (1920)," Eliot's "The Love Song of J. Alfred Prufrock," and Merwin's *The Lice.*

By the end of World War II the consciousness of a cleavage between imaginative life and modern social conditions (popularized by Pound, Eliot, Herbert Read, and others) had taken a particularly dark turn. For behind it lay the pervasive feeling that the vision of a humanistic and liberated mankind, which only a few modern men (for example, Auden and Spender) continued to extol, had already become a cruel delusion. Many of the better young poets turned their attention to political and cultural criticism and, as M. L. Rosenthal has observed,[2] organized their attack around the central perception of the individual (and particularly, of course, the poet) as both the generator and the victim of brutal cultural crisis.

These, then, are the focal issues which conditioned the intense soundings of beat poets in the 1950s. The opening thrust of Allen Ginsberg's visionary-demonic "Howl"—"I saw the best minds of my generation destroyed by madness, starving hysterical naked"—may be taken as emblematic of the beats' self-oriented, despairing perception of the cultural wasteland they saw before them. None of these poets, however, felt more poignantly or recorded as vigorously the pains and desires of his alienated soul than did Imamu Baraka. Every line of his first book of poems, *Preface to a Twenty Volume Suicide Note* (1957–60; hereafter referred to as *Preface*) carries the direct charge, overtone, or echo of self-criticism. For example:

> but this also
> is part of my charm.
> A maudlin nostalgia
> that comes on
> like terrible thoughts about death.
>
> How dumb to be sentimental about anything
> To call it love
> & cry pathetically
> into the long black handkerchief
> of the years.
>
> "Look for you yesterday
> Here you come today
> Your mouth wide open
> But what you got to say?"
>
> —part of my charm
>
> old envious   blues feeling
> ticking like   a big cobblestone clock.
>
> [from "There *Must* Be a Lone Ranger!!!"]

These poems are full of such ironic exorcisms of the "sentimental," the tender, and are infused with a sense of a past ill-used and irrecoverable, which the ticking of clocks and laments of the blues uselessly catalogue. They reveal a tireless descent to the inner spaces of consciousness, resulting in the self-exposing vulnerability and candor that is the mark of the poetic tradition I have just described. Operating by way of a perplexed, exploited, and often curiously withdrawn egocentricity, this solopsistic descent is often revealed by an imaginative fixation upon the concept of microcosm. Selectively viewing the surrounding landscape, the poet makes the ontology of any object of that landscape dependent upon his being, and things gain life only through him. As he surveys the world from within, "locked in with dull memories & self hate, & the terrible disorder of a young man" ("The Turncoat"), increasingly confused and frightened by "the uncertainty / (of what I am saying, who / I have chosen to become, the very air pressing my skin" ("The Insidious Dr. Fu Man Chu"), he constantly admits an essential distrust of public worlds and seeks protection by making a little room, made of words, his everywhere:

> Safe now, within the poem, I make my
> Indiscreet avowals, my indelicate assumptions
> As if this gentle fire that bathed my flesh
> was rancor, or fear, or any other of life's idiot progeny.
> It is the walls of these words protect me
> Throw a fierce cordon
> around me, that I may 'signify'
> to my heart's content.
>
> [from "The A.B.C.'s"]

It is obvious, however, that the "safety" here proposed appears to him a suffocating entrapment, and he mocks the impulses of his shallow 'signifyin' as an "idiot's progeny." Fearful of the external world, dissatisfied with self-generated structures, he attempts a desperate turning away from literally everything:

> The moon
> sits over the North river, underneath
> a blue bridge. Boats & old men
> move through the darkness. Needing
> no eyes. Moving slowly
> towards the long black line
> of horizon. [. . .]
>
> I sit inside alone, without
> thoughts. I cannot lie
> & say I think of you. I merely sit
> & grow weary, not even watching
> the sky lighten with morning.
>
> [from "The Death of Nick Charles"]

The result, of course, is stagnation and an even more intense solipsism. As boats move toward presumed destinations and old men, as if mocking the youthful observer's wasting of time, move easily along darkened paths, the poet, like the lifeless buildings, like the passive moon, merely sits alone; and finally, as the dark sky is lightened by a new day, he wearily slips into the deep, dark, unconscious areas within. The pervading feeling is one of impotence and immobility, brought on, it is true, by a most noble nature ("I cannot lie / & say I think of you") that refuses to take action without the sanctification of some thought.

Yet the speaker heard in these poems is in a state of virtual paralysis, and from this inevitably comes the fixation upon *death* which the very title of the volume evokes. Indeed, we find in an astonishingly large number of these poems what Rosenthal identifies as the "one distinctively modern quality in literature: . . . the centrifugal spin toward suicide in the speaking voice":[3]

> As simple an act
> as opening the eyes. Merely
> coming into things by degrees [. . .]
>
> There are unattractive wild ferns
> outside the window
> where the cats hide. They yowl
> from there at nights. In heat
> & bleeding on my tulips [. . .]
>
> No use for beauty
> collapsed, with moldy breath
> done in. Insidious weight
> of cankered dreams. Tiresias'
> weathered cock.
>
> Walking into the sea, shells
> caught in the hair. Coarse
> waves tearing the tongue.
>
> Closing the eyes. As
> simple an act. You float.
>
> [from "Way Out West"]

Between the simple blink of an eye a whole lifetime passes, "coming into things by degrees," the sweetness of youth imperceptibly swept away amid lies and under the "insidious weight of cankered dreams." The life that lies "outside the window" is wild, fearful, and bleeding its pain upon cultivated beauty: an analogue to the life behind the opened eyes. And with little else observed or achieved, death is chosen, though a final violence accompanies the ultimate relief ("course waves tearing the tongue"). The lemming-like image of suicide by drowning is common in these poems (for example, "The Bridge": "when you touch the water, & it closes, slowly, around your head . . . & you, (when you have let the song run out) will be sliding through unmentionable black") and shows a clear affinity to James Dickey's work of the same period:

> Wait for a coming/And swimming idea.
> Live like the dead/In their flying feeling.
> Loom as a ghost/When life pours through it.[4]

But whereas Dickey conceives of this process as regenerative and a liberation into nature ("Let flowing create / A new, inner being: As the source in the mountain / Gives water in pulses") Baraka can see it only as desperate escape.

If we often find Baraka seeking death in *Preface*, it is in refuge from a dying civilization and ravaged landscape. Beside the essential motif of the self and its confusions and failures, the concern with "the moldy breath" of culture, the uselessness of "beauty collapsed," is the major theme of these poems. In works such as "In Memory of Radio," "Look for You Yesterday, Here You Come Today," and "There *Must* Be a Lone Ranger!!!" Baraka throws together a collage of mythic elements (drawn principally from the popular media of comics, radio drama, and the Hollywood hero cults remembered from the late 1930s and early 1940s) and ironically mourns its defabrication. The Shadow, Kate Smith, the box-top world of Battle Creek, Michigan (home of Kellogg's cereals), Tarzan, Superman, the Lone Ranger—all are rounded together by a "maudlin nostalgia" and are mockingly simpered over. It is with genuine anguish and consequent despair that he registers the death of more meaningful and more painfully developed myths and the ideals they once manifested (see, for example, "The A.B.C.s"). Reinforcing the idea of the death of mythic tradition is the inability to remember, to connect to a past, either individual or collective:

& I have forgotten,
all the things, you told me to love, to try to understand, the
bridge will stand, high up in the clouds & the light.
[from "The Bridge"]

And as the poet attempts to 'only connect' to this past, the ghosts of its now-dead forms tauntingly pass before him, and time indifferently ravishes on:

How can it mean anything? The stop & spout, the
wind's dumb shift. Creak of the house & wet smells
coming in. Night forms on my left. The blind still
up to admit a sun that no longer exists. Sea move.
[from "The Turncoat"]

Baraka describes the death and ruin of culture's myths and heroes with words "blown in the winters, thru windows, lacking sun" ("From an Almanac"). The winter scene viewed through these windows is barren, cold, and desolate. As the poet recoils from rotting corpses strewn along this landscape, he finds only the stench of his own curiously cold sexual impulses (see, for example, "Roi's New Blues"). Many of these poems, as with much of Baraka's poetry generally, are permeated by vivid sexual imagery and freely exploit the senses as the medium of compelling experience; yet in the works of this early period of distraught and disaffected sensibility, the senses cannot suffice to consummate experience, and no poem is freely resolved in the too too solid flesh. The irreconcilability of Goya-esque and sexual images of the flesh in "From an Almanac (2)" is an excellent illustration of this dilemma:

The flesh
hung
from trees. Blown
down. A cold
music. A colder
hand, will grip
you. Your bare
soul. (Where is the soul's place. What is
its
nature?) Winter rattles like the throat

of the hanged man. Swung
against our windows.
                    As bleak
as our thots. As wild
as that wind
we make (between
us).
        Can you dance? Shall
you?

If the landscape of Baraka's early poetry is barren of myth, if the figures found there (principally the poet himself) are, like Kerouac's Rimbaud, "eaten by the disease of overlife," then it is not surprising that the voice of these works is that of an *ironic* speaker. This can best be demonstrated by a brief survey of the poetic style which conveys the temperament elucidated thus far.

The poetic doctrine that directly influenced Baraka in his early "beat" phase was, of course, that of "projective verse" (or "open-field composition") as advocated by Robert Creeley and Charles Olson, the chief documents of which are Olson's *Letters to Origin* and his essay "Projective Verse." The main thrust of this rather confusing and confused theory is the idea of poetry as a vital process of "instant by instant" progression of both meaning and the musical "breathing forward" of the very syllables that, sounded together, create a poem's harmony. This manner of poetic creation, the "energy" by which one perception moves instantly upon another, is placed above any concerns for finished construction or preconceived meaning. "From the moment [the poet] ventures into FIELD COMPOSITION—puts himself in the open—he can go by no track other than the one the poem under hand declares, for itself." [5] These ideas are augmented repeatedly by such maxims as "Form Is Never More Than An EXTENSION OF CONTENT" and "HOW ANYTHING IS SAID is as important as WHAT IS SAID, that it *is* WHAT IS SAID." Such seemingly contradictory statements freely coexist, unresolved, in Olson's writings. These ideas are really the slightly misguided progeny of the Imagist theories, and the Imagists are the projectivist's true spiritual fathers. Indeed, the projectivist doctrine offers little beyond what the Imagists had already conceived, and the original Imagist theory offers a better tool for analysis than the projectivist formulations to which Baraka adhered.

The Imagists play a major role in what Maritain called poetry's "search for the purification of poetry itself of all extraneous or adventitious elements, or of a search after the pure essence of poetry." [6] The Imagist theory, evolved by Poe from his culling of Coleridge and made popular by Pound, maintained that language itself can be reality and advocated its dissolution from the nomenclature and syntax of the practical world. It held that an image should be born and then die into another, that any sequence of images must be, as Dylan Thomas said of his own poems, a sequence of creations, recreations, destructions, contradictions. This is the process occurring in these lines of Baraka's:

> who sees all things
> as love, who sees
> the nature
> of himself, the flatness
> of the room, the evening
> spread against the windows
> soft, who
> stares quietly
> into the shadows
> listening
> to the moon's
> light
> dropping softly
> on the rug.
>
> [from "Duke Mantee"]

The vital tension felt here stems from the poet's obvious desire to create an image that is concrete, exact, a summation of all experience; an image that itself sees and feels, that has all the sense and emotional qualities of the poet himself; an image that acts for him and consecrates the event taking place *now,* the thing which will never be repeated in quite the same way, and which, quite likely, would ordinarily not even be noticed as it happens. Little "meaning" is apparent, but an interplay of emotion and association, a definite feeling that cannot be described in ordinary discursive speech, is achieved by images of an incredible delicacy.

In addition, the beauty of Baraka's early verse seems to answer the *symboliste* aim, expounded by Mallarmé, of "evoking an object in delicate shadow, without ever actually mentioning it, by allusive words, never by direct words." Many of the passages already quoted reveal a most refined use of analogy, suggesting complex emotion by an accumulation of direct images, each perhaps linked to the central idea by only one element, yet, by its interaction with other images, evoking the final synthesis. Many of these images are, in fact, more subtle in aim and technique than the direct and shadowless constructs of the Imagists. Thus, as in *symbolisme,* the poetic symbol in many of these poems means primarily itself in relation to the poem, and the unity of the poem is best apprehended as a unity of mood. Images (for instance, the sitting moon of "The Death of Nick Charles," or "the window's dumb shift" of "The Turncoat") really "point" to nothing beyond the poem, but by pointing to other images in the poem, articulate a predominate emotion or mood. Hence the effect upon the reader approaches the *symboliste* ideal of incantation, a rich harmony of sounds and unrestricted richness of meaning, and the essence of the method is the spontaneity of *improvisation:*

> I love you (& you be
> quiet, & feel my wet mouth
> on your fingers, I
> love you
> & bring you fish
> & oranges. (Before the light fails
> we should move to a dryer place,
> but not too far from water.) I
> Love you &
> you are singing. What song
> is that? (The blinds held up
> by a wind, tearing
> the shadows. I
> Love you [. . .]
>
> & you are singing. What song
> is that The words
> are beautiful. [from "The Clearing"]

Lines such as these realize the ideal of Poe's *Poetic Principle* of the poetic as the lyrical, and they are contained in the discontinuous structures that Frye isolates as the chief form of the ironic age. They utilize several of the most notable methods of the ironic precedure: avoidance of direct statement; mere juxtaposition of images without explanatory linkage, betraying an aversion to the rhetorical; the elimination of punctuation clarifying the identity of the speaker; a baffling, even shocking use of the demonstrative adjective adding to the isolation of the poet by his intentional vagueness and difficulty (e.g. "*that* wind we make," "*those* mad doilies"). The sense of contrast between the internal and external, the individual and social, the mind and nature, which we have noted in these poems, is characteristic of modes closest to the ironic. The language used in revealing these oppositions is, furthermore, the rougher and psychologically charged idiom of the ironic mode; it is the idiom of a passionate naturalism, the record of a microphone held up to nature but edited with the kind of sardonic humor Ishmael Reed was to exploit more systematically a decade later:

> Any kind of sincerity
> Guarantees complete disregard. Complete abnegation.
> "Must dig with my fingers/as nobody will lend me
> or sell me a pick axe!" Axe the man who owns one.
> Hellzapoppin. The stars might not come out tonight . . .
> & who the hell can do anything about that?? Eh,
> Milord/Milady/The kind Dubarry wasn't. Tres slick.
> [from "To a Publisher . . . cut-out"]

Finally, the attitude of the poet toward his activity is that of the ironic author. Words, the entraping "cordon" of "The A.B.C.s," the "clown gods" of "From an Almanac," are often seen as inadequate devices for cutting down to the elemental, the pure. The best statement of this failure is made by the poem "Vice." Here, self-expression is seen as the debris of random perversities and boredom which the poet discharges upon the innocently unconcerned:

> Sometimes I feel I have to express myself
> and then, whatever it is I have to express

falls out of my mouth like flakes of ash
from a match book that the drunken guest
at the grey haired jew lady's birthday party
has set on fire, for fun & to ease the horrible
boredom.

& when these flakes amass, I make serious collages
or empty them (feinting a gratuitous act) out the window
on the heads of the uncurious puerto rican passerby.

The poem continues in the form of a self-mocking drama: after a ludicrous gloss upon the fortuitous events that constitute "Act I," we are told "there doesn't seem to be any act 2. The process is stopped," and the poet deprecates his wasted effort with the realization that "all this means nothing is happening to me in this world." Ultimately, the aesthetic act degenerates into a jungle of observation:

Asked to be special, & alive in the mornings, if they are gray
& I am still alive, (& green) hovering above all the things I
seem to want to be apart of (curious smells, the high-noon
    idea
of life . . . a crowded train station where they broadcast a
    slice,
just one green slice, of some glamourous person's life).
& I cant even isolate my pleasures. All the things I can talk
    about
mean nothing to me.

Organizable experience is dead and meaningless, curiosity deadened by the insipidity of mass culture. In the poems of *Preface* the poet often cannot impel his imagination beyond this harsh accounting of aesthetic energy as little better than "vice."

Much of what characterizes the poems in *Preface* continues in the works of *The Dead Lecturer* (ca. 1960–63): the self-orientation and self-criticism; the obsession with death (both of the individual and of culture); the uses and constructs of image and idiom common to the ironic mode. But alongside these familiar elements there exist three basic new tendencies: (1) the attempt to construct new myths from a new language of symbols; (2) a growing concern with the social or public world; (3) a new tenderness and more freely lyrical tone. The nature of these important developments can be understood by studying just a few of the volume's poems.

In *Preface* there are scattered remarks and allusions that indicate the poet might be black or have a particular interest in black people. However, it is only with the final poem, "Notes for a Speech," that Baraka comes to terms with his isolation and despair as a specifically *black* individual. The poem is a beginning attempt to deal with his relation to and alienation from his roots in the African and American aspects of his blackness. It opens with an explicit rejection of African identity, one that Baraka sees as intolerably foreign:

> African blues
> does not know me. Their steps, in sands
> of their own
> land. A country
> in black & white, newspapers
> blown down pavements
> of the world. Does
> not feel
> what I am.

If the African spirit is no more for him than for any literate Westerner, what of the specific black souls whom Baraka self-consciously calls "my people":

> (And who are they. People. To concern
> myself, ugly man.[. . .]
> My color
> is not theirs. Lighter, white man
> talk. They shy away. My own
> dead souls, my, so called
> people.

The distance established here between Baraka and his "people" is significant: he isn't even of their true color, his language is of another culture—the white man's. Thus a further dimension is added to the stagnation already experienced in preceding poems. He is in limbo between cultures, lured into the language and fantasies of a people from whom he is alien by birth, and thereby severed from his racial roots. Finally, with the possibility of linkage to Africa a vain illusion, he remains, perforce, among the tragic figures of his native landscape:

> Africa
> is a foreign place. You are
> as any other sad man here
> american.

This important poem may be taken as a private collection of fragments, suggestions, and queries in preparation for a more public and definitive statement: *notes* for a *speech.* Perhaps the first version of this statement is the eight-part poem in *The Dead Lecturer*, "A Poem For Willie Best." This is the first sustained attempt by Baraka to answer his own call for black writers to tap "the emotional history of the black man in this country as its victim and its chronicler" and, in doing so, to "propose his own symbols, erect his own personal myths." [7] Willie Best (the Hollywood character actor "Sleep 'n' eat") appears in this poem as the archetypical black victim, at once suffering and chronicling his woe:

> The face sings, alone
> at the top
> of the body. All
> flesh, all song, aligned. For hell
> is silent, at those cracked lips
> flakes of skin and mind
> twist and whistle softly
> as they fall.

The poem stretches for mythic associations, backgrounds, and echoes to give universal significance to the individual shedding of lies and false roles ("those cracked lips . . . as they fall") of this misnamed, misused but spiritually ascendant figure. Thus section 2 is fraught with allusions to the Christian myth, the "born in to death held fast to it" of the Incarnation, the "lover spreads his arms . . . the fingers stretch to emptiness" of the Crucifixion. In section 3, the mythic status of Willie Best, against a background of Oedipal echoes, is strongly established:

> At a cross roads, sits the
> player. No drum, no umbrella, even
> though it's raining. Again, and we
> are somehow less miserable because
> here is a hero, used to being wet.
> One road is where you are standing now
> (reading this, the other, crosses then
> rushes into a wood.
>   5 lbs neckbones.
>   5 lbs hog innards.
>   10 bottles cheap wine.
>   (The contents
> of a paper bag, also shoes, with holes
> for the big toe, and several rusted
> knives. This is a literature of
> symbols. And it is his gift, as the
> bag is.
>   (The contents
> again, holy saviors [. . .]
>   All this should be
> invested.

Actor, musician, performer, trickster, the black hero sits at a crossroads offering, not merely the shallow catharsis of watching a suffering protagonist, but a "literature of symbols," a series of alternatives. No definite answers, no unmistakable directions are proposed: only the meager capital (as much cheap wine as cheap sustenance) needed to develop a future of value, given proper use.

Despite the assurance that this gift of symbols is worth using, Baraka expresses a certain ambivalence toward the role-player. As the history of this character is developed, he is alternately shameful in his "dance of the raised leg. Of the hand on the knee quickly" (section 5), and sensually vital in his "song of the toes pointed inward, the arms swung, the hip, moved, for fucking, slow from side to side" (section 6); the former an act that "punishes speech," the latter "an elegance that punishes silence." Ultimately this "hero" is judged with respect, seen as a man dying in defiance of his oppression, in defence of his dignity; and in so doing, he reveals the grace-in-violence that is the mark of all Baraka heroes:

> The balance.
> He was tired of losing. (And
> his walking buddies tired
> of walking.
> Bent slightly,
> at the waist. Left hand low, to flick
> quick showy jabs ala Sugar. The right
> cocked, to complete,
> any combination.
> He was
> tired of losing, but he was fighting
> a big dumb "farmer."
> Such a blue bright
> afternoon, and only a few hundred yards
> from the beach. He said, I'm tired
> of losing.
> "I *got* to cut 'cha."

Through section 7, Willie Best has clearly remained the sole subject of the myth being erected by the poem. In section 8, however, the poet himself enters the hero's role, or at least the hero's landscape:

> His head is
> at the window. The only
> part
> that sings.
> (The word he used
> (we are passing St. Mark's place
> and those crazy jews who fuck)
> to provoke
> in neon.

Finally, however, the old character actor, whom the poet has not fully penetrated even in weaving the events and costumes of his hero's past into a mythic texture, remains an enigmatic challenge to the future:

> A renegade
> behind the mask. And even
> the mask, a renegade
> disguise. Black skin
> and hanging lip. [. . .]
>
> And he sits
> wet at the crossroads, remembering distinctly
> each weightless face that eases by. (Sun at
> the back door, and that hideous mindless grin.
> (Hear?

"A Poem For Willie Best" is a brilliant poem that ultimately fails in its effort to sift a coherent myth from the varied artifacts and symbols of a most strange and complex part of the Afro-American past. Yet it is a significant move away from the solipsistic and ironic. Baraka is at this point at an identifiable crossroad, and is, moreover, significantly involved in the data of an external, social world. This growing awareness of being "in the world" is self-consciously charted in several of these poems of *The Dead Lecturer*:

> I address
> /the society
> the image, of
> common utopia.
> [from "Short Speech to My Friends"]

There are more images of The Life: "drunk screaming women," "the dozens, the razor, the cloth, the sheen," "porters I ran track with," all take their place among what he now confidently calls "the people of my life" (these lines are from "Rhythm & Blues 1"). He increasingly fears "the deadly idiot of compromise" ("Rhythm & Blues 1"), as the nature of the path he must choose slowly unfolds itself to him. The poem "Black Dada Nihilismus" is, in part, prophetic of the attitudes and values that shape his work in its later phases. The violence, the contempt for a dying West that must be abandoned, the radical dichotomy between black and white, the invocational and prophetic tone, are all major elements of later writings. By the end of the book, the sense of purpose, even if not direction, seems well entrenched; it is the urgency of a revolutionary who senses that, as the German revolutionary, Karl Liebknecht, claimed, "we are all dead men on leave":

> We must convince the living
> that the dead
> cannot sing.
>
> [from "A Guerrilla Handbook"]

He is impatient for the world's improvement; not a day should pass until direction and action can be added to his newfound desire:

> What is tomorrow
> that it cannot come
> today?
>
> [from "Valery as Dictator"]

The pain of the question is accentuated by the fact that, though freshly awakened, he is still bleary-eyed, still unable to act decisively, still at the crossroads. This dilemma is best captured in the following image from "The Measure of Memory (The Navigator)," remodeled from the final lines of "Betancourt":

> The boat's prow angled at the sun
> Stiff foam and an invisible cargo
> of captains. I buy injury, and decide
> the nature of silence. Lines of speed
> decay in my voice.

Though he cannot speak in the language of actual acts, his poetic voice touches areas of tenderness and simple lyricism unexplored in *Preface.* He begins to feel pain, to *scream,* to react to his emotions, not merely record them as they pass over him. The experience of the void, the haunting memories of lost paradises, the despair in being subdued to a craving for a false knowledge—these are the lasting impressions gained from *Preface.* In *The Dead Lecturer*, however, there is increasingly, as Baraka later reflected, "a spirituality always trying to get through, to triumph." [8] Invariably, the form of this spirituality is conceived as a *musical* entity. The musical is always the one incontrovertibly transcendent aesthetic value, free from any taint of vice, and often represented as the ideal projection of all energy and possibility, capable of converting the poet's activity to the most valuable experience:

> I want to be sung [. . .] I want myself
> as dance. As what I am
> given love, or time, or space
> to feel myself [. . .]
>   I am given
> to lying, love, call you out
> now, given to feeling things
> I alone create.
> And let me once, create
> myself. And let you, whoever
> sits now breathing on my words
> create a self of your own. One
> that will love me.
>
> [from "The Dance"]

The poet's plea for musical form, one generated from the private self's aesthetic creativity, expands to incorporate the external world, the reader's aesthetic response called upon as an act of love toward the poet. The "you," though general, is much clearer than any "you" of *Preface*: it is not a feared entity but an other with whom the poet desires to have life-giving intercourse. No other work of the early phase bares so nakedly the belief in the poet's creative powers.

The final impression left by *The Dead Lecturer* is not merely that of an awakened sense of aesthetic purpose; we are given a direct view of the moral and ideological impulses which are to shape Baraka's future artistic acts. The most revealing poems in this regard are the five "Crow Jane" pieces, which remain among Baraka's finest, if most extravagantly complex, creations. These poems are subtle essays on tradition and influence. Their primary subject—which exists as subtext to the surface development of Crow Jane's character—is the relation of Baraka's poetic voice to the competing forces of Western and Afro-American cultures. The former authority is represented by Yeats, specifically the Yeats of the "Crazy Jane" poems; the latter is evinced in the epigram to Baraka's Crow Jane verses:

> Crow Jane, Crow Jane, don't hold your head so high,
> You realize, baby, you got to lay down and die.
> —Mississippi Joe Williams

In Mississippi (Big Joe) Williams's blues poem, "Pallet On the Floor" (from which Baraka is quoting), Crow Jane appears simultaneously as a cleverly veiled personification of Southern racism's Jim Crow and as the typical faithless woman of the blues lament whose cruelty and uppityness drives her man away ("I'm going pretty woman, may get lonesome here / I got nobody, you don't relieve my cares"). Baraka also allegorizes Crow Jane; but in his lyrics she becomes a type of Western civilization, modeled in every significant detail on Yeats's, not Williams's, Jane. Indeed, until the Crow Jane series is understood as a totality, Williams's figure merely casts an ominous Afro-American shadow over an essentially mock-Yeatsian landscape. Baraka's poems thus sequentially explore the character of Western literature before specifically including non-Western elements in a final assessment of poetic influence.

Yeats's Crazy Jane poems exploited violent, sexual, and scatological imagery in an attempt to forge an uncompromising resolution of opposites, of what Yeats elsewhere called "all those antinomies / Of day and night." Crazy Jane, like Yeats's Old Tom, presses the common claims of body, soul, and heart ("love") as she celebrates natural processes. Baraka borrows Yeats's language and intonation but he deliberately inverts or, as Harold Bloom would say, creatively misreads, Yeats's theme. The opening verse, "For Crow Jane," is cast in the haunting idiom of "Crazy Jane and Jack the Journeyman," as Jane is introduced in all of her Yeatsian grotesquerie: "Cold / stuff, placed against / strong man's lips." Baraka then explicitly identifies Jane with Yeats by associating her creations with the Byzantium poems' golden artifices. Moreover, he invokes her career as a precedent for reshaping tradition, while reducing that career's accomplishment to the status of a lifeless, if glittering, artifact:

The wealth
is translated, corrected, a
dark process, like thought, tho
it provide a landscape
with golden domes.
'Your people
without love.' And life
rots them.

Flux, mutability, process—those forces with which Yeats's genius grappled and which later invigorated young LeRoi Jones's spiritual transformation—are depicted as putrefying agents in Yeats's stilled world. Warmth, love, and life itself are incompatible with that world. Crow Jane—like Crazy Jane, an "Old lady [. . .] of useless thighs" ("For Crow Jane")—represents all of Yeats's "people"; in Baraka's second poem, "Crow Jane's Manner," she alone is "without love" and, elevated beyond personality to a principle of being, she is described as the "Dead virgin / of the mind's echo. Dead lady / of thinking." In a rather sharp swerve (or *clinamen,* to borrow Bloom's terminology) from Yeats's true sensibility, Crow Jane's haggard infertility is identified with the worst aspects of Western rationalism as set forth in *Blues People.* Appropriately, in the final poem, "The Dead Lady Canonized," Crow Jane's (again, Western culture's) legacy is pictured as a heap of artifacts, those sterile products of the Western imagination delineated in *Blues People*: "A trail / of objects. Dead nouns [. . .] propose the night's image. Erect [. . .] a grave of her own."

The specific quality of Baraka's revision of Yeats is clearly seen in two particular paraphrases of the Crazy Jane poems that occur in "The dead lady canonized." The poem begins, "(A thread / of meaning. Meaning light"—a direct reference to the lines intoned by Yeats's Jane in "Crazy Jane and Jack the Journeyman":

For love is but a skein unwound
Between the dark and dawn. . . .
I—love's skein upon the ground,
My body in the tomb—
Shall leap into the light lost
In my mother's womb.

Yeats's poem developed from his quasi-mystical notion of "the black mass of Eden"; and his Jane rejects her notion of Blakean utopia for the double-edged reward of sexuality, accepting ghostly isolation as the price for rapture. Baraka now claims the power of revolutionary vision for himself, ironically performing a black mass around Yeats's figure. Crow Jane's "thread" unwinds, not to the intense experience of night, but to the "meaning" of dawn, or rather to the emptiness of "light" which, in Baraka's poems, is identified with disease, futility, and cold sterility. As in "State/meant," Baraka here rejects the West as "death / ly white" and asserts of the true black magicians, "we own / the night."

Yet Baraka's *clinamen* does not rest here; recasting these lines from "Crazy Jane Talks with the Bishop"—

> But Love has pitched his mansion in
> The place of excrement;
> For nothing can be sole or whole
> That has not been rent—

Baraka seeks to kill forever his loveless, infertile Jane and to propose his own image of the (black owned) night:

> may [. . .] Damballah, kind father,
> sew up
> her bleeding hole.

Yeats's lines, with their equivocations "sole" (or *soul*) and "whole" (or *hole*), weld body and soul in a vision of antinomian frenzy producing ecstatic wholeness. Baraka violently inverts this purpose, conjuring the African gods in an effort to repair what is "rent," to close the womb—the creative fount—of his Western protagonist. The "grave" (Yeats's "tomb") of Baraka's Jane is not a door leading toward a pure, illuminated ancestral womb, but a grim end to the "dark process" of her tradition's continuity. Baraka divests Crazy Jane of her sublime madness, leaving only the literal excrementitious mansion of her dead and deadening "images."

Yet this is not all; Baraka does not simply transform—or rather, bomb—the Yeatsian landscape. He is, in fact, a crucial player in this new black mass. He enters the scene in "Crow Jane's

Manner": "Me, the last . . . black lip hung / in dawn's gray wind"; and in "Crow Jane in High Society" he attacks himself as Crow Jane's poetic lackey: "And I tell / her symbols, as the grey movement / of clouds." Like Walker Vessels, the "grey" hero of *The Slave*, Baraka's persona is here venerating Yeats's symbols, thereby investing them with authority and power. He performs for her like a Willie Best; yet (like both Willie Best and Walker Vessels), he is a renegade entertainer ("black lip hung . . ." is an explicit link to this aspect of the Willie Best figure). *Tell* means, of course, "relate"; but it may also mean "understand" or, more radically, "discover." And, indeed, Baraka, as author of the Crow Jane poems, is dis-covering his image of Western culture. His struggling voice within these poems is a prisoner of a foreign language; yet he may say, with King Lear's Fool, "I can tell what I can tell." Ultimately, Baraka-the-author and Baraka-the-persona merge and pronounce Crow Jane's death-sentence in unison.

This complete rejection of Crow Jane joins the end of the series with its opening epigram, forming an African/Afro-American frame to the examination of Western tradition. For, like Williams, Baraka tells Crow Jane, "I'm going . . . you don't relieve my cares." The sequence as a whole is entirely characteristic of Baraka's most revolutionary works: it appropriates a classic Euro-American form, inverts its imagery and themes, and molds it into a new structure by wedding furious critique to traditional Afro-American expressions and the language of Pan-African mythologies. The result is an intriguing paradox, for the product of such rebellion is at once startlingly innovative and thoroughly inextricable from Western tradition itself.

The Crow Jane poems represent more a momentary height of prophetic fervor than a conviction triumphantly sustained throughout *The Dead Lecturer*. By concluding this discussion of Baraka's early poetry with the following lines from the volume's title poem, we gain a proper perspective on where he stands before *Black Magic Poetry*. Hovering between the past and the ability to deal with that past in the language of the present, Baraka faces a considerable gap between his newfound convictions and the form of action he has come to see as necessary. Insofar as he is a poet, this crisis of action is a crisis of expression; insofar as he is beginning to speak as a *black* poet, this crisis of expression is the challenge to deal effectively with the "literature of symbols" bequeathed to him by his racial ancestors. It is a challenge that must be met in the black but now foreign streets of Harlem, where "the life is, all the flesh, to make more than a silhouette, a breathless shadow counting again, his change" (from "Sex, like desire"). Everything must be risked, all must be invested to make life more than a walking shadow, and the sense of insufficiency and possible ruin remains great:

> For all those wan roads
> I am pushed to follow, are
> my own conceit. A simple muttering
> elegance, slipped in my head
> pressed on my soul, is my heart's
> worth. And I am frightened
> that the flame of my sickness
> will burn off my face. And leave
> the bones, my stewed black skull,
> an empty cage of failure.
> ["I Substitute for the Dead Lecturer"]

II *Black Magic Poetry*

"Now that the old world has crushed around me, and it's raining in early summer. I live in Harlem . . . and suffer for my decadence which kept me away so long. When I walk in the streets, the streets don't yet claim me, and people look at me, knowing the strangeness of my manner, and the objective stance from which I attempt to 'love' them." [9] Imamu Baraka wrote these words as LeRoi Jones in the fall of 1965. He had moved uptown, to Harlem. He had left his white wife and their half-white children, his white friends and colleagues. He had not, however, completely cleansed himself of "the old world." The streets remain cold and aloof, and if he is to become a part of their life he must purge himself of remaining decadence, the "dead whiteness":

We turn white when we are afraid.
We are going to try to be happy.[10]

The poems collected in *Black Magic Poetry* (1961–67) document the difficult and often painful period of exorcism, revaluation, and consolidation that was a necessary prelude to the assurance and celebration that mark Baraka's later works. This middle period is distinguished by two distinct phases. First, in the collections *Sabotage* (1961–63) and *Target Study* (1963–65), nearly all of his energy is directed toward the total rejection of "white-Western" values, myths, and obsessions. Second, in the works of *Black Art* (1965–67), the expulsion of white "demons" satisfactorily completed, he turns the full force of his vision toward the development and use of a new mythic apparatus and its relation to black people only. By briefly examining the multifarious poems of *Black Magic Poetry* according to this scheme, one may best observe the aspects of Baraka's aesthetic and emotional evolution necessary to an understanding of his dramatic works.

The whole of *Sabotage* and much of *Target Study* read like a phantasmagoria of past sins, badly remembered and fragmentary truths, and half-created hopes. It is clear from the outset that Baraka is in a spiritual limbo from which he cannot move until the foolish preoccupations of the past are fully denounced and the roots of his black life are recognized and accepted. In "The People Burning," for example, he probes his ambivalence toward both white and black culture. Having tempted himself with various forms of "quietism" and escapism ("Forget the hatred of natural insolence [. . .] march into any anonymous America"), he touches the metaphorical root of his awakening to black consciousness. Characteristically, this rebirth is said to be accomplished by black music; Sonny Rollins's *The Freedom Suite* album (1958), enormously influential among Rollins's contemporary black writers and musicians, is the specific starting point of Baraka's experience:

Got to remember just where I came in. Freedom Suite some five six years ago, Rollins cradling the sun as it rose, and we dreamed then, of becoming, unlike our fathers, and the other cowboys, strong men in our time, raging and clawing, at fools of any persuasion.

[from "The People Burning"]

The poems in these two volumes often express the dream of shedding the burdens of inherited oppression by abandoning the racial heritage which has accepted the weight of injury. However, while he speaks loudly and self-consciously as a black man in all of these works, it is toward his "white" past that Baraka's accusations are directed. The angry question posed in the following lines is whether he can leave his melancholic obsessions with death and the accumulated ruins of a specific culture, and redeem his infidelity to meaningful problems of the living moment:

> Now they ask me to be a jew or italian, and turn from the
> moment disappearing into the shaking clock of treasonable
> safety, like reruns of films, with sacred coon stars. [. . .]
> Forget your whole life, pop your fingers in a
> closed room, hopped-up witch doctor for the cowards of a
> recent generation. It is choice, now, like a philosophy
> problem. It is choice, now, and the weight is specific
> and personal.
>
> [from "The People Burning"]

The poet goes on to claim, "it is not an emotional decision"; but every line of every poem is charged with *emotional* facts. It may be a philosophical problem but he doesn't seek its solution by a cold, determinate logic. The fear of failure remains from *The Dead Lecturer*:

> Your time is up
> in this particular feeling. In this particular throb of meaning.
> Roi, baby, you blew the whole thing,
>
> [from "Citizen Cain"]

and the renunciation of a past in which he never looked beyond given reality is inadequate action for creating a meaningful present or regaining belief in a truer future:

> Shuddering at dusk, with a mile or so up the hill [. . .]
>
> Those days like one drawn-out song, monotonously
> promising. The quick step, the watchful march march,
> All were leading here, to this room, where memory
> stifles the present. And the future, my man, is long
> time gone.
>
> [from "Letter To E. Franklin Frazier"]

At the top of the hill is the sun, the elusive glory and joy of freedom beyond stifling forces that parade collectively and falsely as "reality." Before he can even begin the ascent, he must untangle himself from riddles of imagery created in his days as a "beat" poet. Several unkind references are made to other beats (e.g. he writes, clearly of Allen Ginsberg as well as of himself: "Is sense to be lost, all of it, so that / we can walk up Mulberry Street without getting beat up in Italian"—"The Burning General"); and occasionally the earlier ironic distrust of all art as evil negligence returns with an added attack upon the reader's complicity. Yet Baraka's prevalent attitude now toward poetic activity is utilitarian: the poet must not be a solipsistic adolescent, howling at the discovery that machine civilization has no interest in his having read Whitman; he must speak to the people in the language of the people:

say it straight to be
understood straight, put it flat and real
in the street where the sun comes and the
moon comes and the cold wind in winter
waters your eyes. Say what you mean, dig
it out put it down, and be strong
about it.

[from "Numbers, Letters"]

To "be strong about it" means, in these poems of *Sabotage* and *Target Study*, to be unsparing with the language of hate and condemnation, to exorcise white evil so vigorously that poems themselves become palpable weapons and representative forces of the emerging black consciousness. The desire for an art that is a literal physical tool is best expressed in "Black Art," itself an example of the power and anger generated by this aesthetic:

Poems are bullshit unless they are
teeth or lemons piled
on a step. Or black ladies dying
of men leaving nickel hearts
beating them down. [. . .]

We want live
words of the hip world live flesh &
coursing blood. [. . .]
We want "poems that kill."
Assassin poems, Poems that shoot
guns.

A new vocabulary and a new clarity of belief must be developed. However, before this new style can effectively fill the void left by the purge of the earlier methodology, the content carried by the old language also must be driven out of poetry. Thus the fixation upon death, which in *Preface* and *The Dead Lecturer* had been essentially self-focused, becomes completely centered on the external white world. The familiar language of the wasteland is applied with amazing energy to the Western (but primarily American) landscape; but, unlike the despairing observations of the earlier poems, the poet is now above the scene, the ruins pathetic but objectified:

The magic dance
of the second ave ladies,
in the artificial glare
of the world, silver-green curls sparkle
and the ladies' arms jingle
with new Fall pesos, sewn on grim bracelets
the poet's mother-in-law thinks are swell.

So much for America, let it sweep in grand
style
up the avenues of its failure. Let it promenade smartly
beneath the marquees of its despair.
[from "After the Ball"]

The poet records with changing emotions (bemusement, contempt, and boredom) this grim dance of death, and impatiently anticipates the abandonment of the Western ghost-town by nonwhite survivors. The Western powers progressively die off, but the perversity of their victims worshipping them in the oppressive language of a dead civilization remains; grotesquely, "the dead king laughs, looking out the hole / in his tomb. Seeing the poor / singing his evil songs" (from "Death Is Not as Natural as You Fags Seem to

Think"). Once the clarity of this Western decadence and the absurdity of the fellah's necrophilia is established, the oppressor and the victim will reverse roles.

Not only must the "grey hideous space" of Western civilization be abandoned before it falls but, moreover, its dying gods and worn-out myths must no longer be worshipped by the spiritually endowed oppressed. Utilizing the mask of a Willie Best, the poet plays the humorous (but also deadly serious) bringer of bad news for The Man:

THE LONE RANGER
IS DEAD
THE SHADOW
IS DEAD
ALL YOUR HEROES ARE DYING. J. EDGAR HOOVER WILL
SOON BE DEAD. YOUR MOTHER WILL DIE. LYNDON JOHNSON,
these are natural
things. No one is
threatening anybody
thats just the way life
is,
boss.
[from "Three Movements and a Coda"]

In *The Dead Lecturer* Baraka had often identified with the demise of old values and the despair of the perceptive and hopelessly courageous; in this early work the protestations and laments uttered could have been those of any English-speaking, sensitive white man:

[. . .] despite the rightness, the strength
the brilliance and character, the undeniable idiocy of poets
like Marx and Rousseau.
What we have created, is ourselves
as heroes, as lovers, as disgustingly
evil.
[from "Green Lantern's Solo" in *The Dead Lecturer*]

Baraka stands here in the middle of a solipsistic nightmare, a "disgustingly evil" hero and hero-worshipper, sharing the sense of *nausea* such madness produced among many perceptive white men. But in the verse of *Black Magic Poetry* he clearly divorces himself from the futility of the old mythology. The earlier imagery of sexual perversity and cowardice is transferred to the white man and is, if anything, more intense. In order to attain spiritual fulfillment, to recover himself as a black man, he must leave the dominant culture's assorted corruptions and deaths far beyond him. Having undertaken the systematic ruin of the "white" structures he has acquired—a spiritual destruction symbolizing the inevitable violence by which black men will gain their freedom—he calls for his brothers to move in new directions, to break their chains and leave with him.

The simple alternatives of death in the white man's ways or life in native blackness, which the European Africans of the Negritude movement spoke of so eloquently,[11] indicate, for a man with the immediate past of the Imamu Baraka of *Black Magic Poetry*, the necessity of doing more than simply ecstatically tearing himself from the white world. He must fully discover and become what he is in relation to this immediate past, as well as establish strong bonds to the deeper history of black people.

Thus the search for a sense of place, for security in his newfound ethos, is the solid underpinning of all the militant poses and harsh condemnations struck in poems like "Black Art" and "After the Ball." And thus we find a preoccupation in these poems with recovering something lost or forgotten. What will later find its place in a larger mythic ideal—the return of racial strength and purity—is now cast in terms of a personal miracle, an intimation of love revealed amid the noise and traffic of city streets:

> What I never wanted, came back
> for me to love it. (Above the sirens
> and bogus magic of the laughably damned) Came back
> in a new way, into new heart . . . old things considered
> there light struck me, social songs, racial songs,
> and love, like a versified cliche, came down on me
> hard, in its casual way. Tell me what it looked like.
> And me, who did I resemble? Mute shadow of perfection.
> Blessed and blessed, seeing, smelling, strength alert
> in my weakest parts.

Such a thing of suffering. Yellow girl. Gone
in the subways, my heart
pounding above the train.

["The Visit"]

This momentary perfection and love pass like an overheard and unforgettable song: it cannot now dominate his troubled mind, but it has taken its place in his subconscious and will be remembered when the peace necessary for song is finally attained. Now, however, the questions raised in "Numbers, Letters"—"If you're not home, where / are you? Where'd you go? What / were you doing when gone?"—relentlessly gnaw at his consciousness and force public and complex assessments of his relationship to old and new hierarchies. He speaks, self-consciously, as a black man, but it is his recent role in the white world that aggravates him, and it is the vision of assuming a warm niche in that social order that he despises most:

The place, is the final determination.
What is your place in the order of your feelings?
As the runner for your nation, focused on their needs,
what can you say or dream or float wild copper love in place of,
what you had, which was white and soft, and the vision of the farm
boy, standing in his shit. Replacing the man, and defining his demise.
But that crap is finished. I move with the rest, as strong as they,
knowing my own mind to be the unneeded rationale, the kindly explanation.

[from "Sad Cowboy"]

There is no reservation of intellectual orientation here as in the earlier poetry, where feelings might be withheld behind a screen of tantalizing images. He is obviously unsure of his "place in the order of [his] feelings" and states clearly that this is the most crucial dilemma he faces. Yet, given the admission of unanswered questions and the general undertone of insecurity, the assertions that close the poem—"But that crap is finished. I move with the rest, as strong as they"—are emotionally illogical and certainly forced. The attitude struck at the end is an ambiguous and paradoxical emotional "objective correlative" for the intellectual problems associated with it; Baraka has willfully contracted his material until the attitude serves as an objective correlative only by wrenching both the logic and feeling. Its emotional condition diverges from the poet's intellectual direction; the poet is obviously over-eager to sever himself from a past that is too recent and to which he has been too deeply committed for it simply to fall away. His exorcisms of love for the downtown birthplace of his sensibility, and adamant avowals of newfound love in the somewhat foreign uptown haven, are played out before the audience he claims to have abandoned as well as rejected.

The confusions resulting from the search for place and ease of mind are not surprising: Baraka is, after all, attempting an extremely radical change of feeling. We find this confusion manifested in his temporary dalliance with drugs (see, for example, "Houdini" or "All's Well") and a sinister Prufrockean avoidance of society, though the places of escape are the back-alleys of cities, not sea-bottoms:

> Heart claws
> out into the street. Weak evil eyes
> follow its progress in cabs (with crabs)
> the sky like a drying sore, that progress, swift,
> motherless, away from the normal fact of adventure
> and response. Away from women, heart, rushing
> under cool night air.
>
> [from "Lately"]

But deeper, more painful areas of uncertainty are felt in the growing desire to cleanse himself of the "white and soft," the illusory belief in love against all evidence that "all the world is hatred." This dichotomy was noticed in the earliest of Baraka's poems (for example, "There *Must* Be a Lone Ranger!!!"); but in this period of extreme reorientation, love has become not merely a weakness but an evil, and hate not an unwanted protection but a valuable weapon, even a value. This, at least, is the doctrine of such poems as "Sad Cowboy," and the problem of living with this attitude is the subject of "Air":

> I am lost in hot fits
> of myself
> trying
> to get
> out. Lost
> because
> I am kinder
> to myself
> than I
> need
> Softer
> w/ others
> than is good
> for them.

Yet kindness, softness, and the need for love are certainly all too obviously natural elements of his makeup; the agonizing contortions into which his "softer" parts were twisted to justify their existence in a world of palpable ugliness, a world that seems to demand the callous strength of hatred as the price of survival, push his poetic face into unconvincing masks of racial collectivity.

Though the desperate questions of the following lines are expressed as those of the entire black race—as they may be for many black people—the poet speaks directly of himself, as the last line finally admits:

> Why cant we love each other and be beautiful?
> Why do the beautiful corner each other and spit
> poison? Why do the beautiful not hangout together
> and learn to do away with evil? Why are the beautiful
> not living together and feeling each other's trials?
> Why are the Beautiful not walking with their arms around
> each other laughing softly at the soft laughter of black
> beauty?
> Why are the beautiful dreading each other, and hiding from
> each other? Why are the beautiful sick and divided like
> myself?
>
> [from "Cold Term"]

Until the beautiful can separate hatred of oppression from feelings about themselves, black and beautiful unity—the wholeness presupposed in any mythic ideal of racial strength—cannot possibly be achieved. They, but specifically Baraka, must completely *get themselves together* to be (w)holly TCB: this is the challenge posed by "Cold Term."

As the last stanza of "Air" reveals, the core of Baraka's feeling is lyrical in the sense of songfulness:

> Oh love
> Songs
> dont leave
> w/o me
> that you
> are the weakness
> of my simplicity
> Are feeling
> & want
> All need
> & romance
> I wd do anything
> to be loved
> &
> this
> is a stupid
> mistake.

In a time of organization against oppression, of strengthening against the last struggles of a monstrous West in its death-throes, Baraka, like the theorists of the French and Russian revolutions, finds this lyrical impulse to be a weakness and must, sadly, suspend it:

> I think about a time when I will be relaxed.
> When flames and non-specific passion wear themselves
> away. And my eyes and hands and mind can turn
> and soften, and my songs will be softer
> and lightly weight the air.
> [from "Three Modes of History and Culture"]

It would not be surprising if this were the lament not only of a poet but of a critic as well; for it is as a lyric poet that Baraka writes his most successful poems. One encounters at nearly every stage of his poetry the urge to lead poetry away from excess of thought over image, the arid wastelands of literary and sociological allusion, the will o' the wisp of sardonic wit, toward a natural lyricism, the singing note, and a sensuous imagery deepened in significance by imitations of the hidden life within the mind. To achieve this, of course, Baraka must turn his eye and ear inward and there, communing with himself, imitate the objects he finds and so create images as objectified versions of himself.

This *lyric* urge stands in direct contrast to the concern with external structures and outward representation of imagery which is the *dramatic* impulse.[12] Obviously, as with Faust, two souls dwell within Baraka's breast: the internal, lyrical one that fights for autonomy in his best poetry and the external, rhetorical one that finds a truer home in his drama. The tension between the two motives, which we will surely find in much of Baraka's drama, can be vital and exciting; but when one element, especially the lyrical, is abandoned for the other, the poetic process all but breaks down. Thus, many of the poems in this period of exorcism and absorption into thematic problems are incredibly obscure, the thought itself being overwhelmed by sheer rhetorical mass. An occasional image may be powerful, but it is not usually followed by similarly effective words as a new rhetorical trail is hastily taken up in search of instant revelation.

Some poems are simply bad; any exegesis of "Blank," for example—beyond noting the poet's obvious frustration with delusions and with the sense of the body's being trapped in time—would strain the reader's credulity too much to justify the attempt. Other poems are filled with various sententiae and pretensions to proverbial wisdom. Indeed, the better rhetorical lines arrest one in the manner of Blake's proverbs—now satiric now sincere, but always charged with the energy of antinomian rhetoric: "We are not in danger of being wrong" ("Confirmation"), "We are in love with the virtue of evil" ("Red Eye")—*both* of which may be expressed because "There is no dream of Man that haunts him such as Freedom!" ("Precise Techniques"). But conveying less than full confidence in his vision, and with his lyric voice in exile Baraka's poetry generally suffers the worst effects of the doctrinaire and hortatory.[13]

However bad such rhetoric may be poetically, Baraka clearly found it a necessary tool for rooting out confusion and "evil" inherent in earlier ideas. At the end of *Sabotage*, Baraka is standing halfway up that hill leading toward the transcendent sun (see "The Bronze Buckaroo"). By the end of *Target Study*, Baraka has all but cleared away the bitter memories of his downtown past. He rarely addresses himself to white people, and he is determined to channel his hatred "productively," leaving the force of his love for his black brethren. Finally, as at other points of renewed vigor and clarity of attention, he has become impatient to remake the world:

> The imperfection of the world
> is a burden, if you know it, think
> about it, at all. Look up in the sky
> wishing you were free.
>
> [from "Jitterbugs"]

From now on Baraka's sensibility is quite clearly "Romantic." For at the root of the mythic vision that soon will be spelled out is the idea that man (of course, the black man) is an infinite reservoir of possibilities, and that if one can rearrange society by the reconstruction of oppressive order or the imposition of a new structure upon the withering old, then these possibilities will reap infinite progress. Life and mind, solitude and society, revolution and tradition, progress and culture, no longer appear as logically exclusive or as moral alternatives between which one has to choose, but as possibilities that one strives to realize simultaneously. Baraka has come to see the world in relation to his people as Novalis saw it in relation to himself ("All the accidents of our life are materials out of which we can make what we like, everything is a link in an unending chain"). The people for whom the poet speaks will be his exclusive audience, and his poems will go out to them as the strongest links of the unending chain, no longer the bonds of the slave:

We want a black poem. And a
Black World.
Let the world be a Black Poem
And Let All Black People Speak This Poem
Silently
or LOUD

[from "Black Art"]

The poetry of *Black Art* (1965–67), while certainly involved in the problems that overwhelm the preceding two volumes, essentially establishes the racial myth which the earlier works have been building toward in fits and starts. Much of *Sabotage* and *Target Study* are obsessed with playing the dozens against the white man. By contrast, the poems of *Black Art* are primarily addressed to black men and are about black men. Their words are less satiric and imprecatory; rather, they are an awakening to consciousness.

In an early poem of *Sabotage*, "Leadbelly Gives an Autograph," Baraka demands reparations from the "savage" West. Specifically, he wants the materials necessary for building a new edifice that he will populate with his own "beasts and myths." Gradually he comes to see himself as providing both materials and myths for a new civilization. Thus he devotes himself increasingly to being a spokesman of his people. No longer speaking to another people, he clearly expresses a poetic knowledge which is latent in his own race, now come to articulation in him. His voice is the voice of prophecy, of a seer in the lineage of ancestral visionaries:

My brother, Bigger Thomas, son of
Poor Richard, father, of poor
lost jimmy, locked together all
of us [. . .] all rising, lord, to become the thing you told us.

[from "That Mighty Flight"]

He wants to be, as Sartre said of the French-African poets, "both a beacon and a mirror," [14] half-prophet and half-follower, priest and poet, a literal *vates.* What he offers his people is a vision made of several elements: general paraphernalia of mysticism;[15] the many beliefs, gods, and rituals of Baraka's Nation of Islam faith; Swahili epigrams; and the prevailing pantheistic idea that black people are all members of one body (a general concept as old as Plato's political theory).

At several points in the earlier two volumes, as the image of God as a "white man with a dueling scar" ("Dada Zodji") lost its attraction, the role of divinity was seen as a proper goal for black people. "We Must Become Gods," he declared several times. Finally, in the works of *Black Art*, the goal has been reached:

> Do not obey their laws
> which are against God
> believe brother, do not
> ever think any of that
> cold shit they say is
> true. They are against
> the law. Their "laws"
> are filthy evil, against
> almighty God. They are
> sick to be against God,
> against the animals and sun,
> against thought and feeling
> against the world as it most commonly
> is [. . .] our breathing is harnessed to divinity.
>
> [from "A School of Prayer"]

This is precisely the case set against the Jewish tradition by Christianity and then, in turn, against the Roman Catholic tradition by Protestantism: the necessity of rebellion against old laws that have grown into oppressive and sinful external idolatry. This "will toward righteousness," which Larry Neal identifies[16] as a constant element of Baraka's spiritual quest, is abundantly evident in his pronouncements as an Imamu. It carries with it the arrogance and dignity common to many religious texts.

The heavily religious nature of this myth of black divinity is not surprising. Frye observes that "the return of irony to myth is accompanied [. . .] by a widespread interest in sacramental philosophy and dogmatic theology." [17] Furthermore, as Frye also notes, poets, as poets, are fundamentally more attracted to religion than politics because of the greater freedom of imagination the former allows. Then, too, Baraka's religious orientation takes its place in the strong religious dynamic that informs Afro-American culture, the popular extremes of which might be the Baptist humanism of Martin Luther King and the cults of Voodoo, African-Islamic religions, and other mysticisms. Insofar as Baraka's myth inclines toward the latter, he finds himself in a tradition of the occult that has ranged from Nat Turner to the Nation of Islam, from Father Divine to Sweet Daddy Grace.

But it is as a poet/prophet that Baraka takes dictation from his necessary and incontrovertibly myth-oriented angels, and thus the imagery as well as the content of his visions make them poetically interesting. The sense of something new brought out of destruction of old laws and institutions, of unlimited power in a humanized form ("We are reaching as God for God as human knowing spirit"—from "Human to Spirit Humanism for Animals"), of a world in which everything is potentially identical with everything else as though all were contained within one whole body ("Let the world be a Black Poem")—all of this is essentially *apocalyptic,* and the apocalyptic imagery that permeates Baraka's myth is, as we noted in chapter 2, appropriate to the mythic mode.

Again, Baraka is in a strong Afro-American tradition of apocalyptic ideas, including those of Baldwin, King, and, of course, the late Elijah Muhammad. Moreover, largely under Baraka's influence, many of the better black writers in recent years (as varied a group, in fact, as Ismael Reed, Askia Muhammad Touré, Larry Neal, Henry Dumas, and Don L. Lee) have made greater use of such imagery than ever before. Essential to Baraka's particular utilization of apocalyptic thinking is the central mythic concept of an ancient race of black gods who originally ruled the earth and have "evolved again to civilize the world" (from "Black People: This Is Our Destiny").[18] Reclaiming an identity with African roots so sadly rejected at the time of "Notes for a Speech," the prophet tells of the need to regain the ancient strength and calls for the invocation necessary for apocalypse:

> We have been captured,
> brothers. And we labor
> to make our getaway, into
> the ancient image, into a new

correspondence with ourselves
and our black family. We need magic
now we need the spells, to raise up
return, destroy, and create. What will be
the sacred words?

[from "Ka 'Ba"]

Once the vacancy between the past and present has been closed by the magical words, apocalypse will come.

The interplay of destruction and creation is a feature of nearly every mythic doctrine, from Egyptian, Persian, and Indian myths to the trinitarian concepts of Platonic and Christian beliefs, and devolves from the theory that what is created may be destroyed only in appearance and actually only changes its mode of existence. The most common symbol of the three-personed God that embodies the process of this three-part cycle (creation-destruction-regeneration) is, of course, the sun, perhaps the first object of mankind's adoration.[19] All nature, all energy is called into action by its agency; its return in the spring season renews and increases the animal and vegetable world. Thus the worship of the sun (primarily as energy-giver) is also a central tenet of Baraka's mythic doctrine: "for the sake of, at the lust of/pure life, WE WORSHIP THE SUN" (from "Stirling Street September").

The "lust of pure life" is a natural idea in the imagery of apocalypse; for, as Blake's "Marriage of Heaven and Hell" tells us, apocalypse will begin "by an improvement of sensual enjoyment." The sexual confusions that marked the earlier poetry, and the uneasy dichotomy between impulses of love and hatred, are joyously resolved in this newly made world:

Slide down
the silent woman waits. Her Hands want you, fast, free, wide,
fixed in moving space millions of beautiful shocks she moves
across to pull you. Indians.
Indians. Hey.
Ride, as natural warriors
of the lord. God
touch me in clear

heaven. In free clean
skies, moving quick. A warm wet tongue.
[from "Indians"]

This new celebration is reminiscent of the sexual pantheism of such poets of Negritude as Senghor, Césaire, and Laleau, and stands in contrast to the sexually tormented tradition of Euro-American authors (for example, Wilde, Eliot, and, more recently, Allen Ginsberg) into which several black authors (Baldwin, Cleaver, and as we have seen, the young LeRoi Jones) have been drawn at one time or another. The white stereotype of potent black sexuality, mocked in "A Poem for Willie Best" (part 8), is here accepted and converted into the Romantic impulse of desire and a Puritan-like return to the flesh: to the pure all things are pure.

This celebration brings with it momentary recurrences of the lyricism banished in the beginning of *Black Magic Poetry.* The following lines seem to carry the easy rhythm and energy characteristic of the early verse:

you are the total jazzman
a note on the horn
you are the total fingering
the jawshaking happy hipster waggling at the edge of the stage
you are the perfection the wisdom of the right shaped note-breath-heart
burning all of the world
the universe is close to your lips
blow it out
[from "Death is the beginning of a new form"]

Public and private realms are fused with the heat of this new lyricism, and the inaccessible sky of the earlier period (heaven desired) opens for the black lover. Compare, for example, the coolness and deadly circularity of these lines from an early poem of *Sabotage*:

Rising gate
with disappearing locks.
Thin tingling wind. Sun engines

picking up their whirr, starlings wheeling
across oil and pulling it into clouds. Turning
as a last measure, to scream. But too far away.
The control
is what lifts me. The sky is not open, but curves,
in blue sinking tones
to send us back in the deep flesh of our own places
[from "Morning Purpose"]

with the floating peace, warmth, and socially (and violently) reassured joy of these lines:

Quick Night
easy warmth
The girlmother lies next to me
breathing [. . .]
Night aches
acts
Niggers rage

down the street. (Air
Pocket, sinks
us. She lady
angel brings
her self
to touch me [. . .]
I love &
understand
things.
[from "The World Is Full of Remarkable Things"]

However, the songfulness and beauty of this poem is not entirely typical of *Black Art.* Even in the last of these works the rhetorical didacticism of mythic doctrine prevails, and often the language of Baraka's imposed mysticism literally runs wild and abruptly short-circuits the poetic process.[20] There is, certainly, a noticeable attempt to clarify the use of the many abstractions that together express "the doctrine," and a sense of a ritualistic use of images emerges. But only when an assurance of full transcendence, which these poems never quite project, is reached can the lyrical reclaim its proper place in Baraka's poetry, in the service of celebration of racial myth, not self-obsession. The spirit of *Black Art* has been Faustian, a restless striving after perfection:

> Leans
> we are worlds of leaning, talling, reaching, with
> reaching with, what we reach for already
> in back, of us, reaching
> for and through
> the space
> we take.
>
> [from "The Racist"]

When perfection has been grasped, the poet may sing and cradle the sun. Until then, the prophet of black ascendancy must mix the dance of triumph with the necessity of death, and temper celebration with warning:

> Dance up and down the streets, turn all
> the music up, run through the streets with music, beautiful radios on
> Market Street, they are brought here especially for you. Our brothers
> are moving all over, smashing at jellywhite faces. We must make our own
> World, man, our own world, and we can not do this unless the white man
> is dead. Let's get together and kill him my man, let's get to gather the fruit
> of the sun, let's make a world we want black children to grow and learn in
> do not let your children when they grow look in your face and curse you by
> pitying your tomish ways.
>
> [from "Black People!"]

III *In Our Terribleness* and *It's Nation Time*

By 1970 Baraka has been completely converted to Maulana Karenga's Kawaida doctrine. The apocalyptic myth of black power and triumph that was being developed in the mid-to-late 1960s is now his primary poetic subject; further, this myth has been thoroughly integrated with the political ideal of nationalism that also evolved in this period. The poetic-theologic texts of 1970, *In Our Terribleness* and *It's Nation Time*, reflect the assurance that has finally come to Baraka with the clarification of mythic precepts and ever-growing righteousness of cause. Baraka, like many poets who have suffered similar metaphysical crises, has possessed two Muses, a profane and a sacred. In Baraka's work, the heavenly one is the final victor.

The two works are primarily songs of celebration and prayers for continued evolution toward perfection. The advent of black genius, black strength, and black self-awareness have made the Black Nation an Immanence; the prayer is for its transcendent presence:

> the black man is the future of the world
> be come
> rise up
> future of the black genius spirit reality
>   move
>   from crushed roach back
>   from dead snake head
>   from wig funeral in slowmotion
>   from dancing teeth and coward tip
>   from jibberjabber patme boss patme smmich
> when the brothers strike niggers come out
> come out niggers
> when the brothers take over the school
> help niggers
> come out niggers
> all niggers negroes must change
> come together in unity unify
> for nation time
> it's nation time . . .
>
> [from "It's Nation Time"—*It's Nation Time*]

The transitory stages of black ascendancy—seminal godliness, the slide into slavery, the humiliation of "jibberjabber patme boss," rising black consciousness, ultimate return to godliness—are all duly noted. So, too, are the necessary and holy artifacts of the coming black civilization.

In Our Terribleness is in great part a cataloguing of such sacraments and rituals of piety, as well as a series of clearly stated expositions of the tenets of his nationalistic myth. Its longest distinct section, "Prayer for Saving," is an anatomy of black folklore, cultural heroes, "stereotypical" attributes (for example, athletic prowess); in the breathless pace of a holy chant, the poet calls for their preservation and veneration:

Survive and Defend.
Survive and Defend.
Defend the space you live upon Defend your family your way of
  feeling
  about the world. Defend The Impressions
  and Muhammad Ali
  Defend Ray Robinson and the Songhay Empires [. . .]
let our words and music survive
let the temptations please let their feeling survive
Please Black People Defend John Coltrane and Sun Ra
Claude McKay must survive his long black knowledge walks
in footprint sands of europe america and west indies must stand . . .
  Survive
and Defend all these things in us
All These Things We are
Or Come From
  Defend Defend Survive and Defend
    Spirit of Black Life
    Live in Immortality
    For
    Ever.[21]

The impulse of these late poems, then, is to celebrate not denigrate. The infinite articles of black humanity are its collective "spirit"; the nationalistic tactics needed for the projection of the "Spirit of Black Life" into future greatness are its dogma and affirmation. An essential aspect of this dogma is the Pan-Africanism which began to emerge in the late poems of *Black Art*: "We move from the simple to the many to . . . the nation. And then past there we move to many nations, as one, as Nkrumah and Garvey envision, the many blacks into the One Huge Black Nation, strong as the divinity in us."

The changes of vision undergone between "Notes for a Speech" and these lines from *In Our Terribleness* have obviously been many and diverse. Perhaps the most crucial reversal from the difficulties recorded in "Notes for a Speech" involves Baraka's new attitude toward the black collective that he sadly called "my own dead souls, my so called people" in the early poem. Even in the last poems of *Black Art*, Baraka sometimes fears his words may be useless to a people "rotting for centuries destined to die with the white man" (from "Madness"), and that holy black men may fail their true selves and become "plain dumb niggers with the only quality truly transferable among humans, stupidity" (from "Sisters in the Fog"). In these later poems of celebrated nationhood, however, the black man is no longer a potential "dumb nigger." He is an actual "*bad* nigger," and from do-rag to Afro, from toothpick to swagger stick, from "spirit of the stiff leg" to "music" of the switchblade, the poet consecrates the ethos of his spirit, his badness:

> Ask Me What I Am—
> [. . .] nigger love a magic being
> the dipping interior resurrect constant continuous
> the way the nigger walk
>
> The red hat is a magic hat
> the razor a sword flasher
> the lines of adepts all niggers really
> the pyramid speaks of niggers actually
> the word will be given by niggers
> we are in our most holy selves niggers
> god is a nigger really
> ask who god is and he will answer if you ask right [. . .]
> a nigger is holy.

The strength of the black nation is found on the streets, up the alleys, in the pool-halls, and on the stoops where black men serve their last portion of servitude before passage into the Future City. Judging from the confidence with which Baraka identifies himself with this nucleus of national power, he has finally been claimed by the black streets whose life he chronicles:

> "That's a bad vine that dude got on"
> "Damn."
> "It's a bad dude" [. . .]

This is our leadership
this is our kingdom to come
as it comes out of our hearts
to final strength in the common world.
We will raise it and develop it [. . .]
(on the stoops).

The lines of *In Our Terribleness* present a clear fusion of street life, various mythological abstractions, the several languages of The Life and The Myth, and many other elements. They flow on and on, image evoking image, fragments from one theme mingling with aspects of another, until it becomes obvious that this work is a poetic symphony of verbal association with theme answering theme, an elaborate succession of interwoven analogies and contrasts from all phases of black culture: the elegance of Duke Ellington and the Soul drive of James Brown; the doctrines of Elijah Muhammad and of Maulana Karenga; the rhythm of Swahili and the pulse of jive. Like Pound's *Cantos*, it is an "epic of timelessness," and it realizes the tendency toward extended and encyclopaedic forms characteristic of the mythic mode.

This massive effort is undertaken with a language in which the abstraction of myth and musical cadences of black speech are joined in the full rediscovery of Baraka's natural lyricism. For example, the simply clarity of:

Was this the highest of the physical
I was answering the truth of the whole
She was beautiful in your mind, Halisi, Burnt
full of light. So it is a spiritual blessing
to see eyes and nose and mouth so,
perfect;

the fused bebop-Swahili scatting of:

Ommmm Mane Padme Hummmmmmm
Ooshoobee doo bee
Ashadu an la Illaha Illala
Ooshoobee doo bee
Tuna Jaribu Kuwa Weusi Tu[22]
Ooshoo bee doo bee;
[from "Sermon for Our Maturity"—*It's Nation Time*]

or the rhythmically alluring plea of:

oh lady oh brother, wherever and who ever you are
breathing on
oh please please in the night time
more please in the mewning
we need need you bbbaby man, we need all the blood we gotta
get some blood and
you in your wilderness blood
is the nigger
yes the sweet lost nigger
    you are our nation sick ass assimilado
        please come back
            like james brown say
                please please please
    [from "The Nation Is Like Ourselves"—*It's Nation Time*]

The clear confidence of the poetic voice is matched by a firm belief in the divine sanction of poetic activity. The poet is, indeed, the vatic genius of the spiritual, a harbinger of the universal black soul:

I am a
vessel, a black priest interpreting
the present and future for my people
Olorun—Allah speaks in and
thru me now [. . .] He begs me to
pray for you-as I am doing-He
bids me have you submit to
the energy.

His mission as an intelligence of Allah is to make manifest the link between the complex world of black humanity and Allah, the supreme unifier. He must reveal the nature of the black soul to be both necessity and liberty, fact and value, empirical and moral concept, given reality and archetype.

The words Allah's messengers use to elucidate this reality must themselves become a holy reality. Thus the lines we have been reading must be seen as part of a whole scriptural structure; Baraka is undertaking nothing less than the writing of a new Bible or Koran: "We need our own heavy book. [. . .] We must have our doctrine, our new black quran to save us to lift us." As prophet, priest, genius of black purity, he turns to this massive enterprise.[23] However encyclopaedic the mythic doctrine may become, it will always be most true to its purpose when carried forward by Baraka's energetic lyricism:

> You can dance Nigger I know it
> Dance on to freedom
> You can sing Nigger sing
> Sing about your pure movement
> in space
> Grow
> You pierced the clouds
> of animal ignorance
> you bigger than animal cages
> yr arms cross the serpent of unknowing
> yr heart is Africa and blood line
> sweetens the rest of existence
> w/ color
> All color heat and speed
> are yours
> Salaam Brother
> You still
> gettin up!!

[from "Sermon for Our Maturity"—*It's Nation Time*]

In the title poem of *Preface,* the young LeRoi Jones complained, "Nobody sings anymore." Now he sings a song of black transcendence. The road traveled between these points was long and varied. We come to undertake a similar journey in studying the development of Baraka's drama, that most public embodiment of his artistic quest.

Part 2

The Drama: The Birth of Music out of the Spirit of Tragedy

5 Early Drama: Gestures Toward Liberation

A central preoccupation of Baraka's poetry and prose has been the discovery of a uniquely Afro-American persona and voice:

> The balance.
> He was tired of losing. (And
> his walking buddies tired
> of walking. [. . .]
> He said, I'm tired
> of losing.
> "I *got* to cut 'cha."

This is, in one sense, a dramatic composition: a questioning, ironic rendering of conversation and commonplace observation, and beneath this, the whisper of private crisis. Several of the most successful poems are records of conversation, overheard monologues, or montages of cliché, proverb, and other oral forms. Their structure, from "The A.B.C.s" to "It's Nation Time," is of a dramatized consciousness: juxtaposed scenes, oratorical passages, sudden words and acts. Moreover, various characters, from Willie Best to the street heroes of *In Our Terribleness*, are theatrical figures whose postures and soliloquies help project Baraka's own emotions and thoughts.

The nontheatre works, then, explore a preliminary method of dramatizing values in contrasting rhythms and states of mind. Baraka's concern with linguistic and mental gestures inevitably led him to more overt dramatization during his search for a "post-American form." His plays render corporeal what had otherwise existed as abstract or implied modes of being.

In this effort to dramatize consciousness, Baraka's theatre is in line with a modern European tradition that extends from Hebbel to

Genêt—yet it springs no less naturally from Baraka's concept of the black aesthetic. The "revolutionary theatre" is to be a political weapon; it must communicate a historically valid vision of Afro-American life and, ultimately, galvanize its audience's latent communal spirit. Clearly, the intimacy and immediacy of theatre performance provides the best context for such cultural transformation.

For the Afro-American writer, the call-and-response pattern of oral folk culture—as evinced in such expressions as the toast, dozens, musical jam session, church ritual, and just plain signifying—would appear to offer a basis for a distinctively black theatre. The interdependent relation between the black musician and his audience seems an especially invigorating model for the black playwright. However, given the need to articulate a specific, often didactic message, the problem of form for the black dramatist is not so simple. Though freer than the prose writer from the restrictions imposed on black vocality by the silent finality of a fixed text, the playwright must still face the task of creating a black theatrical idiom with the materials proffered by various dramatic conventions. It is not surprising, therefore, that the story of Baraka's drama, like that of modern black theatre as a whole, is one of ceaseless experimentation and change.

Criticism of Baraka's drama has tended to be primarily thematic, restricting formal discussion to secondary and casual observations. The general inattention to dramatic structure has resulted in much exegesis that reduces the text to mere allegory—usually allegory of "*this* for *that*" (to borrow Charles S. Singleton's phrase). As the plays become subject to one-dimensional schematization and even guesswork, their formal power—and hence the very complexity of their themes—eludes us. Baraka built his plays painstakingly; their structure and content are inextricable. My general aim in interpreting these works is to focus upon this dynamic unity of vision and dramaturgical methods employed by Baraka to give that vision theatrical life. Such analysis is best sustained by examining the plays individually, and I shall handle them chronologically in order to illuminate the evolution of Baraka's "revolutionary theatre."

Dutchman

Dutchman has received continual critical attention since its *succès du scandale* when first produced in 1964. Interpretations of the play have ranged from the initial fear and dismay of the New York critics[1] to triumphant celebrations of the play's "remarkable, stunning poetry." [2] Given the welter of conflicting readings created by explicators of *Dutchman*, it seems necessary to employ a rather rigorous format of interpretation. Accordingly, I shall examine the play in four complementary ways: as a purely formal entity; as a tragic action; as a dialectic between Clay's major speech and the enveloping action; and finally, as historical explanation and ritual. By thus exploring *Dutchman* close to its structural and ideological foundations, I can perhaps arrive at the center of its own "pure heart, the pumping black heart." [3]

I

The story of *Dutchman* is brutal and arresting, true to both the specific quality of tension which typifies urban life and the more universal psychology of human relationships. Each of its two scenes takes place in a moving subway car, "steaming hot, and summer on top, outside." Before scene 1 proper, a short dumb-show takes place: a man sitting in a subway seat uneasily exchanges smiles through his window with a woman standing outside on the platform until the train speeds away. As scene 1 begins, we see this woman (Lula) entering the car and taking a seat beside the man (Clay). Lula is a beautiful, thirty-year-old white woman, Clay a well-groomed, twenty-year-old black man. She immediately instigates a sharp, nervous, and engaging repartee that possesses all the qualities of leanness, economy, accuracy, and consistently ironical understatement characteristic of modern naturalistic drama. Lula and Clay play a game of surface communication, exchanging ritual insults, sexual innuendo, and hip witticisms in the idiom of contemporary urban America:

Clay. Then what happens?

Lula. After the dancing and games, after the long drinks and long walks, the real fun begins.

Clay. Ah, the real fun. (*Embarrassed, in spite of himself*) Which is . . . ?

Lula. (*Laughs at him*) Real fun in the dark house. Hah! Real fun in the dark house, high up above the street and the ignorant cowboys. I lead you in, holding your wet hand gently in my hand . . .

Clay. Which is not wet?

Lula. Which is dry as ashes.

Clay. And cold?

Lula. Don't think you'll get out of your responsibility that way. It's not cold at all. You Fascist! Into my dark living room. Where we'll sit and talk endlessly, endlessly.

[pp. 24–25]

Just beneath the surface of this chatty cleverness, however, lies the sense of ineludible conflict, of impending danger and violence:

Lula. (*Bored and not even looking*) I don't even know you.

Clay. You said you know my type.

Lula. (*Strangely irritated*) Don't get smart with me, Buster. I know you like the palm of my hand.

Clay. The one you eat the apples with?

Lula. [. . .] (*Looks at him*) the same hand I unbutton my dress with, or let my skirt fall down. Same hand. Lover.

Clay. Are you angry about anything? Did I say something wrong?

Lula. Everything you say is wrong.

[pp. 17–18]

For a while, Clay manages to keep pace with Lula's weird shifts of interest and to maintain the superficial interplay. Then Lula bursts into a "rhythmical shudder and twistlike wriggle," dancing up and down the aisle while exhorting an amazed Clay to "rub bellies" and dance with her. She mocks him brutally, calling him a "middleclass black bastard" and "liver-lipped white man," and finally breaks loose into an open, exorcising, insulting tirade:

> There is Uncle Tom . . . I mean, Uncle Thomas Woolly-Head. With old white matted mane. He hobbles on his wooden cane. Old Tom. Old Tom. Let the white man hump his ol' mama, and he jes' shuffle off in the woods and hide his gentle gray head. Ol' Thomas Woolly-Head.
>
> [p. 32]

Finally, Clay slaps her and forces her to her seat, an act of tremendous dramatic impact by virtue of its juxtaposition to both Lula's dance and Clay's former passivity. In control for the first time, he explodes into a long, tortured, emotion-releasing speech that strips him of his "nice-nigger" façade and attempts to put forth a new, powerful identity. He gains the upper hand but decides not to kill her; by thus rejecting the power and violence that would enable him fully to dominate his situation, he reaffirms his vulnerability and suddenly falls victim to the white woman.

Having "heard enough," her voice taking on a "different, more businesslike quality," Lula calmly stabs Clay as he reaches across her to retrieve his belongings. She orders the other passengers to open the door, throw Clay's body off the train, and exit en masse at the next stop. The passengers dump Clay's body from the train. Lula composes herself, "takes out a notebook and makes a quick scribbling note." The train stops and the others leave. Another young Negro enters and sits near Lula; "she turns and gives him a long slow look." An old Negro conductor enters the car, does a soft-shoe dance and mumbles a song, greets the young brother, tips his hat to the lady, and departs. Curtain.

One's primary impression of this drama as a formal structure is that it realizes the naturalists' program for a theater that, as Zola described it, "has to do with the human problem studied in the framework of reality." Zola's words bore fruit in the dominance of the realistic mode in modern drama, with its presentation of the facts of man's existence and environment through a new and rich explicitness. Baraka's *Dutchman* generously partakes of the mimetic urge of realism, and more particularly, of the naturalistic refinement of this style. The props and their placement are made precise and lifelike, the movement and expression of the characters are minutely detailed and psychologically acute. If we open the text of *Dutchman* at random, we find the appearance of ordinary, "ineloquent" language with one cog of thought geared by natural movement or mere chance into another cog. Here we are certainly deep within the ironic mode: a modern, urban reality is presented with verisimilitude of language, scene, and even action, which is perhaps the more shocking because it is remarkably plausible.

The few moments of pure action in the play—the framing dumb-shows, Lula's dance, Clay's murder—stand in stark contrast to the rest of the drama, which consists of the flow of words between Lula and Clay. Indeed, to a great extent we can describe the action of *Dutchman* with Pirandello's phrase, *l'azione parlata:* action-spoken or action-in-words. It is true that this language appears to be that of an idiom alive in the urban street, an accurate reflection of real convention. But if we begin to look more closely, the sound of purely naturalistic speech is countered by a sense of the playwright's subtle but sure shaping of the dialogue into extraordinary meanings and situations:

> *Lula.* Oh boy. (*Looking quickly at Clay*) What a face. You know, you could be a handsome man.
>
> *Clay.* I can't argue with you.
>
> *Lula.* (*Vague, off-center response*) What?
>
> *Clay.* (*Raising his voice, thinking the train noise has drowned part of his sentence*) I can't argue with you.
>
> *Lula.* My hair is turning gray. A gray hair for each year and type I've come through.
>
> *Clay.* Why do you want to sound so old?
>
> *Lula.* But it's always gentle when it starts. (*Attention drifting*) Hugged against tenements, day or night.
>
> *Clay.* What?
>
> *Lula.* (*Refocusing*) Hey, why don't you take me to that party you're going to?
>
> [pp. 12–13]

Where the ordinary contemporary naturalist achieves mere ineloquence and thus ineffective drama, Baraka shows the turbulence and power beneath the surface that makes us realize something much more than a specially edited slice-of-life is being portrayed. This uncanny reproduction of the inflections and rambling irrelevancies of everyday speech sets an unbridgeable gap between the characters, an impenetrable and mysterious space; and as the characters react to each other's random phrases, we gradually sense a poetic dimension, much like that in the drama of Beckett or Pinter, opening before us. The dialogue does start from both ordinary conversation and the kind of rhetoric most closely related to it. The unit remains the actual uttered remark, but the units are then related to each other with poetic implication. Baraka utilizes the understatement, the evasion, the unfinished sentence, and as masterly a combination of clichés as those of Ionesco or Albee to indicate in the linguistic texture of the play a dramatic world much larger than that which pure naturalism can convey.

To what regions, then, does this drama (which seemed at first so clearly naturalistic) take us? The passages quoted above show an affinity with the theatrical category most representative of the ironic mode: the Theatre of the Absurd. It was the Absurdists who ultimately fulfilled the Ibsenite maxim of "poetic creation in the plain unvarnished speech of reality," an achievement to which Baraka adds with *Dutchman.* In *Dutchman*, Baraka shares with many Absurdists a theatre where social criticism and unrelieved, biting satire occur in an enveloping atmosphere of anxiety and despair at the disappearance of solutions, illusions, and purposefulness. He shares, too, the Absurdist sense of humor in the odd, disjunctive, and grotesque.

But perhaps the most important quality that *Dutchman* shares with Absurdist drama is the tendency toward allegorical and mythical modes of thought, and the use of archetypal motifs to deepen the significance of the surface language and action. *Dutchman*, far from making a simple use of random contemporary speech in building the relation and conflict between Lula and Clay, is unified by several subtly organized and highly contrived symbols. In fact, the play is informed by an overall mythic pattern that is not so much secondary as complementary to the main action between the characters.

Here, then, is a work of the ironic mode reaching for the mythic in an effort to universalize, or at least to widen the scope of the particular event it depicts. What is the expression of this mythic impulse? An obvious starting point is to examine the characters Lula and Clay, both of whom suggest Edenic counterparts.[4] Lula, the white temptress, is a composite of many seductresses—Circe, Calypso, Dido, Cleopatra, Duessa, Delilah—but she especially resembles Eve. She enters the car daintily eating an apple, and after sexually arousing Clay she offers him one too:

> *Lula.* (*She returns her hand, without moving it, then takes it away and plunges it in her bag to draw out an apple*) You want this?
> *Clay.* Sure.
>
> [p. 11]

Apples are constantly appearing, both on the set and in the language, and as Lula begins her insulting dance Clay ironically wonders, "Hey, what was in those apples?"

Clay's archetype is, of course, Adam, the victim of seduction whose spiral downward into the Fall brings misery but also knowledge; his name recalls the creation of man: "And the Lord God formed man of the dust of the ground, and breathed into his nostrils the breath of life" (Genesis 2:7). Lula initiates a naming game with Clay, a parody of Adam's naming of the animals and of Eve herself:

> *Clay.* How can I ask you when I don't know your name?
> *Lula.* Are you talking to my name?
> *Clay.* What is it, a secret?
> *Lula.* I'm Lena the Hyena.
> *Clay.* The famous woman poet?
> *Lula.* Poetess! The same!
> *Clay.* Well, you know so much about me . . . what's my name?
> *Lula.* Morris the Hyena.
> *Clay.* The famous woman poet?
> *Lula.* The same. (*Laughing and going into her bag*) You want another apple?
>
> [p. 14]

As Adam's fall from innocence was immediately followed by the shameful discovery of nakedness and consequent lust of the male and female, so Clay's fall occurs in an atmosphere of sexual temptation and rapacious lust. "I saw you staring through that window down in the vicinity of my ass and legs," Lula remarks to Clay just after entering the car, and the sexual flirtation of her dance ("Come on Clay. Let's do the nasty. Rub bellies. Rub bellies") is only the culmination of a long process of enticement.

The dominant mythical pattern, then, is that of the Edenic Fall. The setting, however, is hardly Edenic, the "flying underbelly of the city" no *locus amoenus* worth preserving. Yet, as prosaic as this underground typology seems to the modern urban audience, it is also, as Baraka's stage direction tells us, "heaped in modern myth." As an "underbelly of the city," it is a labyrinthine image of lost direction and, although womblike, is ironically a place of destruction; as the "steaming hot underground," it suggests nothing so much as Hell.

The myth that informs *Dutchman*, then, is actually a *demonic* parody of the Edenic myth. The underground is a perfect symbol of demonic vision, the constant screams of the trains reminding us of the torture associated with the demonic epiphany. The relation of Lula and Clay is a version of the fiendish erotic relationship—a fierce, destructive passion—Lula being the tantalizing harlot or siren who cannot be possessed. Indeed, she seems not so much a human instrument/partaker in Clay's fall as a devil-goddess whose kingdom is the murdering womb of the urban Inferno. She is the femme fatale, the source of evil, and her particular ancestor is less Eve than Lilith, as her name more truly suggests. In another version of the Creation myth, it was Lilith who created Adam and Eve by sacrificing herself to renew life; as Shaw has her say in *Back to Methusalah*, "I suffered unspeakably; I tore myself asunder; I lost my life, to make of my one flesh these twain, man and woman." As a descendant of Lilith, Lula is again a demonic parody, an *anti*-life force who tears apart all around her in order to survive: "I [. . .] control the world," she announces at the start, and it is her search for sacrificial victims that marks the authenticity of her hellish rule.

II

In his analysis of archetypal patterns, Northrop Frye indicates that the mythical tendency which springs from ironic realism is suggestive of the demonic and that the harbinger of mythic reappearance is, as we noted in chapter 2, the "dim outlines of sacrificial rituals." The murder of Clay seems to be just such a ritual victimization, and the mimesis of sacrifice recognizable in his fate is a tragic motif. His is a tragedy of lost direction and lack of knowledge, and the tragic glass through which we view his catastrophe is an ironic perspective, one in which the hero is in a lower state of awareness and freedom than the audience. The action of his story follows the typical tragic pattern: the fall from innocence through harmartia, and from harmartia to catastrophe. Through this downward movement Clay becomes simultaneously assertive and vulnerable, perspicacious and weak, and from it he emerges grown in moral stature, though physically destroyed. This tragic process is perhaps best described as the recovery of "wisdom forgotten,"[5] a painful stripping away of cultivated masks which reveals the naked, unaccommodated knowledge latent in the protagonist. By tracing Clay's developmental pattern, we shall perceive both the dimension of heroism and the necessity of failure that is the special mark of Baraka's early dramatic heroes.

The demonic human world where Clay's fate unravels is a society held together by a special tension of egos, a conflict of loyalties which can only be resolved through violent confrontation. Clay is immediately fascinated by Lula: she is beautiful and weirdly intriguing. He anxiously assumes that her imprecise and leading remarks are sexual teases or suggestions, and is naïvely amazed at the redhead's accurate typification of his background, milieu, and character. In vital opposition to this embarrassed but stimulated absorption with Lula's personality is Clay's attempt to maintain contact with his own impulses and thoughts. The vehicle for this ego-clash is the dominant *ludic* quality of the action. The two are constantly engaged in verbal games, nearly all initiated, controlled, and disengaged by Lula. Her ceaselessly changing moods determine the pace and tone of the action, and from the start she controls Clay's "part" by her own acting:

> *Lula.* (*Starts laughing again*) Now you say to me, "Lula, Lula, why don't you go to this party with me tonight?" It's your turn, and let those be your lines.
>
> *Clay.* Lula, why don't you go to this party with me tonight, Huh?
>
> *Lula.* Say my name twice before you ask, and no huh's.
>
> *Clay.* Lula, Lula, why don't you go to this party with me tonight?
>
> *Lula.* I'd like to go, Clay, but how can you ask me to go when you barely know me?
>
> *Clay.* That is strange, isn't it?
>
> *Lula.* What kind of reaction is that? You're supposed to say, "Aw, come on, we'll get to know each other better at the party."
>
> *Clay.* That's pretty corny.
>
> *Lula.* What are you into anyway? (*Looking at him half sullenly but still amused*) What thing are you playing at, Mister?
>
> [pp. 16–17]

As this passage indicates, the pulse of the play is frenetic, proceeding by the uncertain stops and starts of the games that Lula develops. It is Lula who is "prepared for anything," a protean character who "lies a lot" to help heself control her world. Clay is so taken with her strange elusiveness that he insists she must be an actress, but her manipulation of the language and sequence of events gives her the domineering appearance of the all-determining playwright. It requires all of Clay's mental agility simply to keep pace with Lula's shifts and feints, to understand the rules of procedure, and to participate.

Lula, on the other hand, is quite clearly possessed by a peculiar motivation. While her opponent is struggling at the level of surface meaning or attempting to make the simplest interpretations of their exchange, she is "playing at" a serious ritual of entrapment. By the end of scene 1 she has assumed complete mastery of their relationship; as Clay echoes in painful ignorance a furious crescendo of attacks upon his middle-class, "Uncle Tom" status, "pretending" with Lula that the foul and bewitching air of their underground hell is "light and full of perfume," Lula begins the brutal and dangerous game that comprises scene 2, the agon which ultimately determines the hero's fate:

> *Lula.* And we'll pretend the people cannot see you. That is, the citizens. And that you are free of your own history. And I am free of my history. We'll pretend that we are both anonymous beauties smashing along through the city's entrails. (*She yells as loud as she can*) GROOVE!
>
> [p. 21]

Scene 2 begins with Lula in total command. She has imaginatively removed herself and Clay from their environment and projected them into her own fantasy of the "party" and its consequences. She weaves an alluring tale of a "sophisticated" affair, creating for them a new history where she remains the controller. Even in this fiction she is a death-force, the rooms of her tenement hovel "black as a grave," her hands "dry as ashes," her seduced lover a "tender big-eyed prey." Clay's role has been reduced to that of prompter, his constant questions providing a simple rhythmical motif off of which Lula riffs her main story-line. As Lula brings the conversation to the crucial issue—Clay's *manhood*—his confusion and ignorance reach their zenith: "I don't understand" epitomizes his role of puppet; "You don't know what I mean" summarizes her position of puppeteer.

Lula then abruptly begins her violent, disturbing dance, a last parody of creative activity. It is this wild, Fury-like *danse macabre,* with its obscene sexual challenges and vituperative racial insults, which finally provokes Clay to struggle and calls forth from him the disposition toward action that is necessary for genuine tragic conflict. This abandonment of passivity and arousal of self-assertion reveal Clay's harmartia, his "flaw"; for this flaw is not the weak and ignorant quality of innocence with which he started, but his very willingness to act. Arthur Miller, in "Tragedy and the Common Man," describes such defiant repossession of self-respect and pride as "the flaw, or crack in the character . . . [the] unwillingness to remain passive in the face of what the [tragic hero] conceives to be a challenge to his dignity, his image of his rightful status."

Clay stands here as tragic man, naked and alone, facing the mysterious, the demonic, the difficult truth in himself, and the forces that surround and seemingly control him. Here, with all his prefabricated, protective masks of white philosophy, white religion, white language, and white law stripped away, Clay faces for all black people, as if for the very first time, the essential facts of their existence:

> Shit, you don't have any sense, Lula, nor feelings either. I could murder you now. Such a tiny ugly throat. I could squeeze it flat, and watch you turn blue, on a humble. For dull kicks. And all these weak-faced ofays squatting around here, staring over their papers at me. Murder them too. Even if they expected it. That man there . . . (*Points to a well-dressed man*) I could rip that *Times* right out of his hand, as skinny and middle-classed as I am, I could rip that paper out of his hand and just as easily rip out his throat. It takes no great effort. For what? To kill you soft idiots? You don't understand anything but luxury.
>
> [p. 33]

Taking action against the demons that seek his destruction, Clay speaks as though whole generations of black suffering had occurred in him, yet with no one else being aware of his experience—as though in this moment he were standing alone yet in the center of all the forces that animate his world. He is not "flawed" in the sense of being defective or guilty, but he has chosen the tragic path by choosing to be a man.

It is thus through this explosive speech that Clay enters into the tragic involvement which inevitably must destroy him. What he loses in the process of tragic conflict is not merely his life as concrete existence, but, as his final resignation implies, every concrete embodiment of whatever joy and perfection he conceived possible as a black man:

> Ahhh. Shit. But who needs it? I'd rather be a fool. Insane. Safe with my words, and no deaths, and clean, hard thoughts, urging me to new conquests. My people's madness. Hah! That's a laugh. My people. They don't need me to claim them. [p. 35]

Here, to paraphrase Karl Jaspers, Clay's mind fails and breaks down in the very wealth of its potentialities. The power that had set the conflict in motion—the devil-goddess—is ultimately a "tragic machine" against which Clay can only struggle, and it is the inevitable failure of this struggle that produces the "tragic facts" of experience: death, and the hate and despair of simple life in an oppressive and hostile society. As Larry Neal puts it, "by the time Clay digs himself, it is too late." [6] But against this morbidity of failure stands the balancing and heroic fact of Clay's spiritual triumph; for even defiance to the point of death is an act of transcendence: it is a movement toward the proper black essence which Clay comes to know for himself in the presence of his despair, in the process of his suffering.

The point of the play where Clay's speech occurs might best be labeled the "reversal of the situation," which Aristotle described as "a change by which the action veers round to its opposite." This reversal is plotted in such a way that it is coincident with what Aristotle termed the "recognition" or "change from ignorance to knowledge." By plotting this crucial moment in this way, Baraka has imaged the whole turn of Clay's inner being, from passive ignorance through flashing self-knowledge to exhausted despair. The tremendous excitement of the passage is in great part due to the fact of Clay's conscious recognition of this reversal. And it is due also to the fact that this moment of enlightenment was inherent in the whole texture of the preceding ludic dialogue with Lula.

Thus, the passing of Clay from ignorance to knowledge, the play's mimesis of the action of perceiving, corresponds to Aristotle's model of the best tragedy, the "complex" plot, where recognition and reversal are both included. If we think of the tragic action of the play in more ritualistic and ironic terms, however, we gain additional insight into Clay's character. As already noted, there is much to suggest that *Dutchman* is a shadowy ritual of sacrifice, Lula being the devouring demon, Clay the "tender, big-eyed prey." Seen from Lula's animalistic, hellish point of view, Clay is a scapegoat, a *pharmakos* who is selected for ordeal and death in order to strengthen Lula and her society: "I even got into this train, going some other way than mine. Walked down the aisle . . . searching you out." He is neither guilty nor innocent: in a world of inescapable evil, his fate is harsher than mere existence would seem to warrant. He is Adamic in a double sense: on one hand, he "falls" from the safety of his white mask and is crushed under sentence of death; on the other, he forfeits his innocence and destiny of "success" for moral responsibility and a higher (if momentary) freedom. As tragic *pharmakos,* he is also in the condition of Job: his passionate outburst stands in shocking contrast to a meekness that makes his destruction seem proper, and in itself it vindicates him and makes this destruction morally hideous. And the element in his universe that produces his catastrophe does so without any warning; it is the pure abyss of chaos, the demonic apocalypse of the void: "I'm *nothing,* honey" Lula tells Clay, "and don't you ever forget it" (my emphasis).

If Lula is amorphous, protean, and formless, it is because she is essentially and irreducibly one bare fact, the fact of evil. "I do go on as I do," she says, and her position at the end of the play is no different from what it was in the beginning. In Clay, however, she recognizes a fundamentally opposite principle, the idea of process, evolution, development: "but you change. (*Blankly*) And things work on till you hate them." Though Lula kindles the interaction, Clay is its constant subject, as she realizes:

Lula. . . . we'll sit and talk endlessly, endlessly.
Clay. About what?
Lula. About what? About your manhood, what do you think? What do you think we've been talking about all this time?
Clay. Well, I didn't know it was that. That's for sure. Every other thing in the world but that. (*Notices another person entering, looks quickly, almost involuntarily up and down the car, seeing the other people in the car*) Hey, I didn't even notice when those people got on.

Lula. Yeah, I know.
Clay. Man, this subway is slow.
Lula. Yeah, I know.
Clay. Well, go on. We were talking about my manhood.
Lula. We still are. All the time.

[pp. 25–26]

Clay is continually, if unwittingly, moving toward recognition of his own nature, toward knowledge of the scars and strengths of his black humanity. In a sense his relationship to Lula is similar to that between the hero of Ellison's *Invisible Man* and the whole of that novel. For he must deal with the chaos that surrounds and potentially controls him, must learn, like Ellison's hero, to "step outside the narrow borders of what men call reality," [7] and confront the malignant powers of his universe.

This confrontation releases from Clay's subconscious an imaginative illumination that produces aspects of order. At the moment of greatest breakdown, of sheer unleashed chaos (Lula's dance) Clay meets crisis with a response that represents the memory of truth and black virtue. As Baraka said of this "theatre of victims" in "The Revolutionary Theatre": "it must Accuse and Attack anything that can be accused and attacked. [. . .] It looks at the sky with the victims' eyes, and moves the victims to look at the strength in their minds and their bodies." [8] When Clay begins to look up with assertive pride, he faces a mystery; but it is a mystery that challenges his preconceptions of good, that starkly contrasts what ought to be with what is. His speech is thus a major epiphany of nature itself, of the very ground of black self-awareness, black power, and black freedom. It deserves to be isolated both as Clay's vehicle for self-discovery and as a Barakean manifesto of black liberation.

III

Lula's verbal attacks upon Clay's sexuality, middle-class background, and supposedly half-white manners are all ultimately concerned with, as she says, his manhood, his essential *identity*. Her early jibe, "What thing are you playing at, Mister," is, in fact, the crucial question Clay must resolve beneath his tomish exterior. Lula describes the surface reality of Clay's appearance very well, just as she controls the linguistic surfaces on which she outplays the young man. On this level of being, it is logical that he cannot "understand" her, that her taunt, "everything you say is wrong.[. . .] That's what makes you so attractive," is a feeling shared by the audience. He does appear to be the unreflective, white-aping, neo-Ivy League "dirty white man," comically unaware of how typical and shamefully meek he seems in his smart, three-button suit. But through this surface erupt the anger and truth that had been well submerged within Clay's consciousness, buried by his desire for a false security. He accuses her of being the truly ignorant, of talking idiocy:

> *Clay.* Now you shut the hell up. (*Grabbing her shoulders*) Just shut up. You don't know what you're talking about. You don't even know anything. So just keep your stupid mouth closed.
> [p. 33]

Now the power relationship has been totally reversed. Clay controls the language and the action, and with it the interpretation of his life and identity. Indeed, Clay's long, violent speech may best be viewed as an inversion from the rest of the play, an epiphany of enlightenment set in direct opposition to the demonic epiphany presented within the action Lula controls.

"Let me be who I feel like being," he screams at her through clenched teeth. Whoever that may be, he assures Lula, she cannot possibly understand his true nature, for she is blinded by the very surfaces she controls:

> You don't know anything except what's there for you to see. An act. Lies. Device. Not the pure heart, the pumping black heart. You don't ever know that. And I sit here, in this buttoned-up suit, to keep myself from cutting all your throats. I mean wantonly. You great liberated whore! You fuck some black man, and right away you're an expert on black people. What a lotta shit that is.
> [p. 34]

His three-button suit, proper speech, smooth smile, playful ignorance, are all mere manipulations of an alien style designed to subvert the oppressor's stifling obsession with him. All that the white world sees is a *mask,* and like Willie Best he is a renegade behind it. While Lula's identification of wanton sexuality with the true, unadulterated slave-Negro is shown up as perverse and cruel, she is herself revealed to be sexually impotent, her dance mocked as a gray imitation of true black vitality:

> The belly rub? You wanted to do the belly rub? Shit, you don't even know how. You don't know how. That ol' dipty-dip shit you do, rolling your ass like an elephant. That's not my kind of belly rub. Belly rub is not Queens. Belly rub is dark places, with big hats and overcoats held up with one arm. Belly rub hates you.
>
> [p. 34]

White people believe they can penetrate the pure, pumping black heart by learning a few of black culture's symbols and venerating a few of its more obvious leaders. But they cannot truly go behind the mask and discover the ground of suffering and wisdom that is the necessity of this culture, the home of Clay's true identity.

Earlier in the play, as Clay is attempting to parry one of Lula's verbal thrusts, he gives an account of the genesis of the blues which holds the art form to be a product of lazy and benign tranquility: "Plantations were big open whitewashed places like heaven, and everybody on 'em was grooved to be there. Just strummin' and hummin' all day [. . .] And that's how the blues was born." Now, as Clay is tearing himself away from his own deceptive role, he discovers a truer motive for the blues, which are themselves a defiant mask:

> They say, "I love Bessie Smith." And don't even understand that Bessie Smith is saying, "Kiss my ass, kiss my black unruly ass." Before love, suffering, desire, anything you can explain, she's saying, and very plainly, "Kiss my black ass." And if you don't know that, it's you that's doing the kissing.
>
> [pp. 34–35]

Bessie Smith uses the mask of the blues as a coded language, asking whites to "kiss my ass" to keep herself from murdering them. What we hear her sing is an indication of what we don't hear. It is a necessary avoidance, a hurtful, sly, anguished, and mocking smoke screen, a constant stratagem to cover naked hatred. The blues thus have a violent and almost pathological dimension; they are an artifice imposed upon the bare feelings of wronged humanity:

> If Bessie Smith had killed some white people she wouldn't have needed that music. She could have talked very straight and plain about the world. No metaphors. No grunts. No wiggles in the dark of her soul. Just straight two and two are four. Money. Power. Luxury. Like that. All of them. Crazy niggers turning their backs on sanity. When all it needs is that simple act. Murder. Just murder! Would make us all sane.
>
> [p. 35]

The true madness of a world that worships luxury and enslaving power can be confined only by the simple, purifying force of "murder," what Baraka called "the cleansed purpose" in "Black Dada Nihilismus." As a force patterned by inversion, Clay's speech must expose the attitude of mind exemplified by Lula as a deceiving madness: after all, she appears to have Clay well pegged with her assured typifications and mocking insults. But mental health is manifested only in an act whereby the black man reveals a vision of a better world, a vision concealed from the likes of Lula yet revealed to partakers of The Life in the metaphors of the horn-player, the singer, the musical "screamer." Society would judge a massacring Charlie Parker or Bessie Smith to be mad because it must protect its own madness. When Lula exhorts Clay to burst into a chaotic passion like her own, to "scream meaningless shit in these hopeless faces," she doesn't realize that what he will scream is indeed meaningless only to her own mindlessness and shallowness:

> And the only thing that would cure the neurosis would be your murder. Simple as that. I mean if I murdered you, then other

> white people would begin to understand me. You understand? No. I guess not.
>
> [p. 35]

Lula interrupts Clay only once during his long outburst, to call him a "fool." She knows his action will cost him his life, and in this sense her reaction is correct. But while he stands before her without the mask—the *lie*—that is necessary for them to coexist, he is rational and powerfully sane. It is only by reassuming his former role that he becomes a fool. His is a mask of words, the "fierce cordon" Baraka had feared as a young poet. Clay's major action is linguistic, *l'azione parlata.* Though he comes to know what is pumping deep within his pure black heart, he has grown too dependent upon the methods of discourse common to the white world, the facile allusions to "Juliet's tomb" and the like. He has, after all, once thought of himself as a "black Baudelaire," and his failure to act physically upon what he knows seems anchored in this fact:

> And I'm the great would-be poet. Yes. That's right! Poet. Some kind of bastard literature . . . all it needs is a simple knife thrust. Just let me bleed you, you loud whore, and one poem vanished.
>
> [p. 35]

If Clay could make of the poem a lethal weapon, as Baraka wished to do with "Black Art," he would create a sane, triumphant vision in opposition to the neurosis of his mulatto, or "bastard," poetry. But he is a black man in transition, a prerevolutionary victim of his own miscultivated tastes and inability to act. In his major speech, Clay discovers his revolutionary, deeply spiritual self. But, like the Baraka of "Notes for a Speech," he remains painfully distant from his "people," trapped in an old self which he has nearly, but not quite, outgrown.

IV

Because Clay falls in an "ironic world," a world where his limitations prove all too human, the catastrophe that follows his speech has a far more social than religious or cosmological dimension. In the overall movement of the play, Lula's murder of Clay with the complicity of the other passengers has the effect of isolating him from the enveloping society. He thus has a strong affinity with Richard Wright's Bigger Thomas: his brutalization is in its turn a fierce indictment of American society, and his revolt is stifled because of his peculiar position in the continuum of American history.

The story of *Dutchman* is actually informed by historical interpretation as much as by mythical patterning (more so than in *Native Son*); indeed, historical explanation itself provides interacting mythical motifs in the play. Its very title evokes the historical background of Lula and Clay's relationship; for, as Sherley Anne Williams comments, "it was a Dutchman, a Dutch man-of-war, which brought the first Black slaves to North America." [9] The play offers two powerful and violently opposed interpretations of the history that dates from the first landing in Jamestown: one is Lula's and one is Clay's. Only the latter's is, in the terms of the play, correct or "sane," but the fact that Lula prevails offers a third historical interpretation—a statement on the play's own place in history.

The explanation of American racial history that Lula proposes rests upon a myth of black assimilation, resignation, and cowardice. For her the archetypical and true Afro-American is either a raunchy, overly potent, maniacally belly-rubbing, and mindless "field nigger," or a meek, selfless, helpless, hobbling "Old Tom" who laughably denies his "real" potent self. The one is an outlet for her own erotic fantasies, the other an image that allows her to believe she can control the world. This double aspect of the Afro-American slave past is, in Lula's interpretation, ineradicable. Any given black man, any random Clay, must either embrace a role of sexual super-power and serve the oppressor's neurotic needs, or become a pathetic "Uncle Tom Big Lip," an object of derision and mockery. In any case, he is chained to a submissive, externally determined condition; for him the present and future are only copies of the past, and "history" is a fixed entity. Thus it is natural for Lula to suggest that she and Clay pretend they are free of their own history, for in her view this history is only whatever rendition she chooses to perform of an essentially changeless melody.

It is no wonder, then, that Lula, who does "go on as I do" without meaningful alteration in her manipulative capacity, should fear the possibility of Clay's realizing his ability to change, to let things work on him until he hates them. "You mix it up [. . .] Turning pages. Change change change. Till, shit, I don't know you," she tells him. In order to remain in command she must hold Clay fast to her own constant conception of him, chain him to a role her historical interpretation has created for him. First she forces upon him her idea of the property and cultural rights handed down from slavery:

> *Lula.* A three-button suit. What right do you have to be wearing a three-button suit and striped tie? Your grandfather was a slave, he didn't go to Harvard.
>
> *Clay.* My grandfather was a night watchman.
>
> [p. 18]

Clay's reaction painfully, if amusingly, fuels her attack, and she goes on to say, "I bet you never once thought you were a black nigger." She perceives in him a latter-day "Uncle Thomas Woolly-head," a modern, middle-class updating of the old, head-scratching, compliant slave, an "escaped nigger" who has donned his Ivy League costume and "crawled through the wire and made tracks to my side." It is inevitable that, having once played with the type of control inherent in relating to a "tomish" Clay, she should give vent to her erotic needs and try to convert him to the other role possible for the black man in her scheme, the mindless stud:

> Come on, Clay . . . let's do the thing. Uhh! Uhh! Clay! Clay! You middle-class black bastard. Forget your social-working mother for a few seconds and let's knock stomachs. Clay, you liver-lipped white man. You would-be Christian. You ain't no nigger, you're just a dirty white man. Get up, Clay. Dance with me, Clay.
>
> [p. 31]

Larry Neal sees in this aspect of their relationship a symbolic representation of "the historical castration" of black America by white America.[10] On this level, not only the dialogue between Lula and Clay but the whole play is a constant examination of his manhood, and in this manner *Dutchman* takes its place in an Afro-American literary tradition which is in many ways a long, complex dialectic between the triumph and the emasculation of the black messianic liberator. In *Dutchman* the hero is himself given the capability for this realization or destruction, for it is only so long as he participates in Lula's pretending "non"-history—viewing his ancestors as happy and mindless residents of heavenly plantations—that she can impose any identity upon him. The pain of being torn between two false roles—constructs of Lula's alien historical myth—constitutes Clay's castration (it is also no accident that Lula kills him with a knife). In the process, however, Clay is driven toward recognition of an altogether different identity and historical explanation. In his long speech he in effect stops pretending and steps back into *real* history.

Clay's interpretation of the development from slavery is an inversion of Lula's. Whatever she takes to be the root nature of the black man—pathetic servility or compliant sexuality—is only an "art" that hides the rawbone of hatred he feels toward her. White America has allowed itself to be deceived because it uses the image of a weak, suffering, childish black America to maintain its power, to defend itself from the sanity of justice.

The development of America is thus a history of an oppressive power avoiding sanity at all costs and an oppressed people aping insanity in order to survive. Recognition of this underlying truth of black-white relationships would drive the black man to the action necessary for his liberation, a violently asserted sanity, as Baraka outlines in his essay, "The Last Days of the American Empire":

> To be rational now in this insane asylum, where we are held prisoner by the inmates. They want us to be their keepers. Do you Negroes like being keepers for these sadists? But to be rational. Rational men would do something to stop the mad, before they destroy not only the asylum, but the rest of the world.[11]

Although Clay finds himself incapable of undertaking this mission, he realizes that black men generally are themselves, as Baraka says in "The Revolutionary Theatre," "history and desire"; they will not go on pretending with Clay and Lula, but instead change and change and change, letting desire and history work on them until they hate with all the destructive capacity of "cold logic." Clay thus moves from correction of Lula's version of the past and present to prediction of the future day when black men will rise up and manipulate the rulers' masks for their own liberating purpose:

> And on that day, as sure as shit, when you really believe you can "accept" them into your fold, as half-white trusties late of the subject peoples. With no more blues, except the very old ones, and not a watermelon in sight, the great missionary heart will have triumphed, and all of those ex-coons will be stand-up Western men, with eyes for clean hard useful lives, sober, pious and sane, and they'll murder you. They'll murder you and have very rational explanations.[. . .] cut your throats and drag you out to the edge of your cities so the flesh can fall away from your bones, in sanitary isolation.
>
> [p. 36]

For the black man history can be a dynamic process, a turning of pages that some day reveals the knowledge necessary for freedom. When that time comes the white man will become the isolated victim, dying alone in the ruins of "civilization," in leftover haunts like those of "After the Ball." The oppressor's version of history is only a lie, a pretentious avoidance of historical fact. Thus, Lula needs Clay's participation in that lie in order to live at all:

> *Lula.* [. . .] you'll say, even whisper, that you love me.
> *Clay.* Maybe I will.
> *Lula.* And you'll be lying.
> *Clay.* I wouldn't lie about something like that.
> *Lula.* Hah. It's the only kind of thing you will lie about. Especially if you think it'll keep me alive.
>
> [p. 27]

Her plea that Clay "break out" into a sexual role which will sustain her is couched in terms that actually jeopardize her survival: "Don't sit there dying the way they want you to die." As Williams notes,[12] it is Lula's salvation as much as Clay's that is at stake.

The conflict between these two historical interpretations complements the overall dramatic structure. Clay's speech, by its length and quality of rhetoric, as well as its content, is set apart from the rest of the play. It is a kind of counterplot, a rhetorical inversion of the action that comes before and after it. This action takes on a decidedly *ritual* form, not only in the characters' rigid roles and ludic repartee, but with the reappearance of a Clay-like figure at the end. Indeed, the unstartled collusion of the passengers indicates that they have seen and enacted this ritual sacrifice before, just as Lula's "scribbling note" is merely a statistical observation of an unending, static history. While Clay's speech stands as an act as well as a prophecy of rising black consciousness, Lula's ritual of destruction opposes it as a statement of unchanging evil. The title emphasizes this hideous ritualistic dimension; the "flying underbelly" subway may find its archetype in the Flying Dutchman, the legendary spectral ship which sails the open seas forever without change or a release into death.[13] Clay must utter one tortured scream, but Lula is doomed eternally to hear an infinite number of such cries to the accompaniment of the urban ship's own awful shrieks.

Clay's ultimate failure to act upon the truth he has discovered indicates that he is himself a point in a historical process. He is unable to become the revolutionary he envisions because his black consciousness has not sufficiently developed. Moreover, Clay's temporal limitation indicates that *Dutchman* is itself historically bound, and may perhaps counter the antirevolutionary implications of its ritual structure. Yet, whatever the historical necessity of Clay's defeat, it is memorable as a harbinger of black triumph:

> *Lula.* May the people accept you as a ghost of the future. And love you, that you might not kill them when you can.
> [p. 21]

The Slave

I

The very end of *Dutchman* is a dumb-show which, along with the opening scene, frames the play as a whole. It is the shuffling soft-shoe song-and-dance of the old Negro conductor who bobs his way through the subway car, enigmatically greeting the new young black victim and tipping his hat to Lula. This figure is the prototype of several such characters that Baraka employs throughout his drama. He is a version of the old Negro *slave,* a shrewdly impenetrable mind disguised by a shucking and smiling exterior, what might most accurately be referred to as a Willie Best figure. He is a "renegade behind the mask," a man at the crossroads, who represents both the consequence of what Baraka calls in *Blues People* the "slave mentality" ("the most socially unfortunate psychic adjustments the slave had made during two hundred years of slavery"—*BP,* p. 127), and the transcendent alternative of rebel heroism; a development from the folk-characters Stagger Lee and Shine, who one day, "tired of losing," stand up and say "I *got* ta cut'cha."

In Baraka's second major play, *The Slave*, this Willie Best figure becomes an emblem for the historical phase of black revolution. He is shaped into the role of a contemporary black revolutionary leader, Walker Vessels, who must come to terms with the conflicting impulses implicit in the slave emblem. As Louis Phillips argues in his acute analysis of Baraka's early drama, "[Walker] and his followers . . . are still enslaved by certain ideas and forces they do not understand." [14] And yet, in the complexity of Walker's struggle, two souls dwell within his breast: Walker-the-rebel—isolate, tortured warrior—and Walker-the-slave—spectral embodiment of history, whose gnawing presence Walker Vessels cannot escape. Only by revealing the schism in this disordered personality, by destroying one or the other possibility, can the hero propel himself to some new stance in the historical process. The action of the play is essentially this combat of identities within the psyche of a sophisticated version of Willie Best.

The main action of the play is preceded by a prologue in which Walker, "dressed as an old field slave, balding, with white hair and an old ragged vest," awakens to a child's cry and then delivers a speech. This soliloquy is not so much a summary preface or informational addendum to the main action as a complex, semi-poetic exegesis of its implications. What Walker, as this old slave, delineates are the central questions underlying any interpretation of his behavior as a revolutionary leader.

> Whatever the core of our lives. Whatever the deceit. We live where we are, and seek nothing but ourselves. We are liars, and we are murderers. We invent death for others. Stop their pulses publicly. Stone possible lovers with heavy worlds we think are ideas . . . and we know, even before these shapes are realized, that these worlds, these depths or heights we fly to smoothly, as in a dream, or slighter, when we stare dumbly into space, leaning our eyes just behind a last quick moving bird, then sometimes the place and twist of what we are will push and sting, and what the crust of our stance has become will ring in our ears and shatter that piece of our eyes that is never closed.[15]
>
> [p. 43]

The slave immediately delineates his ambiguous existence: both the "core" and the façade of his personality are undefined, and he lives sedentarily, seeking "nothing but" himself. Whatever the "shape" of this true self, however necessarily unfeeling, the future will render an awesome judgment upon the ensuing revelation of character that "will ring in our ears." Certainly the division between outer and inner, public and private, deceit and core, must be healed. To do so requires a painful balance between the idealism inherent in revolutionary action and the pragmatic sense of public reality needed to complete such action successfully. This balance and unity of self requires a decisive understanding of just what and who this slave will become for those who wish to reveal the core of life.

Thus the actual nature of this old slave of the prologue is elusive, a strange identity of indeterminate age ("I am much older than I look . . . or maybe much younger"), full of the dignity of "filed rhythms" and "great ideas" which he claims and disclaims in one breath ("Ideas. Where they form. Or whose they finally seem to be. Yours? The others? Mine?"). The man only poses the questions, leaving their answers to us and the few choices history offers. As he departs, he cheerily presents to us a "poem [. . .] to divert you . . . in your hour of need. [. . .] Before you get your lousy chance." As his speech dissolves into an old song of "blues people moaning in their sleep, [. . .] growing anxiously less articulate, more 'field hand' sounding, blankly lyrical," the slave assumes the character of Walker, the protagonist of the diversionary "poem" which is the play, and the central plot begins.

Walker Vessels is a "tall, thin, forty-year-old Negro" who has left his career as an academic intellectual and poet and become a leader of a national black rebellion. He has returned to the home of his former white wife, Grace, and her husband, Bradford Easley, a university professor who was once Walker's teacher. Walker's troops are about to take the city where the Easleys live. He has come ahead of them to take his two daughters away and to have a last confrontation with his former white friends. The entire play takes place in the Easleys' living room, where the characters argue about the sanity and purpose of the war, the rights to the children, and various aspects of their past.

After a great deal of debate, Walker finally insists that he has come to take back his children. Grace is horrified and refuses to believe him; Easley is angry and afraid. As the white man prepares to jump Walker, who has been holding a gun but has also become progressively drunk, the soldiers of Walker's army arrive in the city and begin to shell the house. Walker sees Easley's approach in time to recover himself and, in their struggle, manages to shoot and kill his adversary. Soon the rafters begin to fall, one of which strikes Grace. As she dies, she cries to Walker, "See about the girls," who have supposedly been asleep upstairs. After a silence he replies, "They're dead, Grace! They're dead," and as he emerges from the door he again becomes the old man of the prologue. There is a long silence. Then the screaming of a child is heard, followed by explosions that continue "for some time" after the final curtain.

The protagonist of *Dutchman* was a figure less knowledgeable than ourselves, a creature we could judge while looking down on a scene of bondage, frustration, and ultimate weakness. But in *The Slave*, Walker appears to be a man at our level of intelligence and understanding of his environment and, with respect to this environment, a figure of superior power and control. Walker's name suggests an energetic resolve in contrast to the yielding pliancy of "Clay." [16] Yet, like Clay, Walker is presented as a character not yet fully developed. He is a man who must be brought to see the disparate and conflicting forces within his own tormented mind. Although he holds the gun during the long night in the Easleys' home, it is the white couple who are on the attack during the fierce verbal battle. In returning to his old world—particularly to see his former white wife—Walker has come back to face his past, and with it a part of himself that he might have thought long buried. Now that the rebellion has actually begun, this old self has erupted and looms before him, a tempting, treacherous specter of earlier joys, attitudes, and ideas that had been sublimated during his prewar ideological activism. Until he has completely abandoned this older self, he remains slave to a past which had twisted his fundamental concerns, and he cannot wholly embrace his new identity as rebel-leader.

Almost immediately the quality of Walker's action is suspect: "Well, what the hell do you want, *hero?*" (my emphasis), Easley contemptuously demands. Both Easley and Grace deride him as a "racist, nigger murderer," refusing to take him seriously as the commander of a militant insurgency that threatens the core of their lives. Instead, they force upon him a number of roles (or "titles" as Walker mockingly terms them), the most harsh and challenging of which is that of hedonistic individualist, a bitingly antiheroic picture of a man who would destroy all he loves in order to hide from himself his essential nothingness:

> *Grace.* There are so many bulbs and screams shooting off inside you, Walker. So many lies you have to pump full of yourself. [. . .] I don't even think you know who you are any more. No, I don't think you *ever* knew.
>
> *Walker.* I know what I can use.

Grace. No, you never even found out who you were until you sold the last of your loves and emotions down the river . . . until you killed your last old friend [. . .]

Walker. What I can use, madam . . . what I can use. I move now trying to be certain of that.

Easley. You're talking strangely. What is this, the pragmatics of war? What are you saying . . . use? I thought you meant yourself to be a fantastic idealist? All those speeches. [. . .] That the Western white man had forfeited the most impressive characteristic of his culture . . . the idealism of rational liberalism [. . .]

Walker. Yeah, yeah. Now you can call me the hypocritical idealist nigger murderer. You see, what I want is more titles. [pp. 61–62]

Walker defends himself from their onslaught by taking on a number of postures, the "stupid darkie" ("I didn't mean to hit you that hard, Professor Easley, sir . . . I just don't know my own strent"), the pidgin-speaking Japanese torturer ("Oh, don't worry about that, doomed American dog"), the raving-drunk Indian/African ("More! Bwana, me want more fire water!"), the stage Irishman ("sure and they looked well enough"). But these mock-roles are defenses that help Walker only to avoid engaging the white antagonists directly. It is precisely the conflict between "use" and feeling which rages within him, although Grace and Easley cannot perceive it. He has had the strength of intellect and will to undertake a revolution, but the vestiges of passion and sensitivity that once made him love Grace still threaten his ability to lead an army steadfastly.

This dilemma is epitomized in Walker's role as a poet, for it is as failed poet that Easley derides his effort of the past ("Well, once a bad poet always a bad poet . . . even in the guise of a racist murderer!") and belittles his achievement of the moment ("Hah. Poetry? A flashy doggerel for inducing all those unfortunate troops of yours to spill their blood in your behalf"). It is for being a poet at all that Walker feels guilty. Nothing is so repulsive to him as the private cultivation of sensibility—Easley's "high aesthetic disapproval of the political," or what Easley himself admits as his highest value: "life as a purely anarchic relationship between man and God . . . or man and his work."

Easley is shattered by the idea that in Walker's revolution "any consciousness like that is destroyed . . . along with your *enemies.*" What he fails to understand is that, for Walker, just this type of consciousness, this moral solipsism, *is* the enemy; that only things publically "in the world," open to judgment and collective scrutiny, are tenable in a necessarily political world. It was, indeed, Walker's very sensitivity that drove him into his new position of social actor: "I have always found it hard to be neutral when faced with ugliness. Especially an ugliness that has worked all my life to twist me."

Walker, then, understands his ultimate obstacle to be neutrality, the "deadly idiot of compromise"; and it is precisely the continuing memories of his past, of his failed imitative poetry and abandoned relationship with Easley and Grace, that compromise his sense of wholeness and security as a revolutionary. From the beginning of the play, the time in which Walker, Easley, and Grace were all intimately related is evoked; indeed, the motion of the play is in great part the progressive unfolding of this interpersonal history as the characters exchange conflicting interpretations of their collective past. Once the initial shock of Walker's presence has worn off, Grace introduces the question of memory and the past she shared with the black man as his wife:

> *Grace.* (*Furious from memory*) I had enough of your twisted logic in my day . . . you remember? I mean like your heroism. The same kind of memory. Or Lie. Do you remember which? Huh?
>
> [p. 49]

Their memories of the relationship are most sharply opposed on the crucial issue—their break-up. Grace insists that Walker was driven by a need for some false "heroism," a selfish passion that finally led him to an insane search for power. She is certain that because he preached the murder of all white people he necessarily included her, that his drift into black separatism necessitated her separation from him. Yet to Walker, Grace's departure came as a shock, for he tells her, "I was crying out against three hundred years of oppression; not against individuals." Whatever she imagined, she was still his wife and he still loved her because of it:

Grace. You stopped telling me everything!
Walker. I've never stopped telling you I loved you . . . or that you were my wife!
Grace. (*Almost broken*) It wasn't enough, Walker. It wasn't enough.
Walker. God, it should have been.

(pp. 71–72]

It is this failure to separate social from personal history, the "inevitable horror that oppression is not a concept that can be specifically transferable," as Walker once describes it, that produces the crisis of the play—Walker's desire to "retrieve" his daughters. During the course of the action, the girls become objectified symbols of this split historical reality, as Walker recognizes in the following remark: "Those two lovely girls upstairs are niggers. You know, circa 1800, one drop makes you whole?" The tension of trying simultaneously to maintain love for a past that is stained by records of oppression and to achieve revolutionary progress is Walker's central anguish and the driving force of his obsession with the girls:

Walker. [. . .] in spite of the fact that I have killed for all times any creative impulse I will ever have by the depravity of my murderous philosophies . . . despite the fact that I am being killed in my head each day and by now have no soul or warmth, even in my long killer fingers, despite the fact that I have no other thing in the universe that I love or trust, but myself . . . despite or in spite, the respite, my dears, my dears, hear me, O Olympus, O Mercury, God of thieves, O Damballah, chief of all the dead religions of pseudo-nigger patriots hoping to open big restaurants after de wah [. . .] despite all these things and in spite of all the drunken noises I'm making, despite . . . in spite of . . . I want those girls, very, very much. And I will take them out of here with me.

[pp. 66–67]

The pain Walker suffers is that he has willed a world into which he cannot bring anything from the past. Revolution is apocalyptic in its theory and prophetic in its tone; any idea that change can be simply generated out of the past is ultimately conservative, a Wordsworthian concept of going back. To any prophetic poet (Blake, for example) this pastness is anathema. Walker must choose between being a poet of the past, dependent upon the borrowed words of tradition, or a poet of apocalypse, forced into the difficult language of violent acts.

He chooses the latter by murdering his children, a symbolic act which is shown less as an attack upon a virtuous society by a malignant individual than as a symptom of that society's own past sins. It is an act which, like Clay's vision of murder in the course of black liberation, is mad or redemptive depending on one's place in and view toward history:

Grace. You've convinced yourself that you're rescuing the children, haven't you?
Walker. Just as you convinced yourself you were rescuing them when you took them away from me.
Easley. She was!
Walker. Now so am I.

[p. 69]

When, at the end of the play, Walker reveals that the girls are dead, he "looks at his watch" and "listens to see if it is running." By killing his children he has killed his past and is able to resume his place in the inexorable ticking of revolutionary history. He seems to have shed the slave half of the Willie Best image, and to have emerged as a wholly committed rebel leader. If so, he can utter with the Baraka of "Black Dada Nihilismus":

may a lost god damballah, rest or save us
against the murders we intend
against his lost white children
black dada nihilismus.

But the play does not leave us here. As Walker again becomes the old slave of the prologue, we are left with the enigma of his identity. Has Walker truly escaped the hideous past of the "slave mentality" and entered a history of slave rebellion with leaders such as his namesake Denmark Vesey (a free black South Carolinean who led a slave uprising in the first quarter of the nineteenth-century)? [17] Or do the imperatives of history, which the old slave explicated for us in the beginning, make their inevitable mark upon mankind without his intervention? And as the explosions continue and the child's voice screams "as loud as it can," is it a birth or a death shriek that we hear? Are the words of "Black Dada Nihilismus" to be intoned, or are these words of Yeats's, which Walker had known all too well, more appropriate?

> Straddling each dolphin's back
> And steadied by a fin,
> Those innocents relive their death,
> Their wounds open again.
>
> [quoted by Walker on p. 50]

Whatever the answers, they lie between that ominous "sudden aggravated silence" and the intolerable music of the falling bombs.

II

Those few critics who have discussed the form of *The Slave* have been unable to observe more than the obvious: "realism" in the language of contemporary political argument, reinforced by verisimilitude of place and extraordinary "fullness" in the evocation of the characters. *The Slave* is more thoroughly naturalistic than *Dutchman*, yet it too is not simply a slice-of-life depiction of modern racial confrontation. As much as with *Dutchman*, its form is not only a carefully devised medium for the issues the characters confront but, moreover, is in itself a kind of content or message.

The key to *The Slave* as a formal structure lies in Baraka's subheading to the play: "a fable in a Prologue and Two Acts." Indeed, *The Slave* is a *fable* in two formal ways. First, it is a story embodying a moral. One element of this moral certainly resides in the bifurcated personality of its Willie Best figure, the composite of slave and rebel. While Walker sits in the Easleys' living room, discussing and, in effect, reliving his past, he has stepped out of history and into a diverting House of Pride. Grace is a kind of Duessa figure, a beautiful woman who sets Walker off from his quest, a creature from whom he learns but whom he must leave in the wasteland of the past:

> *Grace.* I guess that's the point, now. Is that the point, Walker? Me being alone . . . as you have been now for so long? I'll bet that's the point, huh? I'll bet you came here to do exactly what you did . . . kill Brad, then take the kids, and leave me alone . . . to suffocate in the stink of my memories. [. . .]
> *Walker.* Yeah, Grace. That's the point. For sure, that's the point.
>
> [pp. 83–84]

Unlike Ellison's Tod Clifton, Walker must step back *in*to history to find himself as an individual, to achieve real heroism.

But just as his long evening in the Easleys' house is a temporary escape from the rebellion that rages outside, so our evening in the theatre, watching a poem in our "hour of need," is a diversion from history. The rebellion constantly encroaches upon the isolated living room until it finally blows the play to pieces, ending not only the verbal conflict but the play itself. And as the explosions continue after the curtain has descended, we are forced to contend with a moral crisis as fundamental as that faced by the characters. Grace's constant dismissal of Walker's threat to take the girls is "He's lying," a horribly ironic denial of power reminiscent of Büchner's Danton, who continually scoffs, "They wouldn't dare" until his head rolls in the guillotine's basket. Like Danton, Grace tries to deny the inescapability of historical forces and dies as a result. This is the primary "moral" of Baraka's fable, for the rebellion outside the house is outside the theatre as well, and the play is only a prologue, not an alternative to it.

The second essential feature of *The Slave* as fable is its function as a "little talk" (from the Latin *fabula*). The core of *The Slave* resembles the Platonic symposium, with its issue-oriented dialogue.

Easley's early remark on the "poetry of ritual drama" becomes a recurring appraisal of the action, and he dies thinking of the experience of the evening as "ritual drama. Like I said, ritual drama." Insofar as the play's action is this drama of language, the ritual of dialogue that the characters perform is both its content and its form.[18]

But the precise relation of *The Slave* to the symposium is inversion or parody. Unlike, for example, the High Renaissance neoplatonic manipulation of the symposium form, which conveyed an educational and social ideal of an elite culture, or Plato's own use of the symposium, which attempted an almost sacramental unity of nature and the social body, Baraka's "little talk" is a fierce battle that moves from disagreement within the social fabric to utter destruction of it. What Walker engages in with Grace and Easley (particularly with the latter) is the reductio ad absurdam of what S. I. Hayakawa calls "two-valued orientation" [19]—a debate. In debate the "two-valued orientation," or tendency to see things in terms of two values only, leads to mere confrontation of the "affirmative" and "negative" sides of an issue, each side doing no more than belittling the claims of the opposition and exaggerating its own position. While this kind of "dialogue" is clearly fruitless in any attempt to reach mutual intellectual understanding, the strong emotional truth in the two-valued orientation accounts for its unavoidability where the expression of feelings is inevitable. This essential inability of Walker and the Easleys to exchange meaning, and the violent clash of their linguistic sallies, are apparent from the beginning:

> *Easley.* [. . .] Is *that* why you and your noble black brothers are killing what's left of this city? (*Suddenly broken*) I should say . . . what's left of this country . . . or world.
>
> *Walker.* Oh, fuck you (*Hotly*) fuck you . . . just fuck you, that's all. Just fuck you! (*Keeps voice stiffly contained, but then it rises sharply*)
>
> I mean really, just fuck you. Don't goddamnit, don't tell me about any goddamn killing of anything.
>
> [p. 49]

Easley and Walker are distinctly incapable of communicating. Of the two, however, Easley's rhetoric is especially closed-minded. Whatever beginning Walker and Grace manage to make toward progressive communication is interrupted by Easley's bursts of temper and antagonism. His words have the demagogic ring of a "spread-eagle orator" and are ironically more uncompromising than those of Walker, the professional political polemicist:

> *Easley.* You're so wrong about everything. So terribly, sickeningly wrong. What can you change? What do you hope to change? Do you think Negroes are better than whites . . . that they can govern a society *better* than whites? That they'll be more judicious or more tolerant? Do you think they'll make fewer mistakes? I mean really, if the Western white man has proved one thing . . . it's the futility of modern society.
>
> [p. 73]

Ultimately, even the attempts of Grace and Walker to make contact through language utterly break down. When this happens, language itself seems to lose its commonality, for language is truly little more than a system of agreements:

> *Grace.* You're out of your mind. (*Slow, matter-of-fact*)
> *Walker.* Meaning?
> *Grace.* You're out of your mind.
> *Walker.* (*Wearily*) Turn to another station.
> *Grace.* You're out of your mind.
>
> [p. 82]

When one person's vision of order is another's vision of chaos, each thinks the other is mad and communication becomes impossible. Finally, this battle in mock-symposium form is resolved symbolically in the determination of who attains the ability to hurt the other with language. Grace's failure is signaled by her inability to wound Walker linguistically, to penetrate his feelings with her curse:

> *Grace.* I wish I could call you something that would hurt you.
> *Walker.* So do I.

Grace. (*Wearily*) Nigger.
Walker. So do I.

[pp. 85–86]

Similarly, Walker's defeat of Easley is confirmed by the latter's painful attempts to talk as he dies:

Easley. (*Mouth is still working . . . and he is managing to get a few sounds, words, out*)
Walker. (*Still staring at him, pulling himself up on the chair*) Shut up, you! (*To Easley*) You shut up. I don't want to hear anything else from you. You just die, quietly. No more talk.

[p. 80]

As if to emphasize his superior position, Walker exults in his control of Easley's lines (a reversal of Lula's dictating of Clay's "role" in *Dutchman*) and watches over the inarticulate dying white man in mocking triumph:

Walker. No profound statements, Easley. No horseshit like that. No elegance. You just die quietly and stupidly. Like niggers do. Like they are now. (*Quieter*) Like I will. The only thing I'll let you say is, "I only regret that I have but one life to lose for my country." You can say that. (*Looks over at Grace*) Grace! Tell Bradford that he can say, "I only regret that I have but one life to lose for my country." You can say that, Easley, but that's all.

[p. 81]

As the play ends, with Grace and Easley both dead, Walker escapes the collapsing home as he shouts the last words—"They're dead"—quintessential proof of conquest over his white antagonists in their verbal battle.

In terms of the play's "little talk," then, Walker is a victorious survivor. Yet in the passage just quoted he includes himself among those who will die "quietly and stupidly"; he seems to be another of Baraka's "victim" figures. We can explain this enigma by remembering another, more archaic meaning of *fable*—foolish or idle talk—for Walker's crisis stems largely from his ambivalent relationship to a language which his indomitable troops are extinguishing day by day. As a poet who had imitated the "Western" tradition, Walker had fallen victim to the illusion which Frantz Fanon explored (particularly in *The Wretched of the Earth* and *Black Skins, White Masks*): the belief of the fellah that he can acquire the oppressor's power by assuming his master's traditional masks, the symbols of the dominating culture.[20] Specifically, these symbols are linguistic ones—words. The fact that Walker would rather argue any objective issue with Easley than squarely confront the needs of his current revolutionary stance (as he says in his long speech concerning the girls) leads to a split between his own verbal world and the existential world of his troops, "ignorant motherfuckers who have never read any book in their lives." It is these "ignorant motherfuckers" who save Walker from being destroyed while he is making idle, foolish talk, and this fact constitutes yet another moral perspective of the fable.

Walker, the poet-hero-victim, does recognize the tension between his love of language and his dependence upon an alien, "bastard" lexicon:

> *Walker.* I swear to you, Grace, I did come into the world pointed in the right direction. Oh, shit, I learned so many words for what I've wanted to say. They all come down on me at once. But almost none of them are mine.

These lines recall the old slave's disclaimer in the prologue of his fund of theories and ideas, and especially his conclusion that "we need, ahem, a meta-language [. . .] some thing not included here." In order to achieve complete revolutionary independence, there must be developed new ideas and new linguistic forms for their organization. The idea of a "meta" structure to attain this independence is reminiscent of the famous theoretical ideas of Gödel's proof, the epistemological implications of which seem as relevant to the search for effective revolutionary statement as to the development of mathematical systems: neither can be validated except upon blind faith in its underlying assumptions or recourse to a second model of explanation.

Throughout the play Walker has used the language of revolutionary ideology, just as he had done in precipitating the actual rebellion he leads. But the justification for this language cannot ultimately rest in terms constructed from its own syntax, terms he had utilized in his debate with Grace and Easley; it must reside in some "meta-language," some alternative form of expression. This second mode of meaning—as Walker's bifurcation between private and public selves, between poet and leader, Othello and Bigger Thomas, slave and rebel, points to throughout the play—is revolutionary action itself. In this light Walker is not so much a hero by virtue of having the last word in a ritual exchange of metaphors, or a victim of his own indecision, but an exemplary leader, a Miltonic Sampson who performs a public deed of liberation. And as the Easleys' house—the Philistine, "Western" temple—falls around him near the play's end, one senses strongly that the language of "the idealism of rational liberalism" is being buried along with its last ruined advocates. The fable of *The Slave* is not the Platonic dialectic festivity that moves toward integration of society, a controlling force that holds opposing ideas together, but a crucible of violent controversy, and perhaps an ominous portent of the division and conflict that history will bring.

The Toilet, Jello, and *The Baptism*

In *Dutchman* and *The Slave* Baraka created a world where limitedly heroic characters searched for their true selves within an alien and hostile white world. Clay and Walker are black men in transition, driven by a desire for freedom from the domination of an oppressive culture yet frustrated in their efforts because of a remaining allegiance to this destructive power. The immediate successors to these plays elaborate upon many of the basic problems of identity and effective action faced by the heroes of the earlier two works. *The Toilet, Jello,* and *The Baptism* are particularly interesting as examples of Baraka's experimentation with form and convention in his early phase of dramatic work. A brief survey of these plays, with careful attention to formal technique, should provide a broader context for study of the major works of Baraka's more mature stages of development.

The Toilet is a short, quick-paced piece about a gang of black youths who assemble in their school bathroom in anticipation of a fight between their leader, Ray Foots, and a white boy, Jimmy Karolis. For much of the play they wait gleefully for two of their buddies to bring Karolis down to the bathroom where Foots will later join them and beat him up. Foots is supposedly seeking revenge for a "love" note Karolis had sent to him. But when Karolis is finally dragged in, already bloodied by the boys who deliver him, and the two meet, it is unclear who made the first advance or even who wrote the note. Foots is satisfied with the beating Karolis has already gotten and begs off another fight, but Karolis insists on a battle, which Foots cannot avoid. As Karolis gains the advantage in the fight, Foots's gang members jump the white boy and, while their leader is preoccupied with his own recovery, beat him into insensibility. They all leave the bathroom as Foots begins to revive. Karolis manages to recover a moment later and struggles to one of the toilets but as he tries to stand up he collapses again, unconscious. Foots then enters the toilet, stares at Karolis's body for a second, and after a quick look over his shoulder, cradles the white boy's head in his arms and weeps as the play ends.

This blunt and brutal tale is one of Baraka's most chilling examinations of split identity, crushed sensitivity, and victimization. The whole tone of the play is consistently violent. The gang members are a complete cross-section of the intelligent, somber, stupid but trustworthy, likable, judicious, loud, and ugly individuals whom the difficulties and rhythms of ghetto life can blend into one tough conglomerate. As they anticipate the fight they themselves tussle verbally and at times physically. They are full of the spark of machismo antagonism and their language is flavored by curses, dozens, ritual insults, and braggadocio challenges:

> *Love.* (*Swinging around as if to shoot again he suddenly punches Holmes on the shoulder. Holmes lets out a yelp of pain*): Uhhuh . . . I told you about messin' with me.
>
> *Holmes.* (*Holding his shoulder*): Shit. Why didn't you hit Big Shot, you bastard? He brought the shit up.

Ora. (*Has the door propped open again*): Shit. That narrow head bastid know better than to fuck with me.

[p. 43][21]

Ray Foots is the "possessor" of this "empire," [22] but he does not easily blend into his group of toughs. He is "short, intelligent, manic," and from the moment he enters it is clear that the appearance of control upon which his leadership rests is a mask he wears with great dexterity: "Foots comes in. He is nervous but keeps it hidden by a natural glibness and a sharp sense of what each boy in the room expects, singularly, from him" (p. 51). Underneath this exterior of coolness and practical intelligence is a highly sensitive consciousness, a tender and desiring sensibility that must be smothered as the price for survival. When he sees Karolis lying bloody in the corner of the bathroom, "his first reaction is horror and disgust . . . but he keeps it controlled as is his style, and merely half-whistles" (p. 52). His impulses are clearly to leave the scene and declare the matter finished: "Well, I don't see any reason to keep all this shit up. Just pour water on the cat and let's get outta here" (p. 53).

But the situation cannot rest there. First, the other boys feel they deserve the entertainment of seeing him fight Karolis after their efforts to bring the two together in the bathroom; then, Farrell, a second white boy who came at the invitation of one of the gang members, presses Foots for his reason for wanting to "mess" with Karolis in the first place. At this point the fact of the letter is revealed. Farrell is ejected from the room by the others at Ray's insistence, but as the gang leader himself attempts to leave, Karolis makes his own demand for a fight. Foots is startled, but Karolis is absolutely determined to fight him—in front of the gang. The scene becomes near-hysteria, with Foots screaming curses at Karolis, Karolis awkwardly but determinedly ready to "kill" Foots, and the others shouting, whistling, clapping, and otherwise howling their encouragement.

Amidst this chaos Karolis brings out the central problem of the play: Ray Foots's disjunctive associations. "Foots," the name by which his young black peers call him, belongs to the leader, the tough and clever exterior, the mask. "Ray," the name the white boys use for him, is related to the troubled, sensitive, and lonely adolescent searching for sexual identity and meaningful personal relationships. As Karolis bears down on his opponent, he makes this division clear:

> Did I call you Ray in that letter . . . or Foots? (*Trying to laugh*) Foots! (*Shouts*) I'm going to break your fucking neck. That's right. That's who I want to kill. Foots!
>
> [p. 59]

Karolis is confronted by an inversion of the "Ray" with whom he had communed before and demands from him an appraisal of his *real* name:

> (*Backing up . . . wanting to talk but still moving as if to fight*): Are you Ray or Foots, huh?
>
> [p. 59]

Finally, as Foots remains incapable of facing his internal dilemma, Karolis answers the question with all the bitterness and inflamed antagonism of one utterly betrayed:

> I'll fight you, Foots! (*Spits the name*) I'll fight you. Right here in this same place where you said your name was Ray. (*Screaming. He lunges at Foots and manages to grab him in a choke hold.*) Ray, you said your name was. You said Ray. Right here in this filthy toilet. You said Ray. (*He is choking Foots and screaming. Foots struggles and is punching Karolis in the back and stomach, but he cannot get out of the hold.*) You put your hand on me and said Ray!
>
> [pp. 59–60]

More than any other of Baraka's stage creations, Ray Foots is reminiscent of the kind of tormented and tender being so powerfully evoked in *The System of Dante's Hell* and *Tales*. His sensitivity in a world that demands toughness and strict social allegiances becomes a hated thing; as he reaches out to someone of a different group he appears to himself (perhaps more than to his own peers) a "turncoat," and becomes "locked in with dull memories & self hate, & the terrible disorder of a young man." He is a victim no matter what he does; for if he refuses to fight Karolis his disloyalty to his gang will be disastrous, and when he allows Karolis's beating, the only person he loves is crushed. Karolis, who, interestingly, is attractive only "when he speaks," [23] is also clearly a victim: Ray's betrayal brings him into swift and cruel contact with the enveloping violence of his environment. Both are beaten and alone near the conclusion of the play. As Ray holds Karolis in his arms at the very end, we are shown a painful image of fragility and hopeless compassion in an inescapably hostile, cold, brutal world.

The homosexual union of these two souls in one flesh is, like Clay's relationship to Lula, a kind of demonic parody of marriage. As Frye notes of such demonic alliances, they may be accompanied by an enactment of the social relationship between a mob (associated with some sinister animal) and the victim (*pharmakos*) it seeks for its gratification. This mob is exactly what the gang appears to be as it mercilessly stomps on Karolis, the "ape"-like Knowles "screaming with laughter." The problem of homosexuality is a dominant motif in Afro-American literature, its relations to suffocated feeling being particularly well known in the work of James Baldwin. While Phillips has associated Baraka's use of this theme in *The Toilet* with "escape [from] the traditional matriarchy of the black community," [24] this is only an extraneous and imposed interpretation for which there is no basis in the text. For, as both the whole of Baraka's drama and the text of *The Toilet* itself reveal, Ray Foots's homosexuality is a concrete manifestation of torn allegiances, an accurately conceived image of a natural desire undermined and destroyed by a world that condemns such desire.

The violence depicted in *The Toilet*, unlike that of *Dutchman* and *The Slave*, is entirely specific in context. Like those two earlier works, *The Toilet* takes place in a setting that has a modern, and particularly urban, topography all too recognizable to the contemporary audience. However, this setting is much more naturalistic than those of *Dutchman* and *The Slave*; there are no mythical dimensions to the gray, rough cement, rolls of wet toilet paper, impersonal ugliness, and horrid smells that Baraka minutely catalogues in his description of the bathroom setting, which go beyond whatever automatically accrues to any random "slice" of urban institutional life. In *The Toilet* Baraka has carried the possibilities of fourth-wall naturalism to their extreme. The language of the play is entirely the type of talk actually found in such places, and in this the play touches upon that particular strain of modern art that attempts to make a cult of raw life of any kind, ignoring or denying any differences between art and life. The dialogue of *The Toilet* could well be the unedited accumulation of a tape recorder; only the *situation*, the issue, of the play is contrived. But it is precisely this shaping of plot that saves *The Toilet* from becoming simply realistic and tumbling out of art into life, giving it the vividness of living action rather than the dullness of "art" that is not artful.

The effect of this combination of completely naturalistic language and setting and a carefully chosen situation is the arousing of pathos, the sensations of pity (for the victims) and fear (of their environment and fate).[25] We pity the hero-victims because they are recognizably like ourselves, in power and in temperament; we fear what happens because we are repelled by what we see. The basic root of pathos in *The Toilet*, especially as it relates to Ray, is twofold: first, his inability to articulate any aspect of his own tragic dilemma; and second, his exclusion from the social groups (black gang, white friendship) to which he is trying to belong. In *The Toilet* Baraka has severely taxed the tools of naturalism in his effort to give expression to the black leader's conflict between inner and outer world, between the possibility of tenderness and the reality established by the harsh necessities of the social world.

Jello is an extremely clever exploitation of the old "Jack Benny Show" format. All of the characters are meant to be "as close to what [they are] on TV/radio"[26] as possible: Benny the miser, Dennis the high-voiced underling, Don the robust, smiling announcer, Mary the fussy tagalong. All, that is, except Rochester. His age is the same and his voice is still gravelly, but he has become "postuncletom," with straightened hair, street jive and militant attitude. The play opens with Benny pouting as he waits for Rochester to bring him the car, but when the long-time servant enters, his demeanor has radically altered from the old, familiar TV image:

Roch. (*Comes out, walking very fast, as if HE's going to walk through Benny*) What the hell you want man? Don't be calling me all the time. Damn, can't never get away from you.

Benny. Rochester, what are your talking about? What kind of tone is that? I want my car, and I've been looking all over the place for you. Where've you been?

Roch. Man don't be asking me where I been. Do I ever ask you where you been?

Benny. You don't have to, you know already, you drive me everywhere I go.

Roch. You damn right I do!

[pp. 11–12]

Benny is absolutely startled, and his reaction alternates between dismay and anger as Rochester continues to insult and threaten him. Finally, Benny "fires" Rochester, believing he has found the ultimate weapon in economic sanction.

Rochester proceeds to turn the tables: he is only too pleased to have their "relationship" so severed, because he is going to rip off Benny for every last cent the comedian has stashed away in his shoes, wall safe, etc. The play progresses like a normal Jack Benny routine, Rochester threatening Benny and finding his money step by step, Benny becoming increasingly hysterical as his all-precious gold slips away. Finally, as Rochester is completing his fleecing of Benny, Dennis, Mary, and Don enter one by one, each thinking he or she has walked into a particularly outrageous gag until the more extraordinary truth becomes apparent. Rochester procures their cash, too, and then, the white stars of the show having fainted and collapsed into a pile, Rochester picks up the last money bag (which is tied to one of Don Wilson's Jello boxes) and runs out to a waiting getaway car, "howling with laughter." Three piano chords follow to designate a change of program, and the play ends.

In *Jello*, Baraka has manipulated a naturalistic imitation of a popular culture format to create hilariously effective Theatre of the

Absurd. By keeping all of the white characters in the same rigid roles of the TV show and completely inverting the one black character, Baraka has subjected the white world to a "white-face" parody of its entertainment heroes. Whereas in the traditional "black-face," white actors play "themselves" (i.e. realistic white people) and black characters are reduced to stereotypical roles, in *Jello* precisely the reverse is true. Thus, a comic use of Genêt-like masking produces a new moral logic from the illogical and absurd situation of which we have become aware. Benny is no longer simply a humorous figure with a self-consciously played obsession, but a figure with a "humor" (*vide* Ben Jonson) that has become a ruling passion, a state of ritual bondage.

Hence it is no longer Benny's controlled presentation of miserliness that makes us laugh; rather, it is the repeated motif of his enslavement to money and his surprise at the new situation he cannot control that is comical. His misfortune, which we view with an aloof, critical, and unsympathetic eye, is funny in much the same way as the tricks played on the stupid butts of derisive laughter in the circus or music hall, or the punishments undergone by the obsessed characters in Molière or Ben Jonson. His ungovernable love of money is thus not only funny (as it was in the real Jack Benny skits) but morally reprehensible and censured as well. Money worship is used by Baraka both as a comic "humor" and as an example, both symbolic and literal, of white exploitation of the black community:

Benny. I worked hard for that money boy . . . and don't you forget it.

Roch. Another boy come out of your mouth, you're gonna see permanent stars, JB.

Benny. But I worked hard for this money . . . you know that?

Roch. What you own, one of them appliance stores on 125th Street?

Benny. Ohh, that's just one of my interests.

Roch. Yeh, you own a few butcher stores and stuff too. Prices ten cents higher than downtown too.

[pp. 23–24]

As Rochester goes through Benny's safe he comes upon a human skull (an emblem of Benny's murderous pursuit of wealth) and decides to leave this last piece of "loot" to the fallen comedian, who replies with unconscious self-condemning irony: "Rochester . . . no . . . Rochester you've left me nothing. Please man, have some feeling for another human being" (p. 25). By the end Benny is a slobbering fool; and with his demise the action of the play, the main thrust of which has been to ridicule the absurdity of his passion and expose its underlying cruelty, is complete.

The petty prejudice beneath Benny's avariciousness is revealed as he progressively refers to Rochester as an "unfortunate Negro man" (p. 15), "my chocolate friend" (p. 15), "you savage" (p. 22), "you illiterate swine" (p. 25), and "you crazy coon" (p. 29). Rochester's reaction is calm and amused: he has known his boss's true self all along and has calculated that his own switch to a truer self would unmask Benny as well. Rochester is now in his natural "element," dancing, singing, jiving, as he takes his "back pay." At one point, Benny appeals to him as a "friend" but Rochester strips away that façade with some brutal facts:

> Friend. Damn, man what you talking about? If I'm all that much your friend, why am I the chauffeur? If we so tight, why're you the one with all the money, and I work for you?? That don't sound like friend, to me. Sounds just like a natural slave . . .
>
> [p. 17]

Now he has rejected the slave image and chosen the other half of the Willie Best identity: the signifying, clever, skillful, and proud self-maker. Specifically, he has become a representative of the particularly black life-style of the streetman, the cool, hip, hustling descendant of the Signifying Monkey, John (the trickster slave), and Shine. By reversing roles and turning Benny's world on its head, he has become another in the line of black tricksters who, as Sherley Anne Williams puts it, "knowingly crashes against the conventions and wrests his own versions of right from a system which condemns his every effort toward dignity and self-assertion as moral or legal wrongs." [27]

When Benny is first confronted with the "new" Rochester he gasps, "you must be going mad"; near the point of breakdown he accuses Rochester of being "a mad thief and murderer" and is reduced to shouting "you're crazy" (pp. 26–27). His accusations recall the themes of madness and conflicting visions that are central in *Dutchman* and *The Slave*, at the core of which is the idea of a pulsing black life hidden from the view of whites. Like Clay spitting truth at Lula, Rochester contemptuously mocks Benny's curse of "go back to your horrible life":

> . . . Shiiiit. You don't know nothin' about my life. But I know all about yours. Driving your stinking broken down pennypinchin' short I found out all about your hopeless life, brother. Wait a minute, you ain't my brother. Ha, you must be Mack. That cat that people talk to in gas and train stations, maybe they're carrying the baggage, and a cat like you comes up and says, Hey Mack. Well that's what I'm saying to you now . . . Hey Mack! Where the hell's the rest of your bucks . . .
>
> [p. 19]

Benny continues to call Rochester's private world a "shitty little life" where "illiterate swine" do unimportant, tiny things. But it is Benny's world that is shallow and it is, ironically, the very medium he manipulates that reveals his inner poverty:

> *Roch.* I watch all your little white nasty sterile bullshit imitation life all the time. Drivin' your car. Or lookin' at the TV. (Laughs) Wow. That's where you really show up, my man. That evil tube. All I have to do is sit around and watch The Guiding Light or The Donna Reed Show or Peyton Place, or one of those things, and I find out all about your shallow little lives, and your ugly little needs.
>
> [pp. 25–26]

As Rochester, the happy, "crazy" black trickster makes his getaway with help from a waiting accomplice, he leaves this media-oriented and corrupted culture in a ridiculous heap of chaos. Through a simple change in the regular script, he uses his "white-face" reality as a method of disrupting the complacent white world and achieves a comic triumph for himself.

The Toilet and *Jello* are essentially naturalistic in form, their stories imitative of a reality well known to a contemporary American audience. In *The Baptism*, Baraka begins to feel his way toward a new, freer, more flexible kind of theatre. The play centers around a fifteen-year-old, handsome ("almost to girlishness") boy who comes to a "well-to-do arrogant Protestant church," ostensibly to make a personal confession of past sins and current faith and to receive the rite of baptism. There he meets a "soi-disant intellectual, very queenly" Homosexual and the church's "ridiculous, pompous" Minister. They have been intoning a surreal litany which, though imprecise in meaning, sets the tone of perversity and hypocrisy that characterizes this play:

> *Min.* Lord, in his high place. What creature returns to us, images, the tone of death. Our cloak of color, our love for ourselves and our hymns. [. . .] (*Moans.*) Not love. The betrayed music. Stealth. We rise to the tops of our buildings and they name them after us. We take off our hoods (*removes red hood*) and show our eyes. I am holy father of silence.[28]
>
> [p. 11]

When the boy enters, the Minister and the Homosexual begin to fight for his attention, but they are upstaged by an Old Woman who rushes in screaming that she has seen the boy commit "sins of the flesh." The scene becomes a supremely theatrical spectacle emphasizing the erotic impulses of both those who desire the boy and the boy himself:

> *Old Woman.* He sinned. He sinned. He sinned. (*Screams, jumping and pointing like a witch.*) I saw him. I watched him kneel and blaspheme our God. Sin. Sin. A demon of hot flesh. (*Settling, but still screaming, growing more intent and moved by what she is recounting.*) Sin. He closed his eyes. The lashes fluttered. And I saw how strong he thought to be

[. . .] You blaspheme. The flesh. My God. Those lovely eyelids moving. That hand placed so. [. . .] My lovely, lovely youth. (*She collapses trying to grasp the Boy's legs.*)
[pp. 15–16]

As the Old Woman remains "beseiged with the spirit" and the Minister and the Homosexual continue to tussle, the wild scene becomes even more hysterical when a band of Women ("young sleek 'Village!' types") enters, singing a chant for the boy. They believe he is the reincarnated Son of Man, their "holy husband"; and their hope for "salvation" is also a sexual perversion:

Women. He is the Son of Man. The big Stroker of the universe. It was he who popped us. (*They all moan ecstatically, sinking to their knees, praying.*)
[p. 24]

When the boy admits that he lied to the Women and is not the Christ, everyone but the Homosexual becomes enraged and is swept into a pseudoreligious frenzy. They prepare to exorcise this "demon" from their "holy place" in a ritual of sacrifice, but the boy suddenly turns upon them, shouting: "It is not right that youth should die to cleanse your stinking hearts! I *am* the son of God," and strikes them down with a sword. Then a Messenger enters. He has come from the boy's "father" ("The Man") who has grown angry with his son's failures on earth and wants the boy returned to him before he "destroys the whole works" that night. The boy refuses his father's command and resists abduction, forcing the Messenger (a "Lee Marvin Motorcycle stereotype") to beat him with a tire iron. The Messenger then hoists the boy's body over his shoulders and zooms away with him on his motorcycle. The Homosexual, who was knocked out by the others in their rush to "sacrifice" the boy, revives and closes the play with an enigmatic return to the exact reality the cluttered stage leaves before him:

Good Christ, what's happened in this place? (*Turns Minister's body over with his toe.*) Serves him right for catering to rough trade. All out like lights. [. . .] Damn, looks like some really uninteresting kind of orgy went on in here. (*Looks at watch.*)

> Hmmmmm. 1:30. I got about an hour before the bars close. [. . .] (*Starts to leave.*) Wonder what happened to that cute little religious fanatic? (*Does his ballet step. Starts to sing his song.*) God, Go-od, God, etc. (BLACK)
>
> [p. 32]

The Baptism is a theatrical tour de force, a whirling succession of self-consciously struck poses, "nonsense" patter, surreal images, and exposed perversions. Like the "La Mamma" movement of the past decade, it borrows greatly from the European theatre of spectacle, particularly from elements of Genêt's and Cocteau's work. From Genêt, Baraka has taken the device of figures of monumental and powerful identities who are in reality weak and servile creatures (the Minister, for example, shares a great deal of the role, fantasies, and power obsessions of the Bishop in *The Balcony*). Like Genêt's maskers, Baraka's characters almost seem to be replaced by the symbols they create for themselves: the Old Woman becomes a type of matriarchal dominance, "leaning, leaning"; the Minister, a typical hypocrite who robes his illicit dreams in "our cloak of color, our love for ourselves and our hymns." They are "characters" in appearance only, for as symbols of their own self-projected functions they reflect back upon themselves and thus reveal themselves in their essential nothingness. As Sartre said of Genêt's theatre, "in this pyramid of fantasies, the ultimate appearance derealizes all others."[29] The moment of this "ultimate appearance" in *The Baptism*, as in the theatre of Genêt, is a moment of unleashed evil, the moment when all the unreal fantasies and real obsessions of the characters are fixed upon a sole purpose—possession and then "sacrifice" of the boy. The language of Baraka's characters is also like that of Genêt's: erotic, scabrous, scatological, but at times highly poetic, with a solemn, inverted religious atmosphere representing a world literally turned upside down, a world in which the dedicated pursuit of the abject is carried out with the zeal and devotion of true sainthood.

The Baptism's characters exist in a world of heightened theatricality. Baraka exhibits in this play a remarkable dexterity in the discovery and use of stage effects, a quality that bears a distinct resemblance to the theatre of Cocteau. Extreme attention is paid to the tones of voice, gestures, and timing of the characters as they interact in a series of quickly passing tableaux. As with Cocteau's sense of spectacle, Baraka's theatricality is relentlessly concrete and accurate, linked with the contemporaneous, particular, and realistic. On the altar where most of the action takes place is a speaker-stand with two microphones and a plaque with the inscription "WHBI RADIO" stapled under the letters "IHS." Above the altar is a "huge white cross of glass with the inscription 'IHS' written on the crossbar," and the decor of the altar itself is red velvet and gold. The action played out on this altar is a series of mock-religious rituals, with each figure dancing and chanting his or her own erotic rite, supplicating the false messiah for his "holy" love, and then—showing the underlying cruelty of these desires—joining in a ritual of "sacrifice."

In this manner Baraka unites images of the Sunday-morning commercialization of religious services, the garish bourgeois expression of wealth in religious edifices, and the sexual perversion latent in religious "ecstasy" and "worship," in one sweeping critique of the American Christian church and its cultural, moral, and spiritual failures. The power associated with religious zeal is shown especially to be based upon sexual fantasy (a prominent theme in Genêt's *The Balcony*): the Old Woman in her "ecstasy" pronounces the "instrument" of the boy's sins of masturbation "that hand, where so much life was stilled"; the Minister sees the Women as "virgins of Christ [. . .] my usherettes," and the Women share the general fixation upon the boy as the "Chief Religious jelly roll of the universe." When the boy himself is revealed as a failed messiah, a pouting adolescent who slays in the name of charity and who must be dragged back to "the Man" like a runaway school-child, the apocalypse which the Messenger (a kind of 'gouster' Gabriel) prophesies, seems only too welcome.

What we are left with at the play's end, however, is not a purifying purge of this corruption but a heap of sordid bodies which, ironically, looks like the remains of "some really uninteresting kind of orgy." The Homosexual brings the play into the perspective of a "realistic documentary of unreal events" (as Cocteau described his first film, "The Blood of a Poet"). He has been on the fringe of the other characters' madness, an aloof and witty satirist of their thinly disguised impulses. Yet even this one critical commentator is a man of perversions, aside from his "unselective" homosexuality (as the Minister terms it). He is the spokesman for both Satan ("Satan threw down what was only subjection to become a king") and the "spirit of the Renaissance" ("let no one say we have not fucked everything and everyone we could")—Baraka's vision of the basic force of evil in the modern West. The world of *The Baptism*, then, is finally a totally sterile and corrupted community. Here, like a Genêt character, Baraka has used the medium of theatrical projection to exorcise the petty devils that aggravate his alienated mind.

A Recent Killing

In each of the three plays just examined, Baraka attacked a major institution of American life: the hard-and-cruel school environment, the sterile mass-media culture, and the hypocritical church. Each play has a relentless drive—by turns violent, comic, or surreal—toward expulsion of various forms of madness or weakness that hold down the revolutionary progress anticipated in *Dutchman* and *The Slave.* Even these two early plays are works of exorcism. In *Dutchman* the lure of selling out to middle-class values and accepted meekness is paid for by death in the person of Clay. In *The Slave* the latent attachments to a past involvement with white-dominated society threaten to sever Walker from the revolutionary progress of history. All five of these plays are innovative in form, as challenging to the mainstream of American theatre as to the prominent values of American life. It is after these plays that Baraka makes his only attempt at a traditional type of theatre informed by a less radical content. *A Recent Killing* is, in several crucial ways, a looking back upon Baraka's past involvement with the white community and an "integrated" approach to rebellion against repressive forces in this country. This play is a unique act of exorcism, for Baraka never again returns either to this kind of theatre or to this method of political solution in his search for a vision of black liberation. *A Recent Killing* is a decisive stage in the development of this vision, for with it many bridges to the past are burned forever.

The setting of *A Recent Killing* is an Air Force base in Puerto Rico, the same scene Baraka exploited in "Salute," the story in *Tales.* Three young airmen, distinct outsiders from the regular "cracker" army brigands who rule over them, are the story's "heroes." They are a triumvirate of the fringe American youth that finds itself out of place in the armed forces: Laff, a Jewish photographer from the lower East Side of New York City; T. T. Jackson ("T"), a slick, happy-go-lucky black from a small Southern town; and Lenny, a black would-be poet from Newark, N.J.

The plot is contained in a traditional three-act structure, with exposition and development roughly proceeding through act 2 and climax and resolution occurring in act 3. It concerns the airmen's collective dissatisfaction with military life and the consequences of their unease during a raid upon the base. This raid is carried out by a group of angry Puerto Ricans who want to stop the Air Force from laying tar for a new airstrip over their land. When the raid occurs, Lennie, who is left guarding a plane alone, decides "this is not my stick [. . .] I'm not gonna do anybody's killing for them" (3–9–56)[30] and abandons his post. When he is thrown into jail, Laff and T get drunk and, at Laff's suggestion, decide to liberate their buddy from his confinement. They manage to break into the stockade and get Lennie to the front door, but they are ambushed by an unseen sergeant. Laff and T are killed instantly, but Lennie, who had been trying to talk his stoned comrades out of their foolish "mission," picks up a loose gun during the confusion and manages to kill the officer. He is utterly shaken—everything which he and his friends had fantasized and talked about in vague terms has become suddenly and horribly true. The other guards try to talk Lennie into surrender, but he sees the situation as unalterable. He closes the door, goes to the desk, and places the gun beside the typewriter. He puts a piece of paper in the machine and starts to type: "A Recent Killing," then looks up to say, "and won't nobody know what it means." He "stops for a second to rest his head in his hands," and, as the military police arrive and begin screaming and banging on the door outside, the play ends.

The action precipitating Laff and T's "revolution" (i.e. the attack on Lennie's plane and his abandonment of it) occurs in the nineteenth scene of this twenty-three scene drama. Until then the characters have not faced conflict of any dramatic interest; no real issues have developed up to the point of the Puerto Rican raid (which is not anticipated by the audience any more than by Lennie). The play has proceeded as individual scenes, each quite effective in itself but functionally unrelated to those before or after. These isolated scenes are effective because of Baraka's clever barracks comedy and the flashes of theatrical inventiveness seen in Lennie's psychological projections of Nijinsky, Sebastian Flyte (from Evelyn Waugh's *Brideshead Revisited*), Leopold Bloom, and Sylvia (a "dream girl, masturbation image"). The characters themselves are entertaining: Laff is a master of irreverent Yiddish humor ("mishagases [. . .] that's a Jewish word for Cracker"—3–10–69); T is a jivin', dozens-playing, super-hip slickster ("Boy, I'll slip you so bad you won't know what to do"—3–4–37); and Lennie, the central figure of the three, presents a fascinating combination of coolness, intelligence, sensitivity, self-suffocating seriousness, and redeeming integrity. There is also the interest of a subplot concerning a black NCO "lifer" (Butler) and his wife's adultery with a Southern white lieutenant (Pyle).

The purpose of all this action preceding the last five scenes is to establish an atmosphere of sharp, cynical disaffection, which separates the three crewmen and Sergeant Butler from their environment. This atmosphere provides a plausible background for the swift and violent denouement. But the action of the play is basically unfocused. As was palpable in its premiere in New York City at the New Federal Theatre (directed by Irving Vincent), *A Recent Killing* lacks the central purpose necessary for a play of its ambitious length.

This lack of direction in plot is the play's chief formal shortcoming. It may stem in great measure from the underlying malaise of the characters. Their own lack of meaningful activity is the theme of the play's most interesting scene (3,4). Lennie, Laff, T, and

Butler are guarding a plane. They are busy trying to relieve the boredom of their duty when, in the course of their flippant conversation, Lennie observes that the trouble with evil thugs like Lt. Pyle is shared by most other people: "they don't have anything to do" (3–4–30). The others are baffled, so Lennie explicates:

> None of us wants to go around knocking people off and what not. Well, look, for instance, these jerks send us out here to guard, figuring that's what we're really gonna do. But T listens to his radio, Laff, you're going through your photos . . . I've got my book. (*Making it as light as possible*) Butler, you're the only guy just standing around, that's why you're so . . . nervous."
>
> [3–4–33]

Soon Laff and T begin to acknowledge the simple truth of Lennie's idea. The three young crewmen become absorbed in working out the particulars of what they would like most to do and become, but Butler quietly broods. Then he opens up to them and admits that, while he once wanted to be a soldier more than anything in the world, he now sees that "almost nothing about this [is] the way I thought it would be [. . .] this is bullshit" (3–4–39). Lennie's rhetoric carries him to the extreme of advocating that they leave their guard duty because they all obviously "don't care about the planes," but T scoffs at the suggestion as foolish "jail talk." Lennie relents, but Butler, who has been slowly mulling over the idea of finally just "doing what I want to do," suddenly gets up and announces that he is going to act on Lennie's advice. Lennie, in an ironic and comic reversal, is taken aback: "Whatta you mean? You gotta be out here guarding, with us" (3–4–41), but Butler responds with the learned truth of this emblematic scene: "Why? You just told me the whole thing was a load of shit. I'm gonna take your advice . . . and find me something to do" (3–4–41).

The characters, then, finally *articulate* their basic condition of inaction and misorientation. And the less verbal Butler's willingness to act upon this recognition throws the play itself into dramatically meaningful movement. It is clear that Baraka's uneasiness with so large a framework has led him to belabor the unarticulated inaction in the play's previous two-and-a-half acts. Had this time passed with the characters constantly describing their motionlessness or building a general state of anticipation, the length of the inaction in the plot would have been a more appropriate formal device (as the inactive process of waiting is a truly dramatic action in *Waiting for Godot*).

A good number of the more fascinating scenes concern Lennie. He is another of Baraka's leader-poets ("you're the goddam ring leader of this little bunch of snots," Pyle yells at him—3–2–12), and his psychological growing pains are a major source of interest in the play. Like the play itself, he lacks central purpose, while an array of disparate inclinations struggle for his allegiance. First, his sexual identity is not secure, as the evanescent Sylvia-image indicates. Then, the impulses of intellectual pursuits (symbolized by the admonitions of Leopold Bloom) and the tenderer feelings of poetry (represented by the promptings of Sebastian Flyte) battle for his loyalty. As a sprightly, drunken old Irishman, Bloom dazzles Lennie and leaves him with these words: "I advise you, if you still want to go by the name of Dedalus, to get on the ball, before it rolls right over you. Read or Die. The trickleap summons all definitions" (1–2–13). Flyte is a witty, Oscar Wildean aesthete who is Bloom's enemy in the scenes of Lennie's projected imagination. Scoffing at Bloom's warning that whatever Lennie does should be "educational" (1–2–22), Flyte touts the "images of the wild things a poet could drag into the world" and encourages Lennie's ideal of the poetic:

> *Flyte.* Well you just say the first things come into your mind . . . go ahead . . . poet.
> *Len.* Gold . . . Gold [. . .]
> *Flyte.* Gold? A color? It must be poetry. Poesie, I suppose, is gold [. . .] Well, then, we'll take it as poetry. As the glittery image of life you see. Something to be captured, that is that feeling . . . what gold can make you feel, as color, as something, somehow just beyond your reach, but part of you. Yes. A color, poems are gold. The act of poetry is gold. And the poet himself.
>
> [2–5–19]

Another of Lennie's fantasy images is the swirling, poetic motion of Nijinsky's dancing body, which glides through his mind and across the stage several times. During his first entrance the dancer says: "I do not pretend I am the truth. If I tell the truth, the whole truth, men will kill me" (1–2–10). He is an image of pure beauty, of "God in a body," and Lennie clearly is struggling to resolve desire for such beauty and the ethical impulse of action "in the world." But as it is only "an order of God that tells [Nijinsky] how to act" (1–2–11), Lennie himself remains fixed in his puzzlement until the force of external events throws him, willing and ready or not, into the acting out of his spoken convictions. As he lies in his cell reading Wittgenstein's *Tractatus,* he comes upon the proposition that "ethics and aesthetics are one" (3–12–76). Only the mini-rebellion of Laff and T forces him out of his ambivalence and into an action that begins to realize the unified purpose which he believes this maxim advocates. With his head resting in his hands at the play's end, he seems to be in shock, confusedly contemplating the events that have imposed a "resolution" of his inner torment. The gun and the typewriter lying side by side become a final emblem of the jumbled ethical and aesthetic inclinations which he, like the play, has finally resolved into fragile but welcome unity.

A Recent Killing, like Lennie's final typewritten message, is an enigmatic statement communicated by means of an ineffective technology. For just as Lennie's use of the typewriter is a futile gesture born of frustration, so Baraka's unsuccessful dependence in this play on borrowed dramatic conventions implies a need for a new expressive form. In a later essay entitled "Technology and Ethos," Baraka employs the typewriter image in a more explicit critique of traditional idioms and devices:

> A typewriter?—why shd it only make use of the tips of the fingers . . . If I invented a word placing machine, an "expression-scriber," *if you will,* then I would have a kind of instrument into which I could step & sit or sprawl or hang & use not only my fingers to make words express feelings but elbows, feet, head, behind, and all the sounds I wanted, screams, grunts, taps . . .
>
> [from *Raise Race Rays Raze*, p. 156]

Baraka wishes—with almost self-mocking intensity—to shape a new "kind of instrument," one that allows Afro-American expression to issue from a unity of ethics and aesthetics. Without this "post-American" form he, like Lennie, would remain trapped in a prison not of his own making.

As Lennie begins to accept the brutal reality of his situation at the play's conclusion, he pronounces the scene a "graduation." All of the soul-searching and irresolution of the past are now irrevocably behind him. Similarly, Baraka has, with *A Recent Killing*, taken a last look back to his past associations and experiences in the white world. It is probably fitting that he should use a dramatic form more unwieldy and inflexible than any other in his corpus as the vehicle for his least radical and angry content. After *A Recent Killing*, Baraka begins the task of constructing a transcendent myth of black liberation and discovering a viable dramatic form for its expression. He has now graduated to a truly radical and truly black theatre.

6 The "Black Revolutionary Plays": Experimentation in Form

Baraka's plays from *Dutchman* to *A Recent Killing* represent the first major phase of his development as a dramatist. These works are nearly all formally inventive and offer a variety of theatrical experience unmatched by any contemporary American dramatist. Yet, as Baraka's vision of a liberated and separate black nation became more important in his world-view, his experimentation with dramatic form continued with increased vigor. Before examining the major results of this theatrical experimentation we must understand the nature and the goals of Baraka's efforts.

As different as Baraka's early plays are from one another, we can discern three broad similarities among them: (1) they all utilize naturalistic frameworks; (2) they all (with the exception of *Jello*) depict the limitations of tragic or quasi-tragic heroes; (3) they all are meant for an audience implicitly white. The revolution that occurs in Baraka's dramatic technique proceeds in greatest measure from his desire to change this audience from white to black. The same change occurs in the drama, as we saw earlier in the poetry (chapter 4): after moving uptown in 1965, Baraka began to abandon his white audience and to establish a continuing conversation with black people. The goal was to communicate with and to educate his people, to unite them in one celebration and ideal of unity. Baraka expressed this goal succinctly in his preface to *Black Magic Poetry*: "The whole race connected in its darkness, in its sweetness. We must study each other. And for the aliens we say I aint studying you." The challenge this project poses for the black dramatist is to find a theatrical experience, a dramatic form, capable of integrating audience and vision.

Given this challenge, it is clear why Baraka should abandon the naturalistic and tragic quality of his early drama. The most distinct attribute of naturalism is its guiding sociological and materialistic conception of man. Naturalism takes man to be a part and function of his environment and depicts him as being who, instead of controlling concrete reality, is himself controlled and absorbed by it. The milieu takes a preponderant part in shaping human destiny; all actions, decisions, and feelings contain an element of the extraneous, the external and the material, something that does not originate in the subject and that makes man seem the unalterable product of a mindless and soulless reality. So long as Baraka's drama maintained the element of naturalism he could do little more than express the "plight" of black people; his heroes might declare the madness of reality, but reality inevitably triumphed over them. Furthermore, the precision of naturalism, with its denial of the convention of distortion, is far too restrictive to convey the complex vision of such a playwright. Indeed, Baraka often used naturalistic structures only to overcome their apparent limitations, as we saw in *The Baptism*, *Jello*, and even *Dutchman*. In the subsequent plays, however, the pretensions toward realism are largely discarded in favor of a more visionary conception of "reality."

Naturalism, which makes man appear to be the mere function of his environment, clearly involves the degradation of the hero. Baraka's early heroes are "victims" because their power of action is incapable of realizing their vision and desire. Their "heroism" is a tragic transcendence that can be achieved only because they fail to accomplish revolutionary tasks. Their "triumph" is a spiritual consolation for physical defeat. The interdependence of metaphysical and material victory called for in Baraka's myth of black liberation makes such tragic figures nonviable. Victimization, where it occurs, must now be unaccompanied by pathos; the triumph of black heroes must be unqualified.

The plays studied in this chapter are attempts to find a new dramatic vehicle to replace the kinds used in earlier efforts. It must be stressed that Baraka is not completely shedding the past. In many ways, the revolutionary principles elucidated in his very first drama, *Dutchman*, remain the basic ideas in his art. But now the emphasis has begun to shift from exploration of the problem to realization of the solution. If we can imagine Baraka reviewing his drama in 1965, his reaction might have been expressed in the old man's words from *The Slave*: "we need, ahem, a meta-language. We need some thing not included here." To include that something was the impulse of the new "experimental" period.

Great Goodness of Life

In *Blues People* Baraka wrote: "The black middle-class, from its inception (possibly ten seconds after the first Africans were herded off the boat) has formed almost exclusively around the proposition that it is better not to be black in a country where being black is a liability" (pp. 123–24). Several of Baraka's early characters are members of this black middle class. They become "victims" by being torn between desire for white approval at the cost of blackness and the revolutionary necessity of racial pride. Court Royal, the central character of *Great Goodness of Life*, is another in this line of black middle-class victims; but whereas the earlier heroes were tragic *pharmakoi*, sought and eliminated by the dominant power, Court Royal is a comic figure, an *alazon,* who is shown up as trying to place himself in proper society by slavishly following its decrees. His victimization is humorous and his capitulation is more condemnable than pitiable.

The play opens as Court Royal is ordered from "an old log cabin" (a slave emblem) by a "Voice." [1] This Voice is the controlling power of his world and it has summoned him to stand trial for "shielding a murderer." Court weakly resists the accusation and finally, while entering his "plea," shows himself comically blind to the ways of his world:

> Of course I'm not guilty. I work in the Post Office. (*Tries to work up a little humor*) You know me, probably. Didn't you ever see me in the Post Office? I'm a supervisor; you know me. I've worked at the Post Office for thirty-five years. I'm a supervisor. There must be some mistake.
>
> [p. 47]

Throughout the play, Court frantically seizes upon his role of postal worker as a means of defense, believing that this ultimate status symbol of American middle-class achievement can free him from the Voice's power. He insists he can afford his own attorney, John Breck, but the Voice appoints a "legal aid man," a wind-up, "house-slave" robot who is, in fact, John Breck. The slave tells Court to plead guilty, just as public defenders enter their poor black clients into ruinous plea-bargaining procedures. Court musters his pride and insists on his innocence, so the Voice dismisses Breck. Court is declared guilty but he demands fair play: "What? No. I want a trial. Please a trial. I deserve that. I'm a good man." The Voice booms its reply: "Royal, you're not a man!"

The remainder of the play depicts the black man's gradual acceptance of the Voice's judgment. He is forced to look at a screen upon which are flashed the faces of "Malcolm, Patrice. Rev. King, Garvey. Dead nigger kids killed by the police. Medgar Evers." Court breaks down and calls them "My sons." He begins to realize that the young "murderer," the "prince" whom the Voice's hoods have had "a nigger [kill] for us," is the spiritual warrior of his race. Now the Voice offers him a "way out" of his legal dilemma:

> We have decided to spare you. We admire your spirit. It is a compliment to know you can see the clearness of your fate, and the rightness of it. You are absolved of your crime, at this moment, because of your infinite understanding of the compassionate God Of The Cross. Whose head was cut off for you, to absolve you of your weakness.
>
> [p. 59]

To be released he need only perform a special rite, the murder of the "Myth of the murderer" which is carried within his son's body. Court is momentarily torn, but in the end, desiring the peace of "guiltlessness" and safety, he kills his son. The rite performed, Court is "happy . . . and relaxed," his soul "white as snow." He starts to wander off the stage, mumbling, "I'm free. I'm free. My life is a beautiful thing." But suddenly a "brighter mood strikes him"; he comes toward the edge of the stage and calls to his wife:

"Hey, Louise, have you seen my bowling bag? I'm going down to the alley for a minute. (*He is frozen, the lights dim to* BLACK.)"

On the simplest level, *Great Goodness of Life* is a combination of morality play and political allegory. The white oppressor can kill only black *bodies.* It is necessary to the oppressor that the black man, here the black middle class (Court Royal), murder the black *spirit* (the Young Victim). The determinants of the black man's fate (the Voice) are invisible to him, and the guilt he avoids by killing his own son is merely the oppressor's condemnation. The real crime and guilt are the higher sins of moral and spiritual betrayal. Court, a comic and pathetic slave, believes these sins are really acts of expiation that "free" him to his bowling-alley bliss and "guiltless silence."

But *Great Goodness of Life* is much more clever and interesting than this basic interpretation suggests. To get further in examining the play it is necessary to realize that Baraka wrote *Great Goodness of Life* as an explicit answer to Genêt's *The Blacks.* The themes, structure, and development of Baraka's play all parallel those of Genêt's. Baraka's subtle manipulation of Genêt's devices not only provides the vehicle for his drama but constitutes a critical interpretation of *The Blacks.*

To appreciate fully Baraka's rejoinder to Genêt we must understand the essential design of the Frenchman's play. *The Blacks* is a ceremony presented by a troupe of Negroes which, in the usual manner of Genêt, involves conflicts on several levels of appearance and reality. The first of these is that which pits the white audience against the black actors who devise a masque for their entertainment. Genêt specified that the play must be performed before whites; or that, if it should be presented to a black audience, one symbolic white must always occupy a prominent place in the theatre. A group of eight Negroes appears. They are subservient to the masters of white society (represented by masked Negroes called the "Court"—the Queen, Judge, Governor, Missionary, and Queen's Valet or "poet"), and they are openly hostile to the white audience. Though this anger is real, we are given to understand that the Negroes are merely acting; for, like all of

Genêt's outcast-heroes, they can live freely only in the theatrical dimension: "They tell us we're grown up children," says the Negro "master of ceremonies," Archibald. "In that case, what's left for us? The theatre." [2] The white audience, then, may feel secure in the belief that the Negroes' hatred is part of their role-playing. The Negroes' true bitterness is obscured by outward shows and symbols.

The masque or ritual enacted by the Negroes is the play's main action, and this brings us to the second level of conflict. The masque begins with the Negroes dancing to the strains of Mozart around a catafalque draped in white at stage-center. Upon the catafalque, we are told, is a white woman who has been killed by a Negro. The ceremony is to be a reenactment of the woman's death and a trial of her alleged murderer, the Negro named Village. This ritual murder of the white race is presented before the members of the white court who, sitting on a gallery at the back of the stage, have come to attend their own funeral rites: "They think they are compelling us, but it is owing to our good breeding that we shall descend to death" (The Governor).

This ceremonial murder, however, turns out to be yet another sham: the catafalque is revealed to be merely two chairs and there is no corpse. The stage masque, which celebrates a longed-for state of revolt, has been a pretense allowing for the ridiculing of white values, manners, and institutions. The symbolic vengeance upon white tyranny is again given no physical status but instead exists as pure gesture.

Yet at a third level of meaning the action is removed from the theatrical to the actual. As Village's artificial trial is taking place, an analogous but real trial is said to be happening offstage. A Negro traitor to a rebellion now raging against white society is condemned and executed by an unmasked black court. Thus the first two planes of action—the conflict between Negro actors and white audience, and Village's "trial"—turn out to be diversions from the actual revolt against colonial tyranny. White society is attacked both metaphorically (by the masque and by the eventual slaying of the "white" court) and literally (by the postulated black uprising). We have seen a ritual murder of a white woman, but the reality 'behind the scenes' was the trial and execution of a Negro—a Negro traitor.

Genêt's play is a complex series of play-actions in which illusion gives way to the Negro rebellion that takes place outside the reality of theatre. Baraka exploits this multilayering of spectacle and conflict to great effect in *Great Goodness of Life*. But he has taken each of Genêt's levels of being and reversed them: what is illusion in *The Blacks* is reality in *Great Goodness of Life* and vice versa. Thus the "court" of masked Negroes comes down from the platform to become the black, middle-class Court Royal, who is put on trial. The Voice is the real white world, and its power over those who stand below is likewise real. In *Great Goodness of Life* the ritual murder that occurs offstage is of a hero to the black cause, and although it is physical murder, his spiritual death is only an illusion. The spiritual murder that occurs onstage, of the Myth of the Young Victim or Prince, is the real execution; this is why the Voice so vehemently tries to establish the Myth's—or spirit's—insubstantiality in Court Royal's eyes even after his son is physically slain:

> *Voice.* The rite must be finished. This ghost must be lost in cold space. Court Royal, this is your destiny. This act was done by you a million years ago. This is only the memory of it. This is only a rite. You cannot kill a shadow, a fleeting bit of light and memory. This is only a rite to show that you would be guilty but for the cleansing rite.
>
> [pp. 61–62]

Whereas the Negroes in *The Blacks* take on roles to divert and deceive their white audience while the Negro rebellion is proceeding outside the theatre, Court Royal's acceptance of the role dictated by the Voice is a concession to white society that allows it to crush the leaders of black revolution. In *The Blacks*, the Negroes impersonating the white court remove their masks on the entrance of the Negro messenger who brings news of the traitor's execution, and put them on again only after they have heard that a new revolutionary delegate has been sent to Africa. Once more, precisely the reverse occurs in *Great Goodness of Life*. When Court

Royal realizes his son is physically dead, he becomes for once a true black man and recognizes his real guilt:

> I must be sentenced. I am the one. (*Almost trance-like*) I must be sentenced. With the murderer. I am the one.
>
> [p. 58]

Yet with the false promise of "freedom" given him by the Voice, Court Royal renews his old mask of compliant slave and enacts the murder of his son's spirit.

It may seem from this comparison that Genêt has presented the more radical vision of the two. *The Blacks* involves the condemnation of white society in a series of suffocating illusions while envisaging a triumphant Negro rebellion as reality. *Great Goodness of Life*, on the other hand, is an accusatory exposition of a segment of the black community. Yet there remains in Genêt's play a level of absurdity which is entirely unacceptable in Baraka's vision of a completely liberated black nation. Archibald states near the end of *The Blacks*:

> The time has not yet come for presenting dramas about noble matters. But perhaps they suspect what lies behind this architecture of emptiness and words. We are what they want us to be. We shall therefore be it to the very end, absurdly. Put your masks on again.

The Negroes in this play—the true heroes of Genêt's world—have decided to play out the stereotyped roles assigned them by society, but to play them out even to absurdity, to choose freely to become what they are condemned to be. Baraka rejects the acceptance of this absurdity as being itself absurd. To accept the role devised by the Voice, however self-consciously, can only lead (Baraka seems to be telling us) to utter renunciation of black selfhood and complete acceptance of servility. Genêt's vision of liberation, which proceeds from his own unique experience within society, is seen by Baraka as perhaps the most deceptive of all illusions. Thus, in response to Genêt, Baraka stages the trial of the black traitor (Court Royal) which is the offstage action of *The Blacks*. Genêt subtitled his play "a clown show" to show that the stage action is a farce or practical joke, something not to be taken seriously; he thus renders it bearable to his hypothetical white audience. The subtitle of *Great Goodness of Life* is "a coon show," yet another reversal of Genêt. For Baraka's play, which is meant for a black audience, is no joke. Court Royal is unsympathetically portrayed as a murderer of the black spirit, and the message is deadly serious.

Agit-Prop Plays

Though all art (according to the old Orwellian slogan) may be propaganda in the sense that all writers wish to be persuasive, there remains an immense difference between a merely provocative presentation and an all-out attempt to push an audience from one view to another and thence into immediate and possibly violent action. Because art in general may be held to teach something, it is difficult to say when it is positively "didactic." The plays reviewed in this section are considered didactic in the following sense: every theatrical device is utilized with the primary intention of projecting political ideas in an effort to educate black people to their fundamental tasks. This does not mean that these plays are entirely artless or dramatically uninteresting. On the contrary, they reflect Baraka's search for a dramatic experience capable of reaching large numbers of black people as directly as possible. Hence, like most successful agit-prop, these plays are highly contrived and their appearance of simplicity is often gained with much effort.

In his agit-prop pieces, Baraka's language casts off all ornament. It has become functional, austere, and severely factual and helps make the plays work more like teaching aids than fanciful creations. Baraka meets here the demand for "straight talk" once posed in his poetry (see, for example, "Numbers, Letters," quoted p. 123). It is a measure of his status as a poet that he sometimes achieves the effect of functional elegance, as in passages of the short ritual *Black Power Chant*, which have a monolithic, stark beauty.[3]

Like Brecht's Lehrstuecke, Baraka's agit-prop works are designed to teach certain broad and communal virtues and to make the community face its essential problems. They involve issues of order, discipline, and submission: order and discipline within the community and among black people, submission to the inexorable laws of history and survival. Baraka has used a number of dramatic approaches in these didactic efforts, and those chosen for discussion are selected to exemplify this formal variety as well as Baraka's basic agit-prop themes.

Experimental Death Unit #1 deals with the banality and sexual decadence which the revolution is expected to purge. Duff and Loco are white men who stand on Third Avenue in "late winter,"[4] high on heroin, arguing the virtues of art, knowledge, and intelligence in abstract yet also grossly obscene language. A Negro Woman enters and announces: "I am a groovy black lady . . . fresh outta idea alley. You dig?" The three are "whore and artists [. . .] in this charlieland." Their world is depicted as a dying West consumed by Beckett-like discussions of nothingness and disgusting actions. Screaming insults and jumbled slogans from popular culture, the men fight desperately over the whore who, in turn, spouts such madness as: "Ahhh, man, the old folks talked about spirits. *The* Spirit! I'll go mystical when I goddam please." As they leap onto one another, the soldiers of the black rebellion enter "with drums and marching cadence; [. . .] at the front of the group one boy marches with a pike on the top of which is a white man's head still dripping blood." Duff, who has beaten Loco to death in his effort to procure the whore, is now killed; he dies shouting, "Niggers! Niggers! Niggers!" The woman, who thinks she can save herself by being "cool" with the brothers ("Ahh, honey . . . it's just a soulbrother . . . don't worry"), is also shot. Having imposed a new order, the black army marches off to new missions.

Though *Experimental Death Unit #1* is a rather straightforward comment on the decadence Baraka believes must be expunged by a spiritual war, the play also shows the black playwright responding to European theatre. Duff and Loco are obvious parodies of Beckett's Gogo and Didi and also, with the beating of Loco by Duff, of Pozzo and Lucky. While the play makes a brutally simple moral point, it offers a condemnation of Beckett's "nothingness" to the more sophisticated viewer.

In *Home on the Range* a black burglar enters a white home with the intention of supplementing his "income."[5] To his bewilderment, the people he finds there—a typical American, TV-watching family of father, mother, son, and daughter—speak pure gibberish ("Gimminies. Vathrop. Crouch. Bibble," etc.). The criminal's inability to communicate with the family is broadly farcical; his confusion mounts as the family responds hysterically to the preachings of a concealed loudspeaker ("THIS IS THE VOICE OF GOD, EVERYTHING'S COOL!"), and he finally falls in exhaustion. When he awakens, he abandons his gun for an expansible baton and conducts the family in rousing versions of "America The Beautiful" and the Negro National Anthem, "Lift Every Voice and Sing." As they reach the highest point of the latter song, a crowd of black people pushes through the door. A wild, loud party ensues, with the white people awkwardly trying to dance and finally collapsing. The scene changes to the next morning. A postapocalyptic aura presides as the black party-ers wake and begin to interrogate the father, the only apparent white survivor:

> *Father.* I was born in Kansas City in 1920. My father was the vice-president of a fertilizer company. Before that we were phantoms . . . (*Waving at his* FAMILY.) Evil ghosts without substance.
>
> [p. 111]

The father repeats this methodically then swoons again. A black girl goes to the window:

> Hey look, the sun's coming up. (*Turns around, greeting the three brothers.*) Good Morning, Men. Good Morning.
>
> THE END
>
> [p. 111]

Home On The Range, which was read as part of the 1967 Black Communications Project and performed at a Town Hall rally in March 1968, is a baffling piece. A collage of absurdity, farce, social satire, mythology, and apocalyptic vision, it seems designed to make a series of quick, catching, and only loosely related impressions on a large audience. It is engaging and succeeds in making simple fun of "goofy" white Americans. Yet it is diffuse and unfocused, more entertaining then educational. It is probably the least powerful of Baraka's agit-prop pieces.

Police and *Arm Yourself, or Harm Yourself,* however, are both blunt and powerful examples of street theatre. Both convey simple political lessons and have been acted in community streets. They realize the goals of Ed Bullins's influential program for street theatre: (1) to communicate to masses of black people not ordinarily drawn to the theatre; (2) to employ quick images and symbols that crystallize the crowd's sense of reality.[6] The characters of *Police* all announce themselves as morality-play figures: the traitorous Black Cop, the vicious White Cops, the struggling Black Man and Black Woman. The Black Cop is guilty of killing the Black Man while his Black Woman was hypnotized by a desire for the white world's "soft" luxury. Only when a Young Girl enters screaming for justice does the Black Woman see reality. This recognition is meant to be shared by the audience as the Young Girl runs through the crowd yelling: "Hey people, black white man killed my brother. Please help me!" [7] People then "leap out of [the] audience" and accuse the Black Cop. The players are then meant to take the crowd to a nearby police station "under pretense of play plot." Once there, everyone turns on the Black Cop and orders him to kill himself for his crime. He does so, and as the White Cops assemble around the corpse preparing to feast upon it, the crowd departs yelling comments such as, "Goodbye Savages" and "Let's get out of here and get our own stuff together."

The moral of *Arm Yourself, or Harm Yourself* is even clearer, though its enactment does not include the ritual involvement of the audience. The play opens with White Cops storming a black home and indiscriminately killing most of the inhabitants. Two brothers and a sister survive. The first brother complains of their helplessness while the second argues that so long as he is armed he can fight the devils, protect his family, and survive. The first brother asks why the police shot the sister's husband, eliciting this response from the second: "Why? Man you must be outta your head. Cause he's Black, that's why." [8] The argument between the two resumes and finally they begin to fight each other. As they scuffle they fail to heed the sister's warning of the cops' approach. All three are shot by police shouting racial insults. The second brother dies pronouncing the moral expressed in the play's title: "Shit . . . negro . . . you gon get us killed."

Like all good street theatre, *Police* and *Arm Yourself, or Harm Yourself* are too simple for critical interpretation. They present basic didactic themes comprehensible to large numbers of people, particularly young people. They are full of violent action and involve the audience either directly or by presenting figures thoroughly like them. Unlike the "guerrilla theatre" practiced mainly by white radicals, these plays do not seek to surprise or threaten their audience, and their plots are drawn from typical and recurring community problems rather than from particular historical events. In comparison to the guerrilla theatre, Baraka's agit-prop plays are at once simple and universal.

Baraka may well continue to write such pieces: they are easy and effective. Yet they occupy a limited place in his development as a dramatic artist and contribute little to his search for a form capable of embodying his vision. In agit-prop the conflicts are so coarsely one-dimensional, with the opposition of patently good and patently bad, that little dramatic interest can be generated. Moreover, we must remember that Baraka is primarily a visionary artist and that his natural voice as an artist is lyrical, not flatly rhetorical. Agit-prop is a valuable weapon, but so long as Baraka is a prophet of black liberation, he must produce richer art.

Madheart

Madheart is in great measure as simplistically doctrinaire as any of Baraka's agit-prop plays. Its basic theme—the emancipation of black male identity from sexual bonds imposed by black and white women—is presented in forthright and narrow terms. The black man, the play tells us, must destroy the white female 'demon' (represented here by a grotesquely masked Devil Lady) and create a new relationship with his black woman, who complements him by "submitting" to his essential authority. *Madheart* is, on one level, a self-explicated allegory of this thesis: it depicts Black Man, sometimes aided by his half-afroed/half-geled Black Woman, struggling to slay the Devil Lady and to overcome the slavish efforts of the black Mother and her white-loving daughter (Sister) to save the hated siren. This action is accompanied by Black Man and Black Woman's elementary explanations of the sexual and cultural confrontation that is being enacted. At the play's end, Devil Lady seems to be dead; nevertheless, Mother and Sister have become increasingly possessed by love for the horrible witch-devil, and thus Black Man and Black Woman, now happily reunited, dedicate themselves to the task of rehabilitating or, if necessary, vanquishing their lost kin.

At first sight this play certainly seems crude and un-artfully propagandistic. Yet beneath its obvious message seethes a cauldron of complex issues which find their focus in the blunt and unsophisticated conflict between the faction of Black Man and Black Woman, and that of Devil Lady and her court of neowhite ladies-in-waiting. Moreover, although the vehicle of *Madheart*'s surface theme is roughhewn allegory and ingenuous rhetoric, the play's events actually unfold by a subtle alternation of ritualistic and improvisational actions. What may appear to be merely a piece of agit-prop tour de force is, in fact, a crucial experimental step toward a profoundly effective theatre of collective black liberation.

The use of sexual confrontation as both metaphor and manifestation of broader cultural issues seems an inevitable outgrowth of Baraka's earlier plays. We have noticed that sexual encounter—particularly between black man and white woman—has lent a specific intensity to general racial antagonism in every play from *Dutchman* to the agit-prop works. Lula, who literally 'lulls' or seduces black male victims into her clutches,[9] and Grace, whose intimacy and sexual attraction threaten Walker far more than Easley's effete intellectuality, are clearly forerunners of the femme-fatale Devil Lady. The hysterical Old Woman of *The Baptism* ("strong from years of the American Matriarchy") is an ancestor of the tomish Mother and, by extension, of her daughter, Sister. The latter, in turn, is related to the slavish Women of *The Baptism* and to the cruel prostitute of *Experimental Death Unit #1.*

Homosexuality as a demonic perversion of creative love is featured in *The Toilet*, *The Baptism*, and in the mock-Eucharistic conclusion to *Police.* Clearly, Baraka views the weakening or corruption of black male sexuality as a fundamental aspect of Afro-American subjugation; and, as the restless energy of the desired black nation is a male force, the recovery of black manhood newly inspired by a rising nationalistic consciousness (the trust of the black woman)[10] is an indispensable first step toward Afro-American emancipation. Clay, Walker, Ray Foots, the young Boy of *The Baptism*, Lennie, the Young Victim of *Great Goodness of Life*, and Black Cop of *Police,* are all examples of nascent black manhood twisted, enfeebled, or destroyed. The process of emasculation has been depicted in painful detail (as in *Dutchman*, *The Baptism*, and *The Toilet*) or given as a fait accompli (as in *The Slave* and *Police*); yet in nearly every instance, the specific failure of the young black victim is simply the ultimate and tragic outcome of deformities in both black and white sexuality. And the ubiquitous unnaturalness of American sexual identity is represented, explicitly and implicitly, as both a product and a reproduction of the slave experience.

The dominant action of *Madheart*—Black Man's slaying of Devil Lady—suggests that sexual discord between the races can be viewed as an uncomplicated example of Manichaean good-versus-evil. Yet the misshaping of black sexuality, as Baraka understands it, takes many forms and occurs at several cultural levels. The contrast between Black Man and Devil Lady delineates one of the issue's most important aspects: the relation of black man to white woman and 'white sexuality' in general. Although Black Man declares his intention of killing off Devil Lady in the play's first scene, her opening lines hint that a deep ambivalence preceded Black Man's present determination:

> *DL.* You need pain. (*Coming out of shadows with neon torch, honky-tonk calliope music*) You need pain, ol' nigger devil, pure pain, to clarify your desire.
>
> [p. 69][11]

The "pain" Devil Lady refers to stems from the black man's attraction to the white female, an attraction suffused with guilt and made impure by hatred. Baraka has argued in several essays that the 'possession' of a white female, especially in sexual terms, has always seemed an extremely desirable achievement to black men. Defended by white men with intense and often vicious emotion, the white woman has become an idol, a mythically unspoiled virgin who, whatever her relation to the white male, is above all else not to be violated by black hands. The natural consequence of this protectiveness is that the many angers, frustrations, and desires produced in the black man by white society have been concentrated in his pursuit of the romanticized white female, the Holy Grail in the black man's quest for power and social status. By acquiring the white woman, the black man symbolically overcomes the white man's control by claiming that which white society has defined as most precious. It is an apparent victory over oppression, history, and natural obstacles.[12]

Yet the black man is simultaneously aware that such "victory" is actually mean deception; that beating the Man by taking his carefully guarded goddess is not so much symbolic liberation as a misguided search for denied fulfillment; that, as Clay learned so painfully, attempting to escape history and basic reality is a dangerous, if not fatal, pretension. Thus, the white woman remains essentially unattainable, and the chimera of possessing her only compounds the black man's agony. His bearing toward the white virgin is, as Devil Lady's Petrarchan image of "painful desire" indicates, a self-destructive passion of love-and-hate. Baraka, therefore, in an essay entitled "Black Woman," ironically describes all black men's affairs with the white temptress as "layin up with the oppressor's woe-man." [13]

Baraka, following Frantz Fanon's more inclusive analysis, believes that the black man's pure hatred for his oppressor is perverted into love-hate through the fascination which the ruled have for the rulers, a fascination based on the feeling that revolution cannot succeed. The black male's obsession with the white woman diverts his natural energies and desires, those which would cause him to assert his essential being against the purveyors of falsehood who create an idol of the lily-white *Ewig-Weibliche.* The devastating effects wrought upon the black man who accepts the empty hope of this lie have been seen in several of Baraka's earlier plays, particularly in the cases of Clay and Walker. They become victims precisely because they evade the truth until it is almost uselessly evident, and the revolutionary forces of history blot out their tardy perceptions. Walker in particular can teach us much about what motivates Black Man in *Madheart*: lured away from his roots by the intellectual and sexual prizes of an alien culture, Walker nearly becomes a victim of his own rebels when he attempts to reclaim the products of his sexual bond to white society—the two 'mulatto' girls.

Black Man, then, must be considered a Clay or Walker who has survived his lessons and seeks ultimate exorcism of the corrupting demon. As Charles D. Peavy has noted, the declaration of black manhood in Baraka's plays has previously been "at the expense of the white male."[14] Easley, Karolis, the Homosexual of *The Baptism*, the slobbering white cops of *Police*, Loco and Duff of *Experimental Death Unit #1*, and Jack Benny all possess some dominating passion which alienates them from the truth they cannot evade. They are even less capable than their black foes of grasping the meaning of change and revolt. They are usually either overtly or latently homosexual; all eschew physicality and, concomitantly, natural emotion and visceral expressiveness. At the same time, as representative masters of society, they delight in seeing the black male antagonist surrender his manhood as literally as possible.[15] Asexual, antiphysical, and unnatural, they recognize opposite traits as most threatening to their power.

Yet it is noteworthy that, for all this, the white man does not appear in *Madheart*. Baraka seems to be saying that the effete white male, who is the spiritual negative of Black Man, can only be confronted once the more complex relation to the white female has been resolved. Moreover, Black Man's major task is to see Devil Lady as a projection of his own horrible dreams, an embodiment of a sexual mythology developed during slavery, which conceals flesh-and-blood realities with fanciful lies. The masked Devil Lady is thus presented as hideously lewd and ugly, a complete inversion of the mythic white virgin. Echoing Lula's assertion that she is "nothing," Devil Lady proclaims haughtily, "I am dead and can never die" (p. 70). And Black Man's reply—"You will die only when I kill you"—confirms the fact that to kill this demon is to purge himself.

The presence of Sister and Mother serves as a brutal illustration of the complex effects produced by the prevailing sexual mythology and by mainstream culture in general. The suggestion that Devil Lady exists only by virtue of black people's dependence upon her is rendered theatrically explicit in the relationship between her and Sister. Dressed in "mod style clothes" and covered by a blond wig, Sister epitomizes the black woman who spurns black men ("If I have to have a niggerman, give me a faggot anyday"—p. 76) and her own natural sexual and emotional inclinations, and whose only goal in life is to become white through sheer emulation. In a moment of profound self-awareness, she speaks of the dilemma which Black Man is now overcoming but which plagues her more than ever: "I hate so. I am in love with my hatred. Yet I worship this beast on the floor" (p. 73). Sister's desire to be Devil Lady, subliminally expressed in her clothes and straight, artificial hair, bursts forth in a madness of total identification when Black Man pierces the masked devil with his stake:

> *Sis.* (*Screams as* Black Man *stabs the Devil Lady. Grabs her heart as if the man had struck her*) Oh God, you've killed me, nigger.
>
> *BM.* What? (*Wheels to look at her*)
>
> *BW.* You're killed if you are made in the dead thing's image, if the dead thing on the floor has your flesh, and your soul. If you are a cancerous growth. Sad thing.
>
> [pp. 77–78]

What had earlier been mere envy and heroine-worship soon erupts into quite literal *sympatheia,* as Sister runs about the stage looking for her lost "body . . . my beautiful self" (p. 85). Though mourned by Mother and even, in a brief instant of confusion, by Black Man, Sister is not the phantom she loves. Black Woman, Sister's true spiritual counterpart, explains that "she's not even dead. She just thinks she has to die because the white woman died" (p. 78).

If Sister represents the misguided black woman in search of white society's decadent luxury, Mother is obviously the symbol of the black matriarchy which presumably shares responsibility for the creation of monsters such as Sister. Fifty-ish, attired in a "business suit" and garish "red wig," Mother reveals in her permitted moment of self-revelation that she is "Out of the bowels of the sun. I slap around drunk up Lenox. Stumble down 125th into the poet who frowns at me, lost in my ways" (p. 73). Baraka, like many other writers of the Black Arts Movement, ridicules the image of the awesome black mother holding together her family without male help through pure toughness and unyielding hope. In contrast to matriarchal figures such as Ralph Ellison's Mary (*Invisible Man*) or the relatively recent Mama Younger of Lorraine Hansberry's *A Raisin in the Sun*, Baraka's Mother encourages her child not so much to endure as to succeed at all costs and, further, teaches that 'success' means substitution of white crudity and gaudy riches for black values. Having taught her daughter a religion of assimilation, she falls into drunken obliviousness as the world changes around her. Baraka, ever-suspicious of any ambition dependent upon the power structure, quite evidently considers the black matriarch a serious impediment to the natural aggressiveness and independence of the black male. She and Sister represent the most warped aspects of black womanhood, and Black Man laments their 'sickness' for all his brothers:

> This is the nightmare in all of our hearts. Our mothers and sisters groveling to white women, wanting to be white women, dead and hardly breathing on the floor. Look at our women dirtying themselves.
>
> [p. 76]

Black Woman stands for yet a third dimension of black womanhood: the emerging breed of proud sisters who must become an integral (if male-dominated!) part of the new black nation. Strong black women are notably absent from Baraka's earlier works; even predecessors of Mother and Sister are overshadowed by Devil Lady's ancestors. In the poetry of *Black Magic*, however, we begin to find pleas, tinged by masculine guilt, for a resurrection of Africanesque strength in black women:

> Beautiful black women, fail, they act. Stop them, raining.
> They are so beautiful, we want them with us. [. . .]
> We fail them and their lips
> stick out perpetually, at our weakness. [. . .] her
> sadness and age, and the trip, and the lost heat, and the grey cold
> buildings of our entrapment. Ladies. Women. We need you.
> [from "Beautiful Black Women . . ."]

Energy and heat, basic procreative principles, are as much qualities of the black woman as of the black male. The black man, suspicious from slavery-times of the black woman who associates with whites, must reclaim her by providing the strength and well-being which she has tried to siphon off from the white man for her family. She, in turn, must place her trust in the black man and inspire him "to *be* the new black consciousness, so that we must be defenders and developers of this new consciousness" ("Black Woman").[16] Black men and women are not, Baraka argues, equal; rather, "we will complement each other [. . .] you [black woman], who I call my house, because there is no house without a man and his wife, are the single element in the universe that perfectly completes my essence." To expand upon the notion of formulaic completion, the black nation, like a secret code, is meaningless unless its two discrete halves are brought into perceptible harmony.

Thus Black Woman, whose "soft natural hair" is "caught up in gele," is initially mere possibility, the potential black queen who can finally declare to Black Man:

> (*Her voice goes up to a high long sustained note.*) I am black black and am the most beautiful thing on the planet. Touch me if you dare. I am your soul.
>
> [p. 74]

First she must prove herself. She wages ideological warfare with her damned sisters, Mother and Sister, telling them that they love the

Devil Lady "because you have been taught to love her by background music of sentimental movies. A woman's mind must be stronger than that" (p. 74). When Black Man believes that by killing Devil Lady he may have indeed neglected and even murdered his black female kin, it is Black Woman who remains strong and lucid, bringing Black Man back to his senses:

> *BM.* This is horrible. Look at this.
> *BW.* It's what the devil's made. You know that.
> [p. 80]

In stark and probably deliberate contrast to Lula, who asks Clay to "pretend . . . that you are free of your own history," Black Woman pleads with Black Man to "stop pretending the world's a dream or a puzzle" (p. 81). Questioning his manhood, Black Woman challenges Black Man to renounce past errors and claim her at last: "I am the black woman. The one you need. You know this. Now you must discover a way to get me back, Black Man" (p. 81).

Thus begins a highly formal and foreshortened courting ritual between Black Man and Black Woman, leading from Black Man's violent, machismo-laden assertion of desire and her willing submission to his iron hand, through mutual exorcistic confession of past sins, to the crowning marriage ceremony:

> *BM.* Submit for love.
> *BW.* I . . . I submit. [. . .] (*They both begin to cry and then laugh, laugh, wildly at everything and themselves.*)
> *BM.* You are my woman, now, forever. Black Woman.
> [p. 82]

Together they may form the black nation based on selfless action, which finds its perfect synecdochic analogy in the selfless energies of a pure black sexuality.

Killing the Devil Lady—the simple gesture from which everything else in *Madheart* flows—has allowed for this crucial development toward a complete black communality. We can now properly evaluate the meaning of this action on a broader level of significance. Black Man and Black Woman (who asks her husband to "fill me with your seed" at the conclusion to the "marriage ceremony") are finally prepared to be creative in the fullest sense. At every stage of the play, Devil Lady is portrayed as a witch-goddess of false creation. Sister declares that Devil Lady is "the womb [. . .] the possibility of all creation" (p. 72), but her white goddess is variously described as "a stone pagan," as a diseased creature whose sexuality exists as pure egocentricity and whose womb yields only "cold," and as the mistress of the Western "dark cold cave" which produces only "illusion [. . .] Hatred and Death." Devil Lady herself says that "I am dead. And all my life is me" (p. 73) and claims that from her "dead" womb come "entire civilizations." Hence the attack on her immediately becomes one against the whole of Western culture:

> *BM.* Die, you bitch, and drag your [. . .] newspapers poison gases congolene brain stragglers devising ways to deal death to their people, your smiles, your logic, your brain, your intellectual death . . .
>
> [pp. 83–84]

Christianity is consistently ridiculed by image (a cardboard picture of Christ is pasted on Devil Lady's vagina), symbolic action (Mother and Sister often form a parody of Madonna and Child),[17] irony (as Devil Lady dies, Mother supplicates her cultural patron-saints, Tony Bennett, Beethoven, and Peter Gunn, to "deliver us [. . .] oh please deliver us"—p. 83), and direct statement. Purgation of Devil Lady, then, is clearly intended to be the expulsion of the stifling, arid, and barren value-structure of mainstream Western 'civilization,' which allows for the rise of a fecund people.

In many ways, the conflict between Black Man and Devil Lady recapitulates that involving Clay and Lula, and particularly those aspects which erupted with Clay's speech. For Devil Lady, above all, is the queen of artifice, lies, and the unnatural; masked and luridly painted, she concretely embodies Baraka's idea that "the white man doesn't have time for reality, the white woman uses her leisure to cover it up." [18] She is the quintessential *artifact* of the Western aesthetic, and her rigid movements contrast with the fluid motion of Black Man's lethal blows.[19] While, as Peavy insists,

Black Man's wooden stake is the traditional weapon for killing blood-sucking vampires such as Devil Lady, the death-giving blow plunged through her (mad) heart is also a trenchant reversal of Lula's knife-thrust into Clay, a quasi-sexual penetration that extinguishes her sexual powers and, after help from the ever-obliging Black Woman, his own lust.

According to the scheme of Baraka's essay, "Black Woman," the vanquishing of Devil Lady (the "devil collecting and using our energies to pervert the world") should be an affair producing "no pause, no rhetoric, only action, which is divine." [20] Yet when we consider *Madheart* as a dramatic structure, we find that it is anything but a fluid or pure action. The play presents a series of rituals, ceremonies, and symbolic tableaux which, in the manner of Genêt's *The Maids*, are often interrupted and, as in *The Blacks*, are continually involved in a dialectic of dissolution and reformation. The formless energy of the black nation, embodied in the actions of Black Man and Black Woman, seeks out organization into forms of ritual and power only to be released again into the ever-changing reality of historical process. While *Madheart*'s considerable theatrical impact derives from this tension between stasis and violent change, the play also raises serious questions concerning this particular dramaturgy's efficacy as the vehicle for Baraka's fundamental vision.

The opening scene immediately plunges us into the primordial flux of energy out of which the play's ceremonial and ritual forms are born. Black Man and Devil Lady engage in a highly stylized debate about pain and desire, good and evil, which leads into the first ritual: Black Man prepares to strike Devil Lady and, after a "fanfare of drums, [. . .] the action freezes" and the actors become "fixed" (p. 70). Here, the rite of purgation is arrested into an exemplary tableau, establishing this action as a major icon of the play. Soon, after a musical interlude that evokes present sufferings by progressing from "nasty blues" to screams and a "falsetto howl," the "action continues [and] the actors from the freeze go to life, but never complete the initial action" (p. 70).

The ritual is thus momentarily slowed to a Zenoesque speed

promising no conclusion; and when Black Man finally succeeds in driving his stake through Devil Lady's body, he becomes so obsessed with his conquest that the three black women enter unnoticed. Mother suddenly cries: "No. Madman. Stop!" thereby disrupting complete execution; in contrast, Black Woman wonders if "Perhaps we are intruding" (p. 72). By now the opening ceremony has dissolved and the focus has shifted to antagonisms that arise among the black women and between Black Man and Devil Lady. Within moments the action splits into two contrasting ritual forms: on one hand, Mother and Sister are frozen into an "aggravated pantomimed silence" (p. 74) and, on the other hand, Black Man and Black Woman begin their formal courtship with first touches and an awakening to each other's sensuality. Their mutual wooing is interrupted first by Devil Lady's screams and then by the momentary unfreezing of Mother and Sister's dumb-show. As Devil Lady's power ebbs, so does Mother and Sister's energy, and they soon revert to a silent and pantomimic condition. Black Man delivers a highly didactic explanation of this image, thus completing the play's series of introductory rites and symbols.

Once Black Man has finished his oration, the action again breaks into several moments of free-form dialogue, simultaneously rhetorical and improvisational in nature. Devil Lady is now dead and Mother and Sister mourn her in their sickness. Following Black Woman's emphatic denunciations of the mad women and unflinching praise for Black Man's action, the young couple enters upon the final stages of courting ritual, in which the growth of their love and of their black consciousnesses are coincident. This courtship, as self-consciously patterned as that of any medieval romance and conducted in much the same manner, culminates in the extremely stylized marriage ceremony, in which Black Woman "submits for love."

As they exchange mutual vows, the ritual again gives way to the improvisational action of contemporary conflict, with the newly united defenders of black sovereignty attempting to deal with the growing hysteria of their kin. Black Man assails Devil Lady rhetorically one last time and then throws her "into the pit of deadchange" (p. 84). The play draws to an end as Mother and

Sister grovel after Devil Lady's corpse, Black Man and Black Woman endeavoring vainly to dissuade them. The last scene depicts Black Man and Black Woman standing over the women, vowing to "save them or kill them" (p. 87).

The dialectic between ritual and 'improvisational' moments creates the play's particular rhythm and allows several plot-lines to coexist and to work toward a general harmony. At the ritual moments the plot-lines are gathered together; the issues are held in suspension, and the black audience is reminded of the social values in which they all have some sort of stake. The rituals and symbolic freezes reflect and contrast with each other, gradually working out the general theme of liberated black sexuality. The improvisational scenes, in turn, bear a significant and developing relationship to the rituals. By introducing harsh facts of social and historical dimensions, they throw doubt upon the efficacy of Black Man's "black magic"; yet even the most cutting and disturbing ironies do not repudiate the emotions the rituals celebrate, or reject the purposes that inform them.

Baraka subtitled *Madheart* "A Morality Play," and it is true that the play's allegory, pageantry, and Every-Black-Man quality suggest that it bears resemblance to the medieval form. Moreover, the tension between ironic realism and ritual is reminiscent of the morality play's oscillation between the sublime and the farcical, the transcendent and the tragic, the real and the illusionistic. Certainly Baraka's black aesthetic, which values change and process ("*Voices:* 'We move' "—p. 71) over fixity and the artifact ("the pit of deadchange"), is likely to find an appropriate form in a drama that juxtaposes types of action (relative improvisation/ceremony) embodying such a contrast. In *Madheart*, however, neither the ritualistic nor the improvisational scenes work toward a clarification of Baraka's aesthetic premise; and, further, the methods Baraka employs to reveal the conflict between the Western subjugation to 'illusion' and the Afro-American devotion to the 'real' are not completely successful.

To best consider the dramaturgical dilemmas which *Madheart*'s "morality play" rhythm creates, we must remind ourselves that the ultimate mission of Baraka's art is to project an image of black liberation that will elicit from his audience avid response and even action. *Madheart* calls special attention to this purpose at three striking moments: first, Black Man closes his speech about the fallen Mother and Sister with this sentiment: "Let the audience think about themselves, and about their lives when they leave this happening" (p. 76); second, shocked by Mother and Sister's behavior, Black Man makes a more direct statement to the particular audience *Madheart* was written for: "All this silly rapping and screaming on the floor. I should turn them over to the Black Arts and get their heads relined" (p. 77); [21] and third, Black Man concludes the play by inviting "All of us, black people" to join the struggle to save those like Mother and Sister (p. 87). These addresses to the audience, however cumbersome and unnatural, obviously reveal Baraka's desire to integrate the black spectator and the 'moral' spectacle being presented. But why are these pleas so unwieldy—indeed, why does the attempt to integrate actors and audience fail?

We may gain a clue toward solving this problem by reconsidering what might be the effects of borrowing elements from the quasi-ritualistic theatre of Genêt. We see Baraka's debt to Genêt in several facets of *Madheart*. Devil Lady is very similar to the White Queen of *The Blacks*, who says "I am white, it's milk that symbolizes me, the lily . . . snow," and who is finally vanquished by the Black Queen. Also, the play's form of interrupted ceremony, beginning with Mother and Sister's disruption of Devil Lady's execution, may well be patterned after that of *The Maids*, in which the dramatization of the maids' hatred for the Madame is interrupted by the arrival of the real Madame. And, more generally, the use of masks and of a type of allegory which attempts "to contrive that the characters on the stage are only metaphors of what they . . . represent" (to borrow Genêt's description of his own intentions) connects Baraka's drama to Genêt's Artaudian theatre of doubles, which seeks to link the real and fictitious worlds by simultaneously disguising and revealing reality.

The difficulties engendered by such links to Genêt's drama should have been suggested in our discussion of *Great Goodness of Life*. Genêt's art is forged from paradox and inner conflict. Seeking nothingness, he is pressed into a quest for purity; devoted to reality, he cannot escape from illusion. Thus, in the experience of his plays, what at one moment claims to be ritual ceremony is seen at another as false, sham, pretense. The principal danger of this as it inheres in Baraka's art is that the tangible power of one symbolic action (for example, the marriage ceremony) is set against the ironic hollowness of another (for example, Mother's pathetic "sad dirge" for Sister—p. 80), thereby depicting life as a series of perpetually competing masquerades which finally negate each other and obfuscate altogether the value of ritual activity.

Genêt wishes to plunge through appearances into reality; for him, this means the negation of roles. Baraka also champions the 'real' over the artificial; yet, as the figures of Black Man and Black Woman are intended to illustrate, the black nation functions in great part by virtue of a proper understanding of roles. Such understanding, in fact, is itself the 'reality' Baraka perceives. The use of Genêt in *Madheart* shows that Baraka is, at this stage of his career, still attached to a tradition that possesses no mechanism for reconciling, on one hand, anarchy and freedom and, on the other, organization and order.

The underlying struggle in *Madheart* is one between death and life, between an order in which values exist only in fantasy and perverted ceremony and the attempt to create a new order in which these values penetrate life itself, making it unnecessary to escape into fantasy because living is authentic at last. The makings of a drama which can, metaphorically, resolve this struggle *are* present in *Madheart*. For, as a variety of cultural theorists from Leo Frobenius to Johan Huizinga have argued, one major starting-point of social institutions and communal order is the ritualistic acting-out of a people's rudimentary perceptions about nature, birth, death, evolution (history), etc. The unsophisticated impulse toward sacred ceremony exhibited in Baraka's play betrays his realization that the religious and communal values of the rising black nation can find proper expression in some form of ritual. At the same time, the insistence on prolonged moments of improvisational action bears witness to two enormously important points: that Baraka is aware that ritual celebration requires a strong element of "play" and, more crucial still, that improvisation is for Afro-Americans the primary mode of creation and expression. Clearly, Genêt's amalgam of ritual and improvisation is not a model useful to Baraka, for it seeks a negation of social forms leading to *l'impossible nullité* of pure gesture. Rather, what *Madheart* shows Baraka striving for is a synthesis of ritual and improvisation in which the communality and creativity of black people are mutually affirmed.

Madheart itself, with its awkward blend of allegory and straightforward political rhetoric, remains a complex sermon on black sexuality. Its purpose, as with all propaganda, is to shape the ethos of its audience. While some question must be raised about *Madheart*'s ability to communicate to the mass of black people,[22] a more serious problem posed by the play pertains to Baraka's notions of history and revolution. Devil Lady's death suggests that the tragically cyclical quality of *Dutchman*'s murderous ritual has been, so to speak, interrupted by the Black Man's ever-growing self-awareness. History (as Black Woman urges—as if in response to Lula) is no longer ignored; for if, as Baraka argues in "American Sexual Reference: Black Male," the black man thought he "transcended social history" by associating with the white woman, his renunciation of such desire plunges him back into history's dizzying flood.

The harshness of the Afro-American's history is not transcended during *Madheart*. Indeed, the play has its own deadly circularity, ending more or less as it began: Black Man is attacking (black) women quasi-sexually (here, a firehose replaces the stake), and, though he and Black Woman are now united, the struggle they face appears as difficult as ever. Although *Madheart* moves Baraka closer to a theatre which "shows how we triumphed" by exorcising a major demon within the black consciousness, the drama of purgation has yet to be supplanted by a drama of celebration.

A Black Mass

In several of the agit-prop plays and in parts of *Madheart*, Baraka broadens the attack upon white society begun in *Dutchman* and

The Slave. Though the ideas expressed in the early plays remain the core of Baraka's thought, they are now being expressed in more abstract and mythic terms. Of Baraka's plays to date, *A Black Mass,* though actually written just before *Madheart,* is most infused with mythic doctrine. And of the experimental plays preceding *Slave Ship,* it comes closest to creating a dramatic artifice capable of communicating a universal vision of the black experience.

The myth dramatized in *A Black Mass* is one found in much of Baraka's writing that dates from his conversion to the Nation of Islam. This is the Muslim myth of Yakub or Jacoub, one of the central *topoi* in Baraka's nationalist myth of return to primordial black holiness and power. The Jacoub story was often told by Elijah Muhammad in the Black Muslim paper *Muhammad Speaks.* Here is one of Elijah's versions:

> Today, we live at the end of the world of people who have ruled the black man and his various colors between black and white for the 6,000 years. The world of disbelievers and hypocrites know these are the days and the end of the rule of the white man. I am referring to the rule of the people mentioned by Jesus, Allah, and the Holy Qur-an as being a people who were created (grafted) so that they might be tried at ruling the righteous for the past 6,000 years. Their first 2,000 years were spent in the caves and hillsides of Europe (the only appointed continent of Allah for that people). They suffered divine chastisement for the first 2,000 years on this continent for their trouble-making and for causing war and bloodshed among the original black people, who had not suffered from wars, exploitation and enslavement before the creation (grafting) of this people by their father, Yakub.[23]

A Black Mass begins in the time of peace among the original black races. They are flying through "black endless space" at infinite speeds, creating the "music of eternal concentration and wisdom," celebrating "the beauties and strength of our blackness, of our black arts."[24] Three black magicians, Nasafi, Tanzil, and Jacoub, are practicing their black arts in a room covered with Swahili and Arabic signs, and colored blue and red-violet by glowing potions. Nasafi and Tanzil are humming and keeping time to the music as they work leisurely at their tasks. They are preparing a black mass in which all participants "will dance mad rhythms of the eternal universe until time is a weak thing [. . .] until time, that white madness, disappears. Until we have destroyed it and the animals who bring it into the world."

Decay, transition, and the vicissitudes of historical flux have apparently begun to threaten their world; however, the mock-Eucharistic sacraments of the black mass (symbolized by the brewing "potion") seem potent enough to thwart the demons easily. The greatest enemy grows from within the black nation. For as Nasafi and Tanzil complacently prepare the black mass, Jacoub stands apart, deeply intent upon another project. He is so absorbed in his experiment that he notices neither the music nor the other magicians. Nasafi speaks of Jacoub's work and its dangers:

> You deal in a strange logic, brother Jacoub. You spoke once of time and we forgot about it. Now there are animals who hiss time madness in the air, and into our lives. I had forgotten (*Turns to Tanzil*) but now I'm sure it was you, Jacoub.
>
> [p. 23]

The play, then, takes place in a time of crucial transition. We are not watching the very first black gods but their descendants, magicians who have inherited strengths and myths which they have begun to lose. Thus the characters, in their dual quality of godliness and fallibility, are symbolically identified with the black audience. "Remember the old myths, brother," Nasafi tells Jacoub, "the forbidden fruit of madness." The warning, as the rest of the play proves, is equally for present black visionaries; *A Black Mass* is one of the sacred myths.

Jacoub and the two magicians discuss the nature of his "creation." Jacoub is Faustian; his sensibility is much akin to the Renaissance "overreacher's," which Baraka has elsewhere described as the West's "madness." Jacoub is pursuing all the evils that oppose the sacred humanism of the black nation: "creation for its own end"; "knowledge beyond the human mind"; "compassionless abstractions." What he seeks to create is a being in love with time, what he calls "a neutral being who will not respond to the world of humanity." Nasafi is shocked: "Neutral being. What madness is this? How can a being be neutral?" A band of women, in violation of sacred law, burst into the sanctuary. They are terrified because Jacoub's experiments are so unnatural that they have disturbed the balance of "the elements": "The sky is not the sky. The earth trembles beneath our feet. The sea shudders and rages, and throws strange creatures on the land."

All nature, wisdom, law, and sacredness stand against Jacoub's act, yet he persists. Finally the moment of his creation arrives:

> *Jacoub.* Now is the time of creation. I enter one solution in the other. (*Screaming*) The blood flows in my head and fingers. The world is expanding. I create the new substance of life. Aiiiiieeee. (*Bright explosion flashes and a siren-like laughter blasting. . . . The laboratory is intense red, then hot violent white. The sirens go up to ear-breaking pitch. The women scream.*)
>
> [p. 29]

Here Baraka parodies in Jacoub the "mad scientist" of Romantic and post-Romantic "horror" stories, at once linking Jacoub to a dark aspect of the culture to which the black magician is giving birth and creating an effective and symbolically complementary theatrical spectacle. Jacoub's beast is born:

> (*The figure is absolutely cold white with red lizard-devil mask which covers the whole head, and ends up as a lizard spine cape. The figure screams, leaping and slobberlaughing.*)
>
> [p. 30]

When the beast appears, the "soft peaceful music" becomes "screaming . . . Music of shattering dimension." Jacoub pridefully displays his creature, but the others are horrified. The beast has no "soulheat," "no regard for human life"; it can only slobber about, screaming "White! White! Me! White!" Tanzil cries "Jacoub . . . you have turned loose absolute evil"; Jacoub protests, "How can there be evil in creation, brother?" but Nasafi explains that "this thing is the soulless distortion of humanity." Their argument finally ceases when the beast proves Tanzil and Nasafi correct through its actions. Like other of Baraka's demons, the beast possesses brutish sexual lust. It attacks one of the women; she soon loses her color and is transformed into a slobbering, white, beastly mate. The language of the black mass, "Izm-el-Azam," is impotent now that the monster has been physically realized. Jacoub finally sees that his creation will bring misery and madness, and he asks Nasafi to explain his error:

> Jacoub, your error . . . the substitution of thought for feeling. A heart full of numbers and cold formulae. A curiosity for anti-life, for the yawning voids and gaps in humanity we feel sometimes when we grow silent in each other's presence, sensing the infinite millions of miles in the universe, as finite as it is.
>
> [p. 34]

Jacoub still wishes to try to educate the beast, but again Tanzil explains: "Jacoub. You cannot teach a beast. A blankness in humanity. And we cannot kill. We must set these things loose in the cold north. Where they may find a life, in the inhuman cold" (p. 36). In keeping with the basic Black Muslim myth of Yakub, the beast is banished to the northern caves.

Though the physical monster is sent away, the most horrible evil remains, a kind of wildly devouring Blatant Beast: "this thing is not ourselves. But the hatred of ourselves." Baraka reworks the myth to indicate that the ultimate evil is assimilation of the beast within the black self, and the Jihad can begin only with this recognition. The black women attempt to fight the monster with the old soft songs but, in their terror, they soon shriek their music. The black mass which Nasafi and Tanzil were preparing in the beginning has never taken place. As the beast slobbers amidst the audience, a narrator's voice closes the play with a plea for black people to fight for a renewal of the old strengths and the old myths, to perform finally the long-awaited black mass themselves:

> And so Brothers and Sisters, these beasts are still loose in the world. Still they spit their hideous cries. Let us find them and slay them. Let us lock them in their caves. Let us declare the Holy War. The Jihad. Or we cannot deserve to live. Izm-el-Azam. Izm-el-Azam.
>
> [p. 39]

A Black Mass is an extremely effective dramatic realization of the Black Muslim Fall myth. Baraka uses his considerable abilities of theatricality to create a spectacle in which speech, character, and action are unified toward one purpose. The Jacoub myth offers great opportunity for the use of visual effects, and Baraka exploits them accurately and tastefully; the visual poetry is subsumed in the poetry of a nation's loss of truth and power and in the hope for a cyclical return accomplished by the contemporary black nation (the audience). Perhaps most important is Baraka's suggestion that history can result from ignoring the imperatives of mythology and that, in turn, history is itself a mythological construct. The relation between myth and history and their mutual necessities becomes a major element in *Slave Ship*.

A Black Mass, however, does not quite succeed in integrating form and vision. Specifically, it does not successfully unify its mythic plot and ritual form. In ritual, meaning is expressed by the repetition of symbolic actions. The actors have a sense of awe, of mysterious participation rather than of conceptual communication. In *A Black Mass* ritual occurs on the *conceptual* level; the constant reiteration of the myth's abstract doctrines gives the play its entire substance. Though there is much physical action (the beast's creation and ravings), this does not also take the form of ritual. Indeed, the physical action, while dramatizing the consequences of ignoring sacred myth, is violence against the black characters and inhibits the enactment of their own ritual, the black mass. Furthermore, *A Black Mass* involves the audience only suddenly and only at the end. This is a consequence of the basic obscurity of the myth Baraka has chosen; the audience must learn the myth before it can learn its lessons.

Even with these qualifications, *A Black Mass* is a formidable accomplishment. The play has been performed with great success in the past decade and is one of Baraka's most popular works. Yet, with the writing of *Slave Ship*, Baraka relegated *A Black Mass* to the basic role shared by all the works studied in this chapter: preparation for a masterpiece.

7 *Slave Ship:* Vision Meets Form

When Baraka called for an "anti-Western" theatre in his post-1965 essays, he spoke as both Black Power Nationalist and black visionary artist. The dramatic event he envisaged was therefore one in which black people could experience the growth toward communal identity and solidarity during the theatrical happening itself. In the preceding chapter, we studied principal examples of Baraka's plays written since this project was avowed. We discerned in them the common theatrical problem of communicating to an audience whose members are to be integrated into a new wholeness, of unleashing an emotional response in a community which has been treated and has seen itself as an object in a brutally impersonal system for such a long time as to have been deadened to such an appeal. These plays had only limited success in achieving this goal. But in Baraka's latest major drama, *Slave Ship*, the objectives of the "revolutionary theatre" are fully realized.

Slave Ship has no definite plot. There is very little use of discursive speech and almost no dialogue. Every theatrical device is directed toward creating an "atmosphere of feeling," [1] one appropriate to a slave ship, the attendant horrors of the Middle Passage, and the grim consequences that comprise the history of the Afro-American experience. Baraka transforms the entire theatre into the slave ship whose black passengers' historical journey is from first enslavement to contemporary revolution, and whose mythical journey is from African civilization through enslavement to spiritual reascendancy. With the abandonment of traditional plot, Baraka moves us along these historical and mythical paths by a series of tableaux and symbolic actions. It should be clear from this brief description of *Slave Ship* that any discussion of the play is immediately an interpretation. Accordingly, I shall proceed to analyze its essential motives in the hope that the simple level of action will gradually unfold.

History and Community: The Vision

Baraka calls *Slave Ship* "a historical pageant." From this alone it is clear that the play is a radical departure from the norm of Afro-American theatre which, as Harold Cruse has lamented, tends to be ahistorical.[2] Baraka's abilities as a playwright, so frequently used to mount attacks upon his "grey" brethren (*Dutchman, The Slave*) and to expose the torments of heroes trapped by history (Clay, Walker), are directed in *Slave Ship* toward the formation of a nationalist historical consciousness. The Afro-American historical experience appealed to in *Slave Ship* is the product of event, memory, and communal emotion. Baraka perceives the importance of this history not so much in its "facts" as in their moral significance. For Baraka, *slavery* is the key to interpretation of Afro-American history: it is both the central, finite epoch and the general, persistent condition of Afro-American life. Appropriately, slavery is also, dramatically speaking, the condition of the audience caught with the actors inside the hold of the slave ship. The audience's consequent alienation is a perfect analogy to that of the black slave, the latter's struggle for communal identity becoming ultimately the entire theatre's concern. This struggle, which takes place in the Afro-American psyche as it does in history, accompanies the succession of "images"[3] that identify the origin, evolution, and eventual transcendence of the slave condition.

The glory of the primeval African community is the first image. The African sensibility is depicted as quintessentially religious. We witness a complex fertility rite involving the dances of warriors, farmers, and priests; chants and praises to harvest and protective gods; the whirling dance of the masked fertility goddess; and the culminating expression of social order through a hierarchical procession leading from youngest child to head priest. The ritual is nearly complete when the white slave-trader enters, destroys the tribal harmony, and rounds up his black cargo for the Americas. The black prisoners, proud and once powerful, are dragged from their homeland calling vainly upon their gods and fighting to maintain contact with mates, children, kindred.

In the second image, the slaves are brought aboard one by one. Chains rattle, sea-smell mixes with that of excrement, women moan. Soon suffering begins to overwhelm African strength. A man curses the highest of gods, the creator *orisha* Obatala: "Where you be? Where you now, Black God?" The tribal leader, once holiest of holy high priests, attacks a black girl. Unity dissolves as old people call on God, the young for war; others are merely confused, hurt, and fearful. Worst of all, "families [are] separated for the first time." The community is fractured into an anarchy of individual wills; their isolated cries, rapes, songs, and moans define a moving, tortured existence. Whereas Baraka's earlier plays were characterized by long, illuminating orations, in *Slave Ship* he emphasizes in every way *concrete* aspects of pain, the heavy reality of chains, the screams and smells of degradation. There is horror but there is also life, and we feel it all. The agonized cry—signaling both suffering and survival—echoes in the hold while the white man howls laughter at the condition of the black people.

The third image opens to us the complexity of black life in America. The survivors of Middle Passage are herded onto land. The auction block severs man from wife, mother from child. As in the slave narrative tradition (from which Baraka draws many specific physical details in *Slave Ship*), the break-up of the family is accompanied by the emergence of cultural conflict and debasement. The latter state is portrayed by the archetypical "house-nigger," the grinning assimilationist who predicates his life upon white recognition. The epitome of Baraka's "slave" figures, he dances about the auction block for his master's pleasure and approval:

> Yassa, boss, yassa massa Tim, yassa, boss I'se happy as a brand new monkey, yassa boss, yassa, massa Tim, Yass, massa Booboo, i'se so happy, i'se so happy i jus don't know what to do. Yass, massa, boss, you'se so han'some and good and youse hip, too [. . .] (*Lights flash on slave doing* [*a*] *dance for the boss; when he finishes he bows and scratches*).
>
> [p. 68]

Despite disruption of the community, the African sensibility remains in most others: the tribal rhythms, the pride, the unfetterable urge for freedom. Reverend Turner prepares plantation slaves for rebellion. Some are afraid, but the leader is resolute:

Slave 1. Reverend Turner, sir, what gon' do when the massa come?
Slave 2. Cut his Godless throat.

[p. 69]

Yet the master's Tom betrays the conspiracy for a pork chop and, as the white man laughs in triumph, the others are crushed. The white man seems all-powerful.

The next images deepen the complexity of the African endurance in America. The Tom becomes a modern version of the house-nigger, the comically 'proper' Reverend who preaches a self-negating gibberish devoid of Africanisms, absent of meaning. African chants—"Moshake! Moshake! Moshake! . . . beeba . . . beeba"—are intoned against the preacher's tomming—"We Knee-grows are ready to integrate." African names—Olabumi, Dademi, Aikyele—mingle with slave names—John, Luke, Sarah. The prayer to Obatala, the African God, dies into cries for "Jesus Lord." African rhythms are beaten while spirituals rise up. Historical degradation is overshadowed by spiritual transference; African sensibility fuses itself into Afro-American culture. The call for war, for revolt, comes from the old African warrior with remembered religious invocations: "Beasts. Beasts. Ogun. Give me spear and iron. Let me kill."

The African power, always present and merely molded in the alien land for survival purposes, builds up until the liberating revolt can take place. This is the final image. The chant swells as in tribal ritual:

Rise, Rise, Rise
Cut these ties, Black Man Rise
We gon' be the thing we are . . .
(Now all sing "When We Gonna Rise")
When we gonna rise/up
When we gonna rise/up

When we gonna rise/up
When we gonna rise . . .

[p. 72]

The preacher and the white man (now Uncle Sam) first ignore the rising black anger, then begin to lose confidence. The group converges upon the preacher and kills him. The white Voice's laugh, so powerful throughout the play, as in *Great Goodness of Life*, "gets stuck in his throat." His dying protest—"You want to look like me. You love me. You want me. Please. I'm good"—indicates that the reemerging Africans are killing off the insidious myths by which the oppressor controlled the oppressed.

The revolt has really been immanent throughout, from the first crossing of the gangplank to Reverend Turner's rebellion to final victory. The true victims, symbolized by the heads of the preacher-Tom and Uncle Sam, were always just waiting to be killed. At every stage of his evocation of Afro-American history, Baraka insists upon the survival of aboriginal African communalism in the black slave population. Following the black nationalist thesis of *Blues People*, he shows this survival to be a function of collective separation from the white mainstream. Thus Baraka's energetic revaluation of history does more than prophesy liberation; it teaches the audience that no complete dissolution of the black will has resulted from the inherited burdens of slavery.

Afro-American identity, then, is a function of collective impulses. From African nation practicing holy ritual to the liberating group descending en masse on the two lonely enemies, the entelechy of the black spirit is communality. Mutual concern and reverence for familial forces are the lifeblood of the black nation. A major emblem of the play might be the mother and child, murdered in the village, dying in the slave ship, separated on the auction block, but united (with the male leader) at the end. This communal power of the Afro-American sensibility is sharply contrasted with the oppressive power's individuated sense of self; the latter condition is symbolized by the single actor playing each successive white man from slave-trader to Uncle Sam.

The condition of slavery, which Baraka has chosen as the

metaphor for the Afro-American historical process, is metamorphosed at the end into a celebration of liberation with the audience participating. The actors get the audience to come to the ship's center and dance to the jazz that has continued from the final death-acts. Once everyone is involved in the general festivity, the heads of the preacher and the white man are thrown amidst them. What had appeared to be didactic (if existentialized) historical drama is swiftly transmuted into an integral ritual of triumph involving the entire theatre collective. In the flow of images that comprise *Slave Ship*'s "historical pageant," Baraka has left out one crucial event: Emancipation. By omitting this favorite story of textbook historians, the play tells the Afro-American spectators they are still slaves. As Stefan Brecht put it in his astute review of *Slave Ship*, "by having the slave ship be the stage, it tells [them they are] still on that boat."[4] The scene de-Americanizes the black spectators and returns them to their African roots.

Thus it might be quite helpful to think of the final communal dance in terms of African ritual. When the African dancer puts on his mask, he is divesting himself of his own identity and assuming instead the identity of the spirit for which the mask was created. The demon lives in the mask and, through it, lays a spell on all assembled, sweeps them along, fascinates them even to the point of hypnosis. Such is the nature of *Slave Ship*'s final rite, for the entire assembled black community dons the mask of its ancient spirit and comes to full life as a potent, physical manifestation of the forgotten, but historically nourished, national power. In *Slave Ship*, the black nation promptly transforms itself into history, for the imitation of suffering has conferred on it a collective past and assigned it a triumphant future.

Music and Dance: The Form

In the mid-1960s, strong criticism of the Afro-American playwright's failure to make any progress toward realizing the demands of the new, music-oriented aesthetic began to emerge from various black theorists. It was pointed out that the native Afro-American theatrical form is really not a typically European dramatic form but a musical one that has its roots in such expressions as the minstrel show. Thus Harold Cruse asserted that black originality in nonmusical modes would come when "the blacks in America attempt to reclaim their musical tradition in terms of pantomime, music, movement, dance, in a theatrical form, which is more natural to them because for many years the Negro's chief form in the theatre was a musical form."[5] *Slave Ship* is the most successful dramatic work to emerge from the Black Arts Movement precisely because it "reclaims" and utilizes the musical base of the Afro-American genius. Baraka galvanizes a communal response to his vision by calling upon collective creation and participation in the play's musical life. However, before we can fully appreciate the ways in which music services thought (dramatic and conceptual) in *Slave Ship*, we must first briefly consider music's role in Baraka's earlier poetry and drama.

As a poet, Baraka has seen music as an integral part of the black tradition. As we saw in chapter 4, his verse evolves from the songless deprivation of *Preface to a Twenty Volume Suicide Note* to the transcendent lyricism (both subject and style) of *In Our Terribleness*. Baraka uses musical metaphors in his poetry in several complementary ways. Music is the energy of the black spirit and the bedrock of black strength. In the mythic return to holiness, this musical energy manifests liberty, services prophecy, and signals immanent ascendance:

> Our strength is in the drums,
> the sinuous horns, blow forever beautiful princes, touch
> the spellflash of everything, all life, and the swift go on
> go off and speed. Blow forever, like the animals plants and
> sun. Forever in our universe there is beauty and light, we come
> back to it now.
>
> [from "Distant Hearts"]

Music aids the transformation of reality but it is at the same time the affirmation of this process. Thus Baraka speaks of "the possibilities of music" ("Leadbelly Gives an Autograph") but also, as his concerns move from personal dilemmas to communal issues, of music's confirmation of being itself (see, for example, "Planetary

Exchange"). The pulse of black rhythms (not just musical, but those expressing The Life's total style) cements the multiple aspects of the black soul, communicates a lyric lightness with heavy Dionysian intuitions; rhythm—tom-tom, jazz, field hollers, street shouts, the horns of Armstrong, Trane, and the mythical Probe—represents the temporality of black existence while carrying messages from beyond. When Baraka as black poet prophesies to his brothers a better future, he portrays deliverance as

> the melody, and the rhythm
> of
> the dancing
> shit
> itself.
>
> [from "For All Matter"]

Energy, prophecy, judgment, affirmation, the naked thing itself—black music is for Baraka all of these at once. It is the spark of being and of needing-to-be; it makes the "total jazzman" and he makes it.

In his drama Baraka has constantly used music. In *Jello*, Rochester dances soul-steps while robbing Bennie. In *A Recent Killing*, dances and songs help fill empty dramatic spaces and serve as entertainment. In *Home on the Range*, music becomes a metaphor for judgment and apocalypse in the wild "nigger" party. The most interesting use of music before *Slave Ship* is in *Dutchman*, where Lula's dance, Clay's discussion of the blues and Charlie Parker, and the Negro conductor's final soft-shoe are crucial theatrical and thematic elements of the play.

It is with *Slave Ship*, however, that Baraka elevates music to the dual position of central metaphor and primary theatrical vehicle. While this total unification of drama with music was prepared for in the visions of Baraka's poetry and in the experiments of his plays, the conceptual root of *Slave Ship*'s African/American synthesis can be traced back to the basic music aesthetic that we explored in chapter 3. The drama of *Slave Ship* is fundamentally the same as that of *Blues People*: African Spirit endures Western (specifically, American) oppression and rises to perfection in musical form. The genius of Baraka's play lies in the manner in which the complex black music aesthetic is given precise theatrical embodiment.

These, then, are the primary forces that inform the nature and use of music in *Slave Ship*. As one might expect from this diverse background, music operates on many levels and in many ways to give form to Baraka's thought in the play. Every effect of feeling and every physical condition is portrayed through sound. The props call for ship "noises," ship "bells," sea "splashing," whip and chain "sounds." The slave-characters evoke the state of misery with constant moans, cries, curses—all bare intonations which, rather than describing a condition, become its essence. Baraka's observation in the poem "Ka'Ba," that "our world is full of sound," is concretized in *Slave Ship*: here, sound fully becomes the world.

The experience of the play, then, is less one of watching than of listening. If sound is the world's substance, then the particular organization of sound into music is the world in process. Music in *Slave Ship* is the form of idealized historicity as projected by the successive "pageant" images. Thus religious, civilized Africa *is* the music and dance-oriented rite of the opening image. Africa survives on the slave ship and in America in the incessant drumbeats, ritual chants, and tribal dances that remain a basic means of expression among the slaves. On the slave ship, the life of the black people is assured almost thoroughly through the rising "chant-moan of the women [. . .] like mad old nigger ladies humming forever in deathly patience," and in the percussional beating upon planks and walls. The white man's being *is* his hideous laughter; the entire Middle Passage is composed by Baraka as a sound-war between this laughter and the music of the black collective will (which is also internally threatened by "the long stream of different wills, articulated as screams, grunts, cries, songs, etc."). At times, the "laughter is drowned in the drums," but these moments are always followed by silence (a stand-off) or the rise of white laughter (repression). The tribal humming endures; the African civilization is brought to America with the slaves.

The musical expression of the Afro-American does not simply

parallel history; again, it is the complexity of the slaves' alienated existence. The gospels, presaged by the patient moans of women in the hold, take over as the constant undertone of black resistance. The traitorous Tom's shuffling, jeffing "dance" represents the degradation of the masked dancer of the opening fertility rite. Yet subversively, in darkness, the pure and ancient culture remains, juxtaposed to the Tom image:

> (*Lights off . . . drums of ancient African warriors come up . . . hero-warriors. Lights blink back on, show shuffling black man, hat in his hand, scratching his head. Lights off. Drums again. Black dancing in the dark, . . . scratching his head. Lights off. Drums again. Black dancing in the dark, with bells, as if free, dancing wild old dances. Bam Boom Bam Booma Bimbam Boomama boom beem bam. Dancing in the darkness . . . Yoruba Dance/lights flash on briefly, spot on, off the dance. Then off.*)
> [p. 68]

With the suppression of the plantation revolt, African war drums subside into "the sound of a spiritual," a song of American experience and African spirituality: "Oh, Lord Deliver Me . . . oh Lord." White laughter howls in triumph; for a moment, it drowns out what has now become the complex African/American musical fusion.

Now, modern rhythms: the gibberish of the preacher-Tom takes up the gospel's "Jesus, Jesus, Jesus . . ."; against him, the African/American voices sing new notes—jazz and blues scatting—and "new-sound" horns scream the old war chants. The drums persist as the unvarying keeper of the old rhythms. As the community coalesces once again, the original humming gathers and reaches toward climax. White laughter rises sporadically above the swelling sounds of chant, scream, hum, scat, horns, drums; all is "mixed with sounds of [the] slave ship." History gathers all its imagined moments in an anarchy of sonority and becomes imminently apocalyptic. The chant of "when we gonna rise/up" grows with the music; "the white man's laughter is heard trying to drown out the music, but the music is rising."

Eventually, the chant becomes song; African drums, slave-ship noises, and contemporary visionary jazz (Sun Ra, Archie Shepp) become one poem of black experience, one tangible weapon of black revolt. The preacher's voice "breaks" before he dies; the white man gasps on his laughter as the horde descends. Finally, the triumph—spiritual and physical—is expressed as dance. Again, this is an African/American synthesis, "Miracles'/Temptations' dancing line" merging with African movement in a "new-old dance": what Baraka amusingly but pointedly calls "Bogalooyoruba." The improvisational essence of this Afro-American musical sensibility becomes the ultimate statement of transcendence, and this is the audience's achievement. The quickly created "party" is an ecstasy of "fingerpop, skate, monkey, dog" in which each participant's thing is everyone's thing and individual improvisation becomes communal form: in the words of the street-wise saying, 'everything is everything.'

Music is thus strength, memory, power, triumph, affirmation—the entire historical and mythical process of Afro-American being. The mythical curve of return to primordial power is enacted in the dance, for the final dance of the audience in the womblike hold returns us to the site of the whirling fertility goddess. By integrating the spectator with the opening dance, Baraka has moved *Slave Ship* out of drama and into ritual; that is, he has reversed the process by which the Western (particularly Greek) theatre evolved from rite to drama. In Greek theatre, the spectators became a new and different element added to original ritual. The dance was not only danced but also watched from a distance; it became a "spectacle." Whereas in ritual nearly all were worshippers acting, the spectators added the elements of watching, thinking, feeling, not-doing. The *dromenon* or rite, something actually done by oneself, became *drama*, a thing also done but abstracted from one's doing. The members of Baraka's audience, on the contrary, are transformed from spectators of drama as "a thing done" but apart from themselves, to partakers of ritual, "a thing done" with no division between actor and spectator. Just as the opening African ritual is refashioned at the end into a higher act, one of communal triumph as well as celebration, so the audience is brought to a higher role. No longer merely observers of an oft-forgotten tradition, they themselves now perform a ritual, affirming by their deed the complete communality of the theatrical event. The collectivity of ritual has supplanted the individuation of drama.

The final rite, with its mimed cannibalistic aspect, is apocalyptic in both a mythical and a religious sense. In its mythical dimension, the ending completes the absorption of the natural, historical cycle into mythology. Its mythical movement is one of comic resurrection and integration, completed by the marriage of the spectator into community and the birth of the "old-new" black nation. This fertility ritual clearly has a religious dimension that has been prepared for by the continuous prayers to Obatala and Jesus, curses of the "Godless, white devil," and litanies such as "Rise, Rise, Rise, etc." Indeed, by creating basic images of resurrection with accompanying sensations of magic, charm, and incantation, Baraka returns the black audience to the most fundamental religious ground of tribal ceremony from which sprung the two greatest epochs of Western theatre (Greek and Christian), and which gave life to the archetypical African spirit. The spectators are as integral a part of the work as the congregation of a black Baptist church is of its service, and they function in much the same way. The nationalist myth of African-inspired renewal and Afro-American triumph is taken up by the audience because Baraka has called upon the community's shared aesthetic—the genius for musical improvisation.

This re-creation of the mythical and religious through music points Baraka's art toward the Nietzschean Dionysian state. Here the end of individuation becomes possible, for the Dionysian essence for Nietzsche was a musical one: "In song and dance man expresses himself as a member of a higher community; he has forgotten how to walk and speak and is on the way toward flying into the air, dancing." [6] By claiming African roots in their totality, the black community controls its destiny as Clay, the middle-class greyboy, could not. Now, Baraka's black heroes, not the witch-devil Lula, dance in triumph. The tragedy-burdened slave ship of *Dutchman* has become the dance-filled celebration of *Slave Ship*; musical transcendence has risen from the spirit of tragedy.

Conclusion "Spirit Reach": The Changing Same

Slave Ship attains a synthesis between Western, Aristotelian stress upon the story and 'shape' (development) in drama, and African concentration upon emotional reaction to a single idea or sentiment. A succinct myth or ideology of history and the vitality of black music combine to give Baraka's nationalist vision complete expression. More important than any relationship between Western and non-Western elements, however, is the way in which Baraka's ritual art achieves an emotional and collective intensity comparable to that of traditional Afro-American religious ceremony.

Carlton W. Molette II has drawn a sharp distinction between Euro-American drama, which "seems to emphasize the individual . . . his differentness from the other members of his community," and Afro-American ritual art, which "seems to be based upon the assumption that we who are gathered here to participate in this event are and belong together." [1] Baraka's theatre, from *Dutchman* to *Slave Ship*, has clearly evolved from a concern with the individual cut loose from society to the community itself as victim, rebel, and, finally, triumphant hero. If Molette's thesis is too reductive—especially with respect to the history and principles of Euro-American drama—it does point to a basic difference between the Afro-American and Euro-American dramas as they are today: ritual art based on unity of feeling and total participation is an integral part of the black culture only.

This contrast becomes strikingly apparent when we consider recent attempts at creating 'ritual drama' in the white avant-garde. Living Theatre, rock musicals, the Obie Award winning *Dionysus in '69*, 'happenings,' and other examples of audience involvement and free improvisation theatre all seek to break down established procedures of illusionistic and realistic drama by obliterating distinctions between actor and spectator, theatre and 'real' world, and, ultimately, between art and life. However different the stated aims of these movements may be, at the core of each is an attempt to restore a commonly held religious sensibility to drama, and, further, to make drama itself an instrument of a more pervasive social and spiritual reformation. A tremendous amount of pure energy has been generated from these efforts, but the group transport and complete lyrical attitude achieved at the conclusion of *Slave Ship* have been beyond their power. Walter Kerr delineates the dilemma of the white avant-garde with admirable clarity:

> Drama at the present time has no . . . new mainspring charged with specific religious energy to set the whole vast procreative process in motion. We are trying for a third drama though we do not live in a time of a third religion. We haven't a new impulse to guarantee the birth of a new mode. . . . Drama once grew out of religion. We are trying to grow religion out of drama . . . so that we can grow drama out of the religion once we have got it.[2]

Because the Afro-American community possesses and maintains a shared set of values, one strengthened rather than threatened by exclusion from the dominant culture, Baraka and other black artists can be free from the illusion and failure which plague the radical Euro-American theatre. The Euro-American audience, reflecting the fractured nature of its culture, comes to the theatre out of a network of motives too various for the artist to unify into a common form of expression, whether political, aesthetic, or religious. In modern theatre generally—whether in the neomythic existentialist drama of Camus and Sartre, Giraudoux's theatre of pure poetry, the theatre of games and masks of Genêt and Ionesco, or Beckett's theatre of the Void—one senses the emergence of a sensibility that is dissociated from 'objective reality.' The sense of isolation from milieu (Chekhov), universe (Strindberg), or one's own notions of self and fellow man (Pirandello), is theoretically solved by the new white theatre's fusion of audience and stage experiences. In practice, the results are not so happy nor so whole.

The reasons for this failure are many—the modern embrace of

'freedom' from received religious myth; the 'Romantic' malady of self-consciousness and self-alienation; the consequent disruption of the Enlightenment view of man as a unity and the growth of literature as revelation of personality—and these factors collectively pose the great challenge for the alienated writer: to regain the directness of great visionary poetry, to create, as Yeats put it, "the ritual of a lost faith." Many modern writers reject this challenge as advocating a delusory and impossible goal. Beckett, in fact, seeks to show that the Enlightenment view was indeed shallow, even false, and that the abyss between Self and Other cannot be bridged by any construct of man. Hence, even in the relatively cheery and compassionate *Waiting for Godot*, Beckett takes pains to defy the traditional notions of cycles or curves as suggesting resolution, to show habit and familiarity as increasingly boring and irksome, to use formulae of language only to disparage our "pernicious and incurable optimism," and to deflate the value of cliché sentiments —in short, to create a parody of ritual actions, leaving us with the echo of "reasons unknown" instead of the reverberation of ritual's awesome 'mysteries.' But others have sought to establish an avant-garde which could afford a cure for the cultural disease Beckett is content to document. Unlike Beckett, they seek wholeness and communion through art, and their failure to achieve such ends has a double cause.

The first of these is painfully ironic: the avant-garde bears within it the seeds of its own dissolution (to borrow a phrase from Kierkegaard). The longing for health and restructuring of society fosters a desire to be different, other, *new*. Hence, what begins as an impulse to reform becomes the posture of alienation: faced with a fragmented culture, the artist paradoxically breaks from it as a hope of personal escape. Thus the modern hero is above all else a victim, not a reconciler or saver, of society. This alienation-effect of the Euro-American avant-garde is especially clear in the case of radical American artists who have followed or emulated their black peers. The beats, hipsters, and disciples of bebop were repelled by many of the same facets of white society as were black artists, and they similarly sought release into fresher, newer modes of living. The white radical, however, was rejecting a conformism not readily accessible to the black, and his revolt thus tended to be expressed in negative terms: *not* 'square,' *not* part of the 'industrial-military complex,' *not* a practitioner of traditional art.

On the other hand, the black artist, and particularly the black musician, knew he wasn't any of those things as much as he was aware that he was black. In rebelling against white culture, the black artist also established a deeper relationship to his own community and its traditions: as LeRoi Jones discovered in *The System of Dante's Hell*, the home of black communality is always waiting to be reclaimed by the alienated Prodigal. Afro-American artists are not the only ones to believe that art's power resides in immediacy and spontaneity of expression—most twentieth-century aesthetic revolts have been fueled by the rhetoric of 'feeling.' But whereas for the white artist the search for the original source of unveiled spirituality involves rejection of the world as it now is, for the black artist this recovery is merely a matter of substituting one existent culture for another. For the black artist, the turning away is also a turning toward.

We can see from this difference between black and white radical artists the second reason why the Euro-American theatre cannot create ritual drama such as *Slave Ship*: it seeks to bring man in contact with nature and with the body *as opposed to* society and its 'moral fictions.' This attitude is best illustrated in the work of the avant-garde theatre's ruling deity, Antonin Artaud.[3] Artaud believed that thought and soul were immaterial apart from their "incarnation" or form. This form is the body, and all aspects of spirit, intellect, and emotion must be subservient to the body which is their vehicle. In *The Theatre and Its Double*, Artaud argued that the theatre itself is a body in which function and spiritual condition are united. Pure theatre means the pure, "cruel" act—that is, a gesture without logical origin, intent, or result. Such acts are not only those which society deems monstrous but also such 'ordinary' activities as eating, touching, and smiling.

Opposed to a pure theatre of acts is drama, for drama utilizes the imagination and its cohort, language, in a realm separate from the body's density, creating the illusion of humanistic 'meaning' with its plots, ideas, and values. The theatre is valuable because, by presenting pure acts, it is able to destroy our belief that the natural act can be "redeemed" by social or intellectual systems. Pure theatre is the world in its naked essence—but by "world" Artaud meant nature, not society. Society mediates between man and nature by means of language, thoughts, and rational constructs such as history—it is structured along dramatic lines. Nature, on the other hand, is theatrical: it is a collection of unorganized, gratuitous, immediate gestures. The "theatre of cruelty" is thus antidramatic and therefore antisocial theatre. Artaud called for a theatre of absolute gesture unrefined by social mores, and he therefore felt that the ritual activities of Balinese and Mexican Indian ceremony would furnish helpful stylistic models for a new theatre. But, contrary to many who invoke his name in their effort to produce participatory drama, he did not call for a ritual theatre. Artaud, unlike his followers, was aware that ritual is a deeply conservative action rooted in social custom—the very antithesis of his goal.

Avant-garde 'ritual' theatre is entangled in the contradictions stemming from a desire to unite and heal society by destroying it. Moreover, it is caught in a situation common to much Euro-American literature, what has been loosely designated 'the crisis of language.' All modern art has shown an inclination toward the self-negating state of silence. The "theatre of cruelty," for example, hopes to "abolish the word" and substitute in its place the "concrete reality" of gestures, lights, props, and other tangible things. Some come to feel permanently Hopkins's momentary fear that "our hymn in the vast silence dies." For them, silence is an indication of directionlessness and lack of purpose: linguistic poverty brought on by lack of faith. For others, like Beckett and his tramps, silence is both a welcome respite from the cacophony of meaningless chatter and a metaphysical analogy to the Néant that lies on the other side of the stage. For still others, such as Rilke and Pinter, silence is possibly the province of the mystical and numenous, the true source of the Word from which all other words flow: "Silence. Who fervently remains silent touches the roots of speech" (Rilke). But whether silence be the silence of *kenosis* wherein one empties oneself to then become fuller, or the silence of the Abyss which yields no echo, it cannot give rise to communal celebration and creation.

If the Euro-American attitude toward language is at best ambivalent, in Afro-American culture language and artistic expression are respected as the means whereby life can be positively reshaped in the face of daily hardships. As Roger Rosenblatt recently said, "The association of blackness with art [in black fiction] is an association with a form of freedom."[4] While the symbol and model of the modern Euro-American artist is the Solitary Figure whose consciousness alienates him from life—Faust, Manfred, the Ancient Mariner, Leverkühn, Molloy—the typical Afro-American artist is the leader of a call-and-response composition: the Louis Armstrong whose horn is heard above but not apart from the musical ensemble; the Martin Luther King who preaches with and not simply to his choric congregation; the blues improviser who shifts his song according to the directions suggested by his signifying audience.

Afro-American art is vital because it proceeds from a common field of creative activity and aesthetic principles. As Molette says of Afro-American religious ritual, art in general has a functional value to black people because it sustains and nourishes a sense of community while touching upon specific aspects of their lives. While Euro-American art may ask its audience to act it does not first present a common canon of values capable of generating the concord necessary for meaningful response. Afro-Americans, on the contrary, have always been concerned with communicating to each other essential values based on shared experience which can affirm the collective sensibility. For this reason, language has maintained a central role in Afro-American life, and hence in Afro-American art. We have already noted that black poetry tends to emulate music and demands to be read aloud. This is due not only to the essential vocality of black life at its most expressive, but also to the traditional regard for oratorical modes and the spoken word—to (as Alvin Aubert says) "living in and through language when language was all the world the black man had to move around in, to inhabit."[5] While the words of the Euro-American artist grow ever more faint, the Afro-American is enjoying the pulsing sounds of a thriving art. In the words of jazz bassist Willie Ruff: "Ours is the only culture now enjoying its Golden Age."

II

The strength of contemporary Afro-American culture derives, in great measure, from the black artist's recognition that art and life are not separate entities, that all dimensions of black existence need to be joined into a whole life vitalized by the saving power of Soul. Art, therefore, must not be stifled by preestablished requirements of beauty, proportion, or ideal form. Like life, it is mutable and subject to a complexity of ever-changing influences, and thus the creative process or "attitude" is valued over the particular, concrete product. As James T. Stewart writes: "We know . . . that man cannot create *a* forever; but he can create forever. But he can only create if he creates as change. Creation is itself perpetuation and change is being." [6]

Baraka's literary career, more than that of any other Afro-American writer, has illustrated the ethic/aesthetic of "change." The impulse to harness the energy of black life's chaos is consonant with the desire for political and cultural transformation. Thus "the revolution = change," [7] and Malcolm X, the exemplar of cultural revolution, "was killed, for saying, / and feeling, and being / change" (from "Poem for Black Hearts"). At the core of Baraka's art is the insistence upon the formlessness of life-giving energy and the energetic or fluid nature of all form. It is no wonder that events in his work are violent, his images often alarmingly brutal. The only fruition or finality honored is that of death, which produces a sudden enlargement of vision—the realization that personality, or the "deadweight" of any fixed idea or being, is inevitably annihilated by history's progress: "The only constant is change." [8]

In the purgatorial domain of his "ever-blacker" life, the artist learns to submit to his people's pure energy. He must surrender the shape of his own life, freeing his soul to flow into the black nation.

The most extreme form of such identity-loss is the ceremonial dismemberment of the poet, so that he is no longer a man but instead becomes his singing, his fateful words and purest deeds, a man reduced to the barest of essences:

> When I die, the consciousness I carry I will to
> black people. May they pick me apart and take the
> useful parts, the sweet meat of my feelings. And leave
> the bitter bullshit white parts
> alone.
>
> [from "leroy"]

This poem had begun in a pastoral dimension, a realm of accomplished forms and stilled gestures, a realm suffused with sadness:

> I wanted to know my mother when she sat
> looking sad across the campus in the late 20's
> into the future of the soul.

The violent ending is a stunning reversal of the poem's opening: the history of black consciousness is a generation-by-generation stripping of "sweet meat" from "bitter bullshit white parts." Here, Baraka sustains the hope that a static resolution of black experience can be avoided by willing the collective purification of his specific personality: "leroy" dies and Imamu is born.

The restless search for forms which Baraka's literary corpus exhibits—engendered by an aesthetic of process and the belief in inevitable change—links him to a similar motive in all modern art. He partakes, with the modern Western artist, of the quest for a proper idiom or voice, although his desire to control some manner of expression is conceived in political as well as aesthetic terms. Yet his sense of continual challenge, of the constant need to test positions, is specifically Afro-American in its deliberately improvisational thrust and, concomitantly, in its persuasion that life is essentially *dramatic*. Baraka's creed of black Being as Ideal yet everchanging calls to mind Zora Neale Hurston's suggestion that "acting out" or "drama" is the black man's fundamental trait:

> something that permeates his entire self. . . . Every phase of Negro life is highly dramatised. No matter how joyful or how

sad the case there is sufficient poise for drama. Everything is acted out.

[from "Characteristics of Negro Expression"][9]

Baraka would agree with Hurston as well as with his own character, Walker, who said (but nearly forgot) that "right is in the act!" His career reveals that he is making the continuous, open-ended epic that will end with his death: it is endlessly exploratory, continually forming, disintegrating and re-forming. This epic-dramatic impulse led him at first to stage himself in thinly veiled guises: Clay, Walker, Ray, and Lennie are all products of Baraka's own experience and they embody a sensitivity and torment common to the young LeRoi Jones.[10] The emphasis on individual character—the subject of the early poetry and drama—is gradually replaced by a focus upon passions, motives, events, and moments of ritualistic violence and beauty.

Yet as the revelation and exorcism of self have given way to a communal orientation, Baraka has not abandoned his theatrical sensibility. On the contrary, he has sought an increasingly expansive theatre—the stage of world politics. His shifts—often perplexing and contradictory—leading from uncompromisingly separatist black nationalism to a more inclusive Pan-Africanism, and most recently to the embrace of international socialism,[11] may be taken partly as an attempt to gain a broader world forum, and partly as reflecting the need to fabricate new ideological roles for each change wrought by contemporary history.

Baraka has shown at every instant of his public career an intense commitment to those ideas and ideals he felt were integral to his motivating vision of life. Like James Brown, he has always been "an actor that is now." And it is by way of this ethos, with its equation of passion and significance, that Imamu Amiri Baraka creatively identifies himself with the evolving spirit of his people:

play on play on in the warm blue road
know you doin it. Cant get far from indigo whispers.
Our love is here its grown so full. Our hearts from Be have
become what they must be. Be. we say, for the coming
revelation. BE

we say, as the black hearted revolutionaries. BE, we say to the epoch of
tomorrow. And tomorrow is now. And Now is when we mean.

[from "Love Is the Presence of No Enemy," in *Spirit Reach*]

Notes

CHAPTER ONE

1 See Walter A. Strauss, *Descent and Return* (Cambridge, Mass.: Harvard University Press, 1971), pp. 140–217.
2 James Hollis, *The Poetics of Silence* (Chicago: Southern Illinois University Press, 1968), p. 18.
3 For a survey of the circles of Jones's *The System of Dante's Hell* and some parallels between Jones's novel and Dante's *Inferno*, see "From Brother LeRoi Jones Through *The System of Dante's Hell* To Imamu Ameer Baraka," by Paulette Pennington-Jones, *Journal of Black Studies* 4, no. 2 (December 1973): 195–214. See also Michael G. Cooke's article, "The Descent into the Underground and Modern Black Fiction," *The Iowa Review* 5, no. 4 (1974): 72–90, on the relationship of Baraka's novel to a literary tradition in which, as Cooke notes, "a special isolation and disorientation would seem to be associated with the underground."
4 Gerold Weales's judgment that "the middle-class boy wants a glimpse into the deep, mysterious underworld"—*The Jumping Off Place* (New York: Macmillan, 1969), p. 318—typifies erroneous interpretations of passages from Baraka's work which fail to deal with the language *in context* rather than as filtered through the critic's prior attitude toward the author.
5 *Home: Social Essays* (New York, 1966), p. 76.
6 On the significance of the gyre in Dante's *Commedia*, see John Freccero, "Dante's Pilgrim in a Gyre," *PMLA* 76, no. 3 (1961): 168–81.
7 William C. Fischer, in "The Pre-Revolutionary Writings of Imamu Amiri Baraka," *The Massachusetts Review* 14, no. 2 (1973): 259–305, discusses Baraka's concept of the scream at length. I explore these ideas further in chapter 3.
8 Quoted in Mel Watkins, "The Lyrics of James Brown," *Amistad 2* (New York: Random House, 1971), p. 25.

9 Ibid., p. 30.
10 Quoted by Cecil Brown in "James Brown, Hoodoo and Black Culture," *Black Review No. 1* (New York: William Morrow & Co., 1971), p. 184.
11 *Blues People* (New York, 1963), p. 29.
12 *Invisible Man* (New York: New American Library, 1952), p. 434.
13 "The Music of Invisibility," *City of Words* (New York: Harper and Row, 1971), pp. 50–63.
14 Cf. Esther M. Jackson's idea that Baraka's early work exhibits a "preoccupation with consciousness in crisis"; "LeRoi Jones (Imamu Amiri Baraka): Form and the Progression of Consciousness," *The CLA Journal*, 17, no. 1 (March 1973): 34.
15 See Strauss, *Descent and Return*, p. 176.
16 On the relation between Belacqua and Beckett's tramps, see Walter A. Strauss, "Dante's Belacqua and Beckett's Tramps," *Comparative Literature* 12 (1961): 56–71.
17 See the Sinclair edition, p. 121.
18 See Freccero, "Dante's Pilgrim," p. 176 on Dante's concept.
19 Some helpful sources are: Sherley Anne Williams's *Give Birth to Brightness* (New York, 1972); Stephen Henderson's "Survival Motion," in *The Militant Black Writer* (Madison, Wisc.: University of Wisconsin Press, 1969); Don L. Lee's *Dynamite Voices* (Detroit, 1971).
20 *The Souls of Black Folk* (Chicago: A. C. McClurg and Co., 1903), p. 3.
21 "Revolutionary Nationalism and the Afro-American," in *Black Fire*, ed. LeRoi Jones and Larry Neal (New York, 1968), pp. 39–63.
22 All quotations from Malcolm X are from *Malcolm X on History* (New York: Pathfinder Press, 1967), pp. 3–17.
23 See "Hidden Name and Complex Fate," in *Shadow and Act* (New York, 1972), pp. 144–66.
24 Kenneth Burke, in "Lexicon Rhetoricae," *Terms for Order* (Bloomington: Indiana University Press, 1958), pp. 34–46, wrote: "ideology is the nodus of beliefs and judgments which the artist can exploit for his effects."
25 Henderson, *Militant Black Writer*, p. 110.
26 Quoted in an editorial in *Liberator* (December 1963), p. 3.
27 For a representative selection of this work, see *For Malcolm X*, ed. Dudley Randall (Detroit: Broadside Press, 1967).
28 Lee, *Dynamite Voices*, p. 34.
29 Ibid., p. 33.
30 A fine sample of the new poets reading their work is available on the

record "Black Spirits: An Anthology of New Black Poets," Motown Records, s4536.

31 *Raise Race Rays Raze: Essays since 1965* (New York, 1971), p. 145.

32 These lines of Edward Spriggs's are quoted by William Keorapstse Kgositile in "Paths to the Future," in *The Black Aesthetic*, ed. Addison Gayle, Jr. (New York: Doubleday, 1972), p. 243.

33 Larry Neal, "Some Reflections on the Black Aesthetic," in Gayle, p. 14.

34 *Raise Race Rays Raze*, p. 126; the emphasis is Jones's.

35 Addison Gayle, Jr., "Introduction," in Gayle, p. xxii.

36 Henderson, *Militant Black Writer*, p. 102.

37 Fischer, "Pre-Revolutionary Writings."

38 See Jackson, "LeRoi Jones," p. 53 and C. Lynn Munro, "LeRoi Jones: A Man in Transition," *The CLA Journal* 17, no. 1 (1973): 68; both point to the influence of Malcolm X upon Jones's development.

39 *Raise Race Rays Raze*, p. 112.

40 *From LeRoi Jones to Amiri Baraka* (Durham, N.C., 1973), p. 182.

41 "An Interview with LeRoi Jones," by Marvin X and Faruk, *Negro Digest* (January 1969), p. 79.

CHAPTER TWO

1 All quotations from "Brief Reflections on Two Hot Shots" are from *Home*, pp. 116–20.

2 All quotations from "The Revolutionary Theatre" are from *Home*, pp. 210–15.

3 *Preface to a Twenty Volume Suicide Note. . . .* (New York, 1961), pp. 39–40.

4 *Tales* (New York, 1967), p. 111.

5 *Four Black Revolutionary Plays*, pp. 26–27.

6 Cf. DeWitt H. Parker, *The Principles of Aesthetics* (New York: Burdett and Co., 1946), pp. 275–76.

7 Quoted in *The Black American Writer, Vol. I* (*Fiction*), ed. C. W. E. Bigsby (Baltimore, Md., 1969), p. 10.

8 Ibid., p. 12.

9 "Africa" by Langston Hughes, quoted in ibid., p. 11.

10 "Revolutionary Nationalism and the Afro-American," *Black Fire*, ed. LeRoi Jones and Larry Neal (New York, 1968), pp. 39–63.

11 Cf. "Black Art, Nationalism, Organization, Black Institutions," *Raise Race Rays Raze*, pp. 97–101; *Blues People*, p. 135; "The Legacy of

Malcolm X, and the Coming of the Black Nation," *Home*, pp. 242–43.

12 See *Harlem Renaissance* by Nathan Irvin Huggins (New York: Oxford University Press, 1971), pp. 65 ff.

13 "Blueprint for Negro Writing," *The Black Aesthetic*, ed. Addison Gayle, Jr. (New York, 1969), p. 320.

14 "That Same Pain, That Same Pleasure," *Shadow and Act* (New York, 1973), p. 22.

15 All quotations from "The Myth of a 'Negro Literature'" are from *Home*, pp. 105–15.

16 This attitude is not at all uncommon in traditional Afro-American thought. For example, Richard Wright declared that "the Negro is America's metaphor," and Dr. King's movement was predicated on the assumption that the civil rights struggle was the key to the future of American democracy. Albert Murray's writings are perhaps the most insightful in this vein (see especially *The Omni-Americans*).

17 All quotations from "The Legacy of Malcolm X, and the Coming of the Black Nation" are from *Home*, pp. 238–50.

18 Ibid., p. 245.

19 "STATE/MEANT," *Home*, p. 251.

20 "The Fire Must Be Permitted to Burn Full Up," *Raise Race Rays Raze*, p. 121.

21 "The Need for a Cultural Base to Civil Rites & Bpower Mooments," ibid., p. 46.

22 "The World You're Talking About," ibid., p. 37.

23 "Work Notes—'66," ibid., p. 14.

24 "Black Art, Nationalism, Organization, Black Institutions," ibid., p. 98.

25 Harold Cruse writes, in *The Crisis of the Negro Intellectual* (New York, 1967): "with LeRoi Jones and his young Afro-American nationalists, anti-interracialism was equated not only with anti-whiteness, but with *hatred* of whiteness" (p. 364).

26 "The Need for a Cultural Base," *Raise Race Rays Raze*, p. 47.

27 Cf. "The Legacy of Malcolm X," ibid., p. 247.

28 "The Revolutionary Theatre," ibid., p. 211.

29 "Work Notes—'66," ibid., p. 15.

30 "Nationalism Vs PimpArt," ibid., p. 127.

31 "Black Art, Nationalism, etc.," ibid., p. 98.

32 Lucien Goldmann, "The Sociology of Literature," *The Sociology of Art and Literature: A Reader*, ed. Milton C. Albrecht, James H. Barnett, and Mason Gniff (New York: Praeger, 1970), pp. 582–609.

33 See *Anatomy of Criticism* (Princeton, N.J., 1957) or "Myth, Fiction, and Displacement," in *Fables of Identity* (New York: Harcourt, Brace, & World, 1963), pp. 21–38.
34 "The Need for a Cultural Base," *Raise Race Rays Raze*, p. 44.
35 *Black Magic Poetry*, pp. 173–74. *Sonni Weusi Akbar* means "All praises to the black man."
36 "Black Art, Nationalism, etc.," p. 101.
37 "The Revolutionary Theatre," pp. 211–12.
38 This is a phrase of Aristotle's which Blake notes in making a similar point. Cf. Northrop Frye, "Blake's Treatment of the Archetype," *Critics on Blake*, ed. Judith O'Neill (Miami, Fla.: University of Miami Press, 1963).
39 "The Revolutionary Theatre," p. 213.
40 "What the Arts Need Now," *Raise Race Rays Raze*, p. 33.
41 "Work Notes—'66," pp. 14–15.
42 "What the Arts Need Now," p. 33.
43 "Poetry and Karma," *Raise Race Rays Raze*, p. 24.
44 Frye, *Anatomy of Criticism*, p. 137.
45 Ibid., p. 42.
46 Ibid.
47 Ibid., p. 33.

CHAPTER THREE

1 The best discussion of the relationship between black music and black poetry is that of Stephen Henderson, *Understanding the New Black Poetry* (New York, 1973), pp. 46–61.
2 Some further exceptions to this general attitude may be found in James Weldon Johnson's work (see esp. his preface to *The Book of Negro Poetry*) and, more obscurely and surprisingly, in Booker T. Washington's preface to *Twenty-Four Negro Melodies*, transcribed for the piano by Samuel Coleridge-Taylor (Boston, 1905).
3 *Give Birth to Brightness*, p. 145.
4 *"Ark of Bones," and Other Stories* (New York: Random House, 1974), pp. 109–15.
5 "Black Cultural Nationalism," in *The Black Aesthetic*, ed. Gayle, p. 37.
6 "The Development of the Black Revolutionary Artist," in *Black Fire*, ed. Jones and Neal, p. 10.
7 This and the other quotations in this paragraph are from *Black Music*

(New York, 1967), pp. 13–14. All other quotations in this chapter, unless otherwise noted, are from *Blues People* (New York, 1963). Page numbers for quotations from *Blues People* will be given in parentheses.

8 This is what Baraka calls Yacoub in "The Fire Must Be Permitted To Burn Full Up," in *Raise Race Rays Raze*, p. 119. A more complete explanation of the Yacoub myth is given in chapter 6.
9 Fischer, "Pre-Revolutionary Writings," p. 294.
10 *Home*, p. 174.
11 *Black Music*, p. 176.
12 Albert Murray, *The Omni-Americans* (New York: Avon Books, 1971), p. 88.
13 Ibid., pp. 91–92.
14 *"Blues People,"* in *Shadow and Act* (New York, 1964), p. 256.
15 *Urban Blues* (Chicago, 1966), p. 39. Kiel's phrase "myth of the Negro past" refers to the title of Melville J. Herskovits's famous study of African-derived cultures in the New World.
16 Ellison, *Invisible Man*, p. 253.
17 Kiel, p. 43.
18 Jackson, "LeRoi Jones (Imamu Amiri Baraka)." Jackson's interest is with Hegel's effect on Baraka's ideas about form in art; I am more concerned with the Hegelian nature of Baraka's historiography and mythology.
19 *Hegel* (Edinburgh and London, 1883), p. 52.
20 Ibid., p. 114.
21 *Prolegomena to the Study of Hegel's Philosophy, and Especially of His Logic* (Oxford, 1894), p. 160.
22 *Black Music*, p. 72.
23 *Raise Race Rays Raze*, p. 117.
24 "Mwalimu Texts," in ibid., p. 166.

CHAPTER FOUR

1 *Creative Intuition in Art and Poetry* (New York, 1953), p. 177.
2 *The New Poets* (New York, 1967), p. 13.
3 Ibid., p. 7.
4 This and the following quotation are from Dickey's poem "Inside the River," in *Drowning With Others* (Middletown, Conn.: Wesleyan University Press, 1962), pp. 91–92.
5 This and the following quotation are from Olson's essay "Projective

Verse," in *Human Universe* (New York: The Averhann Society, 1967), pp. 52–61.

6 *Creative Intuition*, p. 255.

7 "Myth of a 'Negro Literature,' " *Home*, p. 112.

8 From "An Explanation of the Work," the preface to *Black Magic Poetry*.

9 From the short story "Words," *Tales*, p. 89.

10 Ibid., p. 91.

11 For example, these lines from Césaire's *Les armes miraculeuses*:

> My negritude is not a stone with its deafness flung
> out against the clamor of the day
> My negritude is not a dead speck of water on the
> dead eye of the earth
> my negritude is neither a tower nor a cathedral
> it plunges into the red flesh of the ground
> it plunges into the ardent flesh of the sky
> it perforates the opaque pressure of its righteous patience.

Quoted in Sartre's "Black Orpheus," *The Black American Writer, Vol. II* (*Poetry and Drama*), ed. C. W. E. Bigsby (Baltimore, Md., 1971), p. 18.

12 Frye, *Anatomy of Criticism*, p. 250.

13 Of course, no poetry can exist without abstractions, poetry itself being an abstraction from ordinary speech. But in Baraka's early poems the presentation of abstract ideas was nearly always accompanied by qualifying imagery. We may recall these lines of "Way out West," where the idea of time is followed a few lines later by the image of creeping shadows:

> Unable to mention
> something as abstract as time [. . .]
> shadows will creep over your flesh
> & hide your disorder, your lies.

14 Sartre, "Black Orpheus," p. 11.

15 For example, the letters *OM* appear repeatedly in these poems. *M* is in many religious systems (including the Islamic) a monogram for the never-to-be-spoken or unknown God. *O* is commonly "total." They appear, e.g., in "MO-hammed," and in this context may also be related to the idea of divine love, which found its way into Latin as *Amo*. Cf. Godfrey Higgins's *Analcalypsis* (London, 1878), a text with which, Larry Neal tells me, Baraka is familiar.

16 This observation was related to me in an interview with Mr. Neal.

17 Frye, *Anatomy of Criticism*, p. 65.

18 Higgins believed in this mythic idea: "a black race, in very early times, had more influence over the affairs of the world than has been lately suspected," *Analcalypsis*, p. 39.

19 This has been the observation of anthropologists from Payne Knight to Frazier and, in more recent times, Eliade.

20 For example, the poem "Part of the Doctrine" literally ends thus:

> Huge Breast of the Night, awake to the whole
> of creation, the thing breathing, a breast silhouette,
> under supercool
> new moons of turning into[.]

21 Passages from *In Our Terribleness* (New York, 1970) cannot be referred to by poem titles, page numbers, or line numbers because the text is a continuous commentary accompanying photographic illustrations of black people by Fundi (Billy Abernathy). All quoted passages that follow are from *In Our Terribleness* unless otherwise indicated in the text.

22 A rough translation of this line from the Swahili is: "Experience, be, swell with black destiny."

23 Baraka's effort to use any available avenue of expression at the service of vision, to find, in the words of "Sermon for Our Maturity," a "language at celestial altitudes [sounding]/like bloods scattin at hightempos," established new directions for modern black poetry to explore. Several young poets, such as Don L. Lee, Askia Muhammad Touré, Michael Harper, and Sonia Sanchez, have begun to realize a few of these possibilities, and Baraka's influence upon the current generation of black poets is incalculable.

CHAPTER FIVE

1 See, for example, Susan Sontag's discussion of *Dutchman* in "Going to Theater," *Partisan Review,* 31 no. 3 (1964): 392–94.

2 Clayton Riley, "On Black Theater," in *The Black Aesthetic*, ed. Gayle, p. 301.

3 All references to *Dutchman* are from the Morrow Paperback edition, pp. 3–38.

4 Tom S. Reck first noted edenic imagery in *Dutchman* in his article "Archetypes in LeRoi Jones' *Dutchman,*" *Studies in Black Literature*, 1

no. 1 (1970): pp. 66–68. Cf. Hudson, *From LeRoi Jones to Amiri Baraka*, p. 148.

5 This phrase is borrowed from Martin Mueller's unpublished essay, "The Children of Oedipus: Some Reflections on Ancient and Modern Tragedy," delivered at The University of Rochester, March 16, 1971.

6 "The Black Arts Movement," *The Black American Writer: Vol. II*, p. 195.

7 *Invisible Man* (New York, 1952), p. 498.

8 *Home*, p. 211.

9 *Give Birth to Brightness*, p. 107.

10 "The Black Arts Movement," p. 195.

11 *Home*, p. 192.

12 Ibid., p. 65.

13 Several critics have noted this analogy. See, for example, Reck, "Archetypes," p. 68; Williams, *Give Birth to Brightness*, p. 106; Hudson, *From LeRoi Jones to Amiri Baraka*, p. 152.

14 "LeRoi Jones and Contemporary Black Drama," in *The Black American Writer: Vol. II*, p. 208.

15 All references to *The Slave* are from the Morrow Paperback edition, pp. 43–88.

16 This contrast was first noted by John Lindberg in "*Dutchman* and *The Slave:* Companions in Revolution," *Modern Black Literature*, ed. Dr. S. Okechukwu Mezu, p. 102.

17 See Williams, p. 120.

18 Cf. Richard Lederer, "The Language of LeRoi Jones' *The Slave*," *Studies in Black Literature* 4, no. 1 (1973): 14–16. Lederer argues that the play is a war between "linguistic basics" which ultimately reduce themselves to "non-verbal absolutes."

19 *Language in Action* (New York, 1940), p. 168.

20 Cf. Neal's application of Fanon to *Dutchman* in "The Black Arts Movement," p. 195.

21 All references to *The Toilet* are from the Grove Press edition, pp. 34–62.

22 This is quoted from Baraka's character descriptions, p. 35.

23 This is quoted from Baraka's character descriptions, ibid.

24 Phillips, "Jones and Contemporary Black Drama," pp. 212–13.

25 I draw here from Samuel H. Butcher's analysis of Aristotle's conception of pathos in *Aristotle's Theory of Poetry and Fine Art* (New York: Dover Publications, 1951).

26 All references to *Jello* are from Baraka's Jihad publication.

27 Williams, p. 76.

28 All references to *The Baptism* are from the Grove Press edition, pp. 9–32.
29 "Introduction" to the Evergreen edition of *The Maids* and *Deathwatch.*
30 The references are to act, scene, and page number. *A Recent Killing* has not yet appeared in print; I am fortunate in being able to use an unpublished version of the script, procured and authenticated for me by Larry Neal.

CHAPTER SIX

1 All references to *Great Goodness of Life* are from the Bobbs-Merrill edition, *Four Black Revolutionary Plays*, pp. 40–63.
2 All references to *The Blacks* are from the Grove Press edition, trans. Bernard Frectman.
3 *Black Power Chant* is printed in *The Drama Review* 16, no. 4 (1972): 53.
4 All references to *Experimental Death Unit #1* are from *Four Black Revolutionary Plays*, pp. 1–16.
5 All references to *Home on the Range* are from *The Drama Review* 12, no. 4 (1968): 106–11.
6 See "Short Statement on Street Theatre," *The Drama Review* 12, no. 4 (1968): 93.
7 All references to *Police* are from *The Drama Review* 12, no. 4 (1968): 112–15.
8 All references to *Arm Yourself, or Harm Yourself* are from Baraka's Jihad publication.
9 This point is made at greater length by Charles D. Peavy in "Myth, Magic, and Manhood in LeRoi Jones' *Madheart*," *Studies in Black Literature* 1, no. 2 (1970): 14.
10 The role Baraka envisages for the black woman in the new black nation is discussed in his essay, "Black Woman," *Kawaida Studies* (Chicago, 1972), pp. 23–32.
11 All references to *Madheart* are from *Four Black Revolutionary Plays*, pp. 66–87.
12 This notion should not be thought of as necessarily the product of an extreme nationalist ideology. Charles W. Chesnutt's short story, "Uncle Wellington's Wives" (the sixth story in *The Wife of His Youth*), for example, turns upon a black man's false hope that marriage to a white woman will constitute the epitome of social freedom.
13 "Black Woman," p. 29.

14 Peavy, "Myth, Magic, and Manhood," p. 13.

15 See, for example, the end of *Police* and Baraka's discussion, in his essay "American Sexual Reference: Black Male" (*Home*, pp. 229–30), of a story his grandmother once told him about a black alleged rapist who, when caught by a white posse, had his genitals cut off and stuffed in his mouth.

16 This and the following quotation are from "Black Woman," p. 25.

17 See Peavy, pp. 16–17.

18 "American Sexual Reference: Black Male," p. 223.

19 The whole procedure by which Black Man kills Devil Lady is executed as though it were very precisely choreographed. See *Madheart*, p. 70.

20 "Black Woman," p. 23.

21 The play was written for members of the San Francisco-based Black Alliance and was first performed by that organization in May 1967.

22 Theodore Hudson, for example, asserts that "*Madheart* is a bit more poetic and a bit more intellectual in language than Jones' plays intended for audiences from the black masses" (Hudson, *From LeRoi Jones to Amiri Baraka*, p. 167). More important, perhaps, is the elitist and dangerously messianic thrust of the final invocation to "save or kill" errant black people.

23 *Muhammad Speaks*, July 15, 1960, p. 26.

24 All references to *A Black Mass* are from *Four Black Revolutionary Plays*, pp. 17–39.

CHAPTER SEVEN

1 My discussion of *Slave Ship* is based upon the text published in *Negro Digest*, April 1967, pp. 63–74 (from which all following quotations are drawn) and a performance of the play by Detroit's Concept East Theatre on November 18, 1973. Having seen Concept East's brilliant realization of the script, I can confidently assert that the possibilities and objectives evident from the text have been fully achieved where they count: in the theatre.

2 "Harold Cruse: An Interview," conducted by C. W. E. Bigsby (*The Black American Writer: Vol. II*, p. 229).

3 I borrow this term to describe *Slave Ship*'s episodic scenes from Stefan Brecht's "LeRoi Jones's *Slave Ship*," *The Drama Review* 14, no. 2 (1970): 212–19. Though I identify a few more such "images" than does Brecht, his tripartite division of the play ("deprivation of

identity, alienation, retrieval of identity") is a provocative and informative approach to which I am much indebted.

4 Ibid., p. 218.
5 "Harold Cruse: An Interview," p. 236.
6 *The Birth of Tragedy*, trans. Walter Kaufmann (New York: Vintage Books, 1967), p. 37.

CONCLUSION

1 "Afro-American Religious Ritual," *Black World* (April 1973), p. 10; p. 9.
2 "God on the Gymnasium Floor," *Theater* (New York, 1968–69), pp. 14, 16.
3 My understanding and description of Artaud's theory is deeply indebted to Tom F. Driver's excellent analysis of Artaud in *Romantic Quest and Modern Query* (New York: Delacorte Press, 1970), pp. 353–68.
4 *Black Fiction* (Cambridge, Mass.: Harvard University Press, 1974), p. 158.
5 "Black American Poetry: Its Language and the Folk Tradition," in *Modern Black Literature*, ed. Dr. S. Okechukwu Mezu (Buffalo, N.Y.: Black Academy Press, 1971), p. 79.
6 Stewart, "Development of the Black Revolutionary Artist," p. 4.
7 *Raise Race Rays Raze*, p. 103.
8 Ibid., p. 132.
9 "Characteristics of Negro Expression," in *Negro Anthology*, ed. Nancy Cunard (New York: Negro Universities Press, 1934), p. 39. Several other Afro-American writers have echoed Hurston's idea. See, for example, Richard Wright's observations about Asian-African and Negro "acting" in *White Man, Listen!* (New York: Doubleday & Co., 1964), pp. 17–20.
10 Another fascinating instance of LeRoi Jones's self-dramatizing occurred at his 1967 trial for allegedly carrying firearms unlawfully. He and the judge (Leon W. Kapp of New Jersey's Essex County Court) felt that the charges were intimately related to Jones's activities and works as a *poet*. Judge Kapp read excerpts from Jones's poems and essays, attempting to establish guilt by rhetorical association. A look at the trial's transcript shows that Jones was completely aware of the implications of this procedure and that he "played" it to the full. For a representative sample of the transcript see Hudson, *From LeRoi Jones to Amiri Baraka*, pp. 27–31.

11 This latest position was expressed by Baraka at the 6th Pan-African Congress; see "Toward Ideological Clarity," *Black World* (November 1974), pp. 24–32, 84–95, for his most recent theoretical statement. Baraka has been taken to task recently by other black nationalists who see him as straying from the "purely black" fold; a notable example is Harold Cruse's article, "The National Black Political Convention, Part II," published in the same issue of *Black World*, pp. 4–21.

Bibliography

General Criticism

Bentley, Eric. *The Life of the Drama*. New York: Atheneum, 1967.

———. *The Playwright as Thinker*. New York: Meridan Books, 1955.

Breman, Paul. "Poetry into the 'Sixties." In *The Black American Writer, Vol. II*, edited by C. W. E. Bigsby, pp. 99–110. Baltimore, Md.: Penguin Books, 1971.

Clurman, Harold. *Naked Image: Observations of the Modern Theater*. New York: Macmillan, 1966.

Frye, Northrop. *Anatomy of Criticism*. Princeton, N.J., Princeton University Press, 1957.

———. *Fables of Identity*. New York: Harcourt, Brace, & World, 1963.

Hayakawa, S. I. *Language in Action*. New York: Harcourt, Brace and Co., 1940.

Hunninger, Benjamin. *The Origin of the Theater*. New York: Hill and Wang, 1955.

Maritain, Jacques. *Creative Intuition in Art and Poetry*. New York: Pantheon Books, 1953.

Parone, Edward, ed. *New Theater in America*. New York: Dell Publishing Co., 1970.

Peacock, Ronald. *The Poet in the Theater*. New York: Hill and Wang, 1960.

Rosenthal, M. L. *The New Poets*. New York: Oxford University Press, 1967.

Theater, 1968–1969. New York: International Theater Institute of The United States, 1970.

Afro-American Criticism

Bigsby, C. W. E., ed. *The Black American Writer, Vols. I and II*, Baltimore, Md.: Penguin Books, 1971.

Bullins, Ed. "A Short Statement on Street Theatre." *The Drama Review* 12, no. 4 (Summer 1968): 93.

Cade, Toni. "Black Theater." In *Black Expression*, edited by Addison Gayle, Jr., pp. 134–43. New York: Weybright and Talley, 1969.

Cook, Mercer, and Henderson, Stephen E. *The Militant Black Writer*. Madison: University of Wisconsin Press, 1969.

Cooke, Michael G. "The Descent into the Underground and Modern Black Fiction." *The Iowa Review* 5, no. 4 (1974): 72–90.

Couch, William, ed. *New Black Playwrights*. New York: Avon Books, 1970.

Cruse, Harold (with C. W. E. Bigsby). "An Interview." *The Black American Writer: Vol. II*, pp. 227–39. Baltimore, Md.: Penguin Books, 1971.

———. *The Crisis of the Negro Intellectual*, New York: William Morrow & Co., 1967.

———. "Revolutionary Nationalism and the Afro-American." *Black Fire*, edited by LeRoi Jones and Larry Neal, pp. 39–63. New York: William Morrow & Co., 1968.

Davis, John Preston, ed. *The American Negro Reference Book*. Englewood Cliffs, N.J.: Prentice-Hall, 1966.

Ellison, Ralph. *Shadow and Act*. New York: Vintage Books, 1972.

Gayle, Addison, Jr., ed. *The Black Aesthetic*. Garden City, N.Y.: Doubleday & Company, 1972.

———. *Black Expression*. New York: Weybright and Talley, 1969.

Gibson, Donald B. *Five Black Writers*. New York: New York University Press, 1970.

Gibson, Donald B., ed. *Modern Black Poets*. Englewood Cliffs, N.J.: Prentice-Hall, 1973.

Henderson, Stephen E. *Understanding the New Black Poetry*. New York: William Morrow & Co., 1973.

Hill, Herbert, ed. *Anger and Beyond*. New York: Harper & Row, 1966.

Huggins, Nathan Irvin, *Harlem Renaissance*, New York: Oxford University Press, 1971.

Jahn, Janheinz. *Neo-African Literature: A History of Black Writing*. Translated by Oliver Coburn and Ursala Lehrburger. New York: Grove Press, 1968.

Jones, LeRoi, and Neal, Larry, eds. *Black Fire*. New York: William Morrow & Co., 1968.

Keil, Charles. *Urban Blues*. Chicago: University of Chicago Press, 1969.

Kgositsile, K. William. "Towards Our Theater: A Definitive Act." In *Black Expression*, edited by Addison Gayle, Jr., pp. 146–48. New York: Weybright and Talley, 1969.

King, Woodie, and Milner, Ron, eds. *Black Drama Anthology*. New York: New American Library, 1971.

Kofsky, Frank. *Black Nationalism and the Revolution in Music*. New York: Pathfinder Press, 1970.

Lee, Don L. *Dynamite Voices*. Detroit: Broadside Press, 1971.

Littlejohn, David. *Black on White*. New York: The Viking Press, 1966.

Mitchell, Loften. *Black Drama*. New York: Hawthorn Books, 1967.

Neal, Larry. "The Black Arts Movement." *The Drama Review* 12, no. 4 (Summer 1968): 29–39. Reprinted in *The Black American Writer: Vol. II*, edited by C. W. E. Bigsby, pp. 187–203. Baltimore, Md.: Penguin Books, 1971.

Sartre, Jean-Paul. "Black Orpheus." In *The Black American Writer: Vol. II*, edited by C. W. E. Bigsby, pp. 5–40. Baltimore, Md.: Penguin Books, 1971.

Wagner, Jean. *Black Poets of the United States*. Translated by Kenneth Douglas. Chicago: University of Illinois Press, 1973.

Williams, Sherley Anne. *Give Birth to Brightness*. New York: The Dial Press, 1972.

Baraka Criticism

The following is a list of works which I believe to be especially valuable in studying Baraka's writings. A more thorough bibliography of Baraka criticism is given by Letitia Dace in *LeRoi Jones: A Checklist of Works by and About Him*, and by Theodore R. Hudson in *From LeRoi Jones to Amiri Baraka*, pp. 201–09.

Adams, George R. " 'My Christ' in *Dutchman*." *CLA Journal* 15, no. 1 (September 1971): 54–58.

Brecht, Stefan. "LeRoi Jones' *Slave Ship*." *The Drama Review* 14, no. 2 (Winter 1970): 212–19.

Brown, Cecil M. "Black Literature and LeRoi Jones." *Black World*, June 1970, pp. 24–31.

Coleman, Larry Grant, "LeRoi Jones' *Tales*: Sketches of the Artist as a Young Man Moving Toward a Blacker Art." *Black Lines* 1, no. 2 (Winter 1970): 17–26.

Costello, Donald P. "LeRoi Jones: Black Man as Victim." *Commonweal*, June 28, 1968, pp. 436–40.

Dace, Letitia. *LeRoi Jones: A Checklist of Works by and About Him*. London: Nether Press, 1971.

Dennison, George. "The Demagogy of LeRoi Jones." *Commentary*, February 1965, pp. 67–70.

Faruk and Marvin X. "Islam and Black Art: An Interview with LeRoi Jones." *Negro Digest*, January 1969, pp. 4–10, 77–80.

Fischer, William C. "The Pre-Revolutionary Writings of Imamu Amiri Baraka." *The Massachusetts Review* 14, no. 2 (Spring 1973): 259–305.

Hudson, Theodore R. *From LeRoi Jones to Amiri Baraka*. Durham, N.C.: Duke University Press, 1973.

Hughes, Langston. "That Boy LeRoi." *Chicago Defender*, January 11, 1965, p. 38.

Jackson, Esther M. "LeRoi Jones (Imamu Amiri Baraka): Form and the Progression of Consciousness." *CLA Journal* 17, no. 1 (September 1973): 33–56.

Jackson, Kathryn. "LeRoi Jones and the New Black Writers of the Sixties." Freedomways 9, Third Quarter (1969), pp. 232–46.

Jacobus, Lee A. "Imamu Amiri Baraka: The Quest for Moral Order." In *Modern Black Poets*, ed. Donald B. Gibson, pp. 112–26. Englewood Cliffs, N.J., 1973.

Jeffers, Lance. "Bullins, Baraka, and Elder: The Dawn of Grandeur in Black Drama." *CLA Journal* 16, no. 1 (September 1972): 32–48.

Lederer, Richard. "The Language of LeRoi Jones' *The Slave*." *Studies In Black Literature* 4, no. 1 (Spring 1973): 14–16.

Lindberg, John. "*Dutchman* and *The Slave*: Companions in Revolution." *Modern Black Literature*, edited by Dr. S. Okechukwu Mezu, pp. 101–07. Buffalo, N.Y.: Black Academy Press, 1971.

Margolies, Edward. "Prospects: LeRoi Jones." In *Native Sons: A Critical Study of Twentieth-Century Negro American Authors*, pp. 190–99. Philadelphia: J. B. Lippincott Company, 1968.

Miller, Jeanne Marie A. "The Plays of LeRoi Jones." *CLA Journal* 14, no. 2 (March 1971): 33–39.

Mootry, Maria K. "Themes and Symbols in Two Plays by LeRoi Jones." *Negro Digest*, April 1969, pp. 42–47.

Munro, C. Lynn. "LeRoi Jones: A Man in Transition." *CLA Journal* 17, no. 1 (September 1973): 57–78.

Neal, Larry. "The Development of LeRoi Jones." *Liberator*, January 1966 (pp. 4–5) and February 1966 (pp. 18–19).

Peavy, Charles D. "Myth, Magic, and Manhood in LeRoi Jones' *Madheart*." *Studies In Black Literature* 1, no. 2 (Summer 1970): 12–20.

Pennington-Jones, Paulette. "From Brother LeRoi Jones Through *The System of Dante's Hell* To Imamu Ameer Baraka." *Journal of Black Studies* 4, no. 2 (December 1973): 195–214.

Phillips, Louis. "LeRoi Jones and Contemporary Black Drama." *The Black American Writer: Vol. II*, edited by C. W. E. Bigsby, pp. 204–19. Baltimore, Md.: Penguin Books, 1971.

Reck, Tom S. "Archetypes in LeRoi Jones' *Dutchman*." *Studies In Black Literature* 1, no. 1 (Spring 1970): 66–68.

Schneck, Stephen. "LeRoi Jones, or Poetics & Policemen, or Trying Heart, Bleedin Heart." *Ramparts*, July 13, 1968, pp. 14–19.

Taylor, Clyde. "Baraka as Poet." In *Modern Black Poets*, ed. Donald B. Gibson, pp. 127–34. Englewood Cliffs, N.J.: Prentice-Hall, 1973.

Works by Baraka

The following is a bibliography of works by Baraka discussed in the text. A thorough bibliography of Baraka's work is given by Hudson in *From LeRoi Jones to Amiri Baraka*, pp. 198–201.

Arm Yourself, or Harm Yourself. Newark, N.J.: Jihad Publications, 1967.

The Baptism and *The Toilet*. New York: Grove Press, 1966.

Black Magic Poetry. New York: Bobbs-Merrill Company, 1969.

Black Music. New York: William Morrow and Co., 1968.

Blues People: Negro Music in White America. New York: William Morrow and Co., 1963.

The Dead Lecturer. New York: Grove Press, 1964.

Dutchman and *The Slave*. New York: William Morrow and Co., 1964.

Four Black Revolutionary Plays. New York: Bobbs-Merrill Company, 1969. (This volume includes *Experimental Death Unit #1, A Black Mass, Great Goodness of Life: A Coon Show*, and *Madheart*.)

Home: Social Essays. New York: William Morrow and Co., 1966.

Home on the Range. The Drama Review 12, no. 4 (Summer 1968): 106–11.

In Our Terribleness (Some Elements and Meaning in Black Style). New York: Bobbs-Merrill Company, 1970.

It's Nation Time. Chicago: Third World Press, 1970.

Jello. Chicago: Third World Press, 1970.

Kawaida Studies: The New Nationalism. Third World Press, 1972.

Police. The Drama Review 12, no. 4 (Summer 1968): 112–15.

Preface To A Twenty Volume Suicide Note. . . . New York: Totem Press, 1961.

Raise Race Rays Raze: Essays Since 1965. New York: Random House, 1971.

A Recent Killing. Unpublished manuscript.
Slave Ship: A Historical Pageant. Negro Digest, April 1967, pp. 62–74.
Spirit Reach. Newark, N.J.: Jihad Publications, 1972.
The System of Dante's Hell. New York: Grove Press, 1965.
Tales. New York: Grove Press, 1967.

Index